A SHAKESPEARE WORKBOOK

Other books by Bertram Joseph

ACTING SHAKESPEARE

CONSCIENCE AND THE KING

ELIZABETHAN ACTING

SHAKESPEARE'S EDEN

THE TRAGIC ACTOR

A Shakespeare Workbook

Volume 1: Tragedies

by BERTRAM JOSEPH

THEATRE ARTS BOOKS
New York

First Published in the USA 1980
by Theatre Arts Books
153 Waverly Place
New York, New York 10014

Library of Congress Catalog Card No. 80-50211
ISBN 0-87830-566-1

Designed by Bernard Schleifer
Printed and bound in the United States of America

In Memory of

Robert M. MacGregor

in gratitude
for his
friendship, wisdom and integrity

PREFACE

THE SCENES treated in this book have been selected simply to give practice in meeting the different demands which Shakespeare makes on the actor. I hope thereby to make it possible for anyone working through the scenes (or a selection from them) to gain some experience of the fact that problems solve themselves when the words of the text are understood accurately and are read precisely as part of the action of each character trying to obtain a specific objective in relationships with others.

For convenience, references to the text may be made to *The Complete Works of Shakespeare* (revised edition), edited by Hardin Craig and David Bevington (Scott, Foresman and Company, 1973). From time to time I have emended this where there are grounds for believing that the editors may not have grasped Shakespeare's meaning. I have added my own glosses and explanatory notes where necessary.

February, 1979
Glen Cove,
Long Island

B.L.J.

INTRODUCTION

THE ACTOR'S TASK with Shakespeare is exactly the same as with any other dramatist, to behave as if he were the imaginary character whom he represents. He has to perform the actions of that character, think his thoughts, want his wants, feel his emotions, all as if they were his own in relationships with other imaginary characters.

But Shakespeare presents the modern actor with two difficulties encountered in comparatively few other dramatists. First, Shakespeare's plays are written for the most part in "poetic" language, in blank verse, rhyme and unrealistic prose. The dialogue tends to obstruct the actor who is trying to perceive motive and thought processes which allow him to imagine his role; for he has to play the role with the appropriate actions which such a person would perform in real life if he were to exist, while speaking dialogue which such a person would not speak in such circumstances.

The second great difficulty which the actor encounters with Shakespeare is one of language. Shakespeare wrote in the language of some four hundred years ago; it is now in many respects virtually a foreign language to us, with the added difficulty that many words are still in use, but with different meanings. When Kent tells Lear to let his sword strike *the region of my heart,* the modern mind tends to imagine a vague area in the vicinity of the heart. But in Elizabethan English, Kent is telling the King to strike exactly where his heart is and nowhere else.

The actor needs to know the exact sense of every word so that he can think his character's thoughts as if they were his own. Precise knowledge of Shakespeare's words is essential for another reason; he uses words very exactly, and to mistake their meaning, even slightly, can be to hide the truth about an intention, a relationship, an action. To know the exact sense of a word is often not enough, however; we also need to understand its implications in the particular context in which it is used by a character. For instance, when Ophelia tells how Hamlet came into her room with *no hat upon his head*, each of those five words has the same dictionary sense today as it had in the early seventeenth century. But to play Ophelia at this moment an actress has to imagine herself affected as Ophelia is by the absence of Hamlet's hat. This means imagining herself in a society in which noblemen wore hats indoors as part of their ensemble, a society in which men removed their hats only in the presence of superiors. Ophelia must be imagined as a noblewoman who expects the Prince of Denmark to wear his hat indoors and certainly in her presence. To her the absence of Hamlet's hat is just one more disturbing piece of evidence of his psychological degeneration.

In this book an attempt is made to familiarize the student with processes of study which enable him to read Shakespeare's text with full recognition of its quality as literature, but in such a way that he can imagine and play the actions of the character who speaks this text. In addition the aim is to accustom the student to the need to understand the words precisely and, with historical information in mind, to imagine a society and culture of four hundred years ago. Each of the scenes or incidents chosen for study is accompanied by a full vocabulary and adequate comments and notes, with suggestions for their use by the actor in preparing his role. He must learn first to think in the English of his role as one thinks in a foreign language without translating from it into his own and vice versa; then comes the task of recognizing why this character thinks these thoughts, which leads us to perceive his motives and feelings, the action which he is performing, what he is doing in the fullest meaning of the word. One of the great obstacles to acting Shakespeare lies in the ease with which we hide from ourselves the fact that we do not understand a word, a phrase, a line clearly and precisely. Consider for instance these lines of Macbeth's:

> I have supp'd full with horrors;
> Direness, familiar to my slaughterous thoughts,
> Cannot once start me. (V, v, 13–15)

He is not saying that he has eaten his fill of horrors, but that "with horrors," despite their presence, he has been able to eat all he wanted, not disconcerted or turned from his food by them. *Direness* means horror. *Familiar* means acting as a familiar, or constant companion to; i.e., "Horror, the constant companion of my slaughterous thoughts, cannot even make me twitch once with terror."

The aim of providing a copious vocabulary and relevant notes is paradoxically that of making the student less, not more, dependent on this book. For his own experience tells him the difference between understanding and not understanding every word; and, as a result, he gradually becomes alert to an inability to think the sense of individual words clearly. This alertness will protect him from mistaken assumptions and will send him to the research which is needed if he is to play the role.

The precision of Shakespeare's language is an advantage to the actor who learns how to use it. Nevertheless, it is also in part responsible for difficulties which arise from the playwright's ability to express a wealth of meaning in very few words. Take, for instance, Juliet's couplet:

> Prodigious birth of love it is to me,
> That I must love a loathed enemy.

If other words are used to express the sense of these lines we shall have to use far more than Shakespeare has needed here: "The love that has been born to me is an unnatural monster, in that I am unable to stop myself loving a person whom I detest as an enemy." The actress must think this sense as she speaks Shakespeare's words; he has used fifteen words to express what has needed twenty-nine, almost twice as many, in my version.

This ability to say much in few words is a characteristic quality of poetic statement as such, both in and out of drama.

The fact that Shakespeare retains this quality in his dramatic dialogue means that his actor has more to play in a given number of words than in the same number of words of nonpoetic statement.

Again a passage from *Romeo and Juliet* serves as illustration. I have treated these lines elsewhere, but make no apology for calling attention to them once more here, for they show so clearly how the actor should study Shakespeare when preparing to play him. Romeo is trying to convince Juliet that dawn is on them, that he must leave her:

> Look, love, what envious streaks
> Do lace the severing clouds in yonder east;

Shakespeare has imagined him looking at streaks of light crisscrossing over a split in the darkness in the east where the light from the sun is beginning to shine through a rift in the clouds. The clouds are separating *(severing)* and the streaks look like lacing, used to hold together two parts of a garment; the surface sense implies that this lacing does not hold together the *severing clouds,* for it comes from the light of the sun which will split them farther apart. Finally the word *envious* implies that the streaks seem to begrudge Romeo and Juliet these last moments together. Romeo's meaning can be put into unpoetic language as: "Look, love, at those streaks of light, crisscrossing like laces over the separating clouds there in the east, as if they envy us our time together; for while laces usually hold severing things together, these are pushing the clouds of darkness farther apart." This restatement of the sense of Romeo's lines requires forty-three words; Shakespeare uses no more than thirteen. But the actor playing Romeo must express all that sense in those thirteen if he is to think Romeo's thoughts. In playing the role he communicates those thoughts in an attempt to achieve his objective, which is to convince Juliet that she must let him go.

The key to playing Shakespeare lies in understanding the nature of his art as a dramatist. He imagines characters in action, doing things to one another in relationships. Nevertheless, while he imagines dramatically he uses his verbal art to communicate his characters' actions. He often uses the techniques which other poets use in nondramatic poems, but whenever he does this he always imagines every word as essential to the action of the character who speaks it. In the lines of Juliet referred to above, the rhyme is perfect as such, but each rhyming word is also part of the action of the character. Juliet needs it in what she is doing at this moment in her relationship to her parents, to her hereditary enemies and to Romeo, whom she loves and hates:

> Prodigious birth of love it is to me,
> That I must love a loathed enemy.

Similarly in their first meeting, she and Romeo have just spoken to one another inside the rhyme scheme of a sonnet. But the rhyming words are dramatic because they are all part of the action of the speaker. So long as the actor remembers that this is true of all Shakespeare's words he will find that to prepare to act Shakespeare, as to prepare to act any other playwright, is a matter of recognizing the actions which he has imagined and which he has communicated in the dialogue. He is a dramatist because he imagines characters in relationships with one another in action. All his words are part of the action of the respective characters, who need them to try to achieve an objective in action.

So far as his words are part of the action of the respective characters Shakespeare is like all other dramatists in the use of words. Where he differs from the majority of Western dramatists of the last two hundred years is not only in his ability to use his words for the needs of the characters, but also in his virtuosity with the verbal techniques appropriate to nondramatic writing.

As we can see in imagery, in rhyme and in other sound patterns, and in verse itself, Shakespeare's words conform to two requirements simultaneously. Nevertheless, the more important task for the actor is to find the intention and emotion of the character, created in imagery, sound pattern or in meter. When he has done this, however, he must not ignore the verbal skill of the playwright. Invariably the actor will find that skill inseparable from the creation of character.

Literary criticism of Shakespeare pays much attention to

elements of his art which are also to be found in the art of nondramatic poets, to his imagery, complexities of meaning, verbal patternings (of sense and of sound), his meter and rhythm. All these elements are important for the actor, too; he will find that, properly understood, this side of the dramatist's art contributes to the ability to imagine and play a role. If we consider Shakespeare's imagery we note that traditionally it has been praised for its beauty, for the fact that it makes the audience imagine what could not be represented on the Elizabethan stage, whether that be an incident taking place in the present or narrated as past, or a description of a place or a person. It has also often been emphasized that Shakespeare's images can communicate to us the implications of what takes place, and that both images and implications are repeated and organized coherently to make us grasp a theme of some importance to our understanding of the whole work.

Nevertheless, while it is true that no actor should close his mind to these qualities of Shakespeare's images, what is most important for any performer's playing of a Shakespearian role is that every image always derives from the character's motive; the image is always part of the action by which the character seeks to achieve a goal. This is true, for instance, of the famous "poetic" line of the First Murderer in Act Three, Scene Three, of *Macbeth,* a line which literary criticism has been so ill-advised as to call "pure poetry":

> The west yet glimmers with some streaks of day (l. 5).

The actor's main concern is with the Murderer's intention. Macbeth has already told him and the Second Murderer that Banquo and Fleance must be murdered that night, that the crimes must not be traced back to him *(I require a clearness),* that these must be done in secret (III, i, 127–38), that he will let them know the exact time and place. Macbeth has already ascertained that Banquo and Fleance will be returning from their ride at nightfall. In Act Three, Scene Two, he makes the actual decision for them to be murdered as night falls completely (ll. 46–53).

When the First Murderer utters his famous line, his task has been to make his way to the place of ambush in secret, using the gathering darkness to hide his approach. He and his companions are now in position; but it is so dark that he has a sudden fear that they might have come too late, that the intended victims might have passed by already on their return to the palace for the *solemn supper* in Banquo's honor. To reassure himself the Murderer looks at the sky in the west, where some remaining *streaks of day* satisfy him that no mistake has been made. The image expresses the satisfaction fused to a determination to have his revenge.

Of course, this line spoken by an actor who imagines himself in the dark place of ambush also paints for the audience a scene of night falling. The words are also beautiful, and in addition they make us respond to Shakespeare's emphasis of one of his themes, the conflict between evil and good in this play, which is expressed in images of a struggle between darkness and light, night and day, respectively. Even so, the actor's main concern is with what the line does for his role; and only when he plays it as a part of the role's action is he able to communicate its other qualities to his audience.

The words are also related to the character's intention in the account given by Enobarbus of the first meeting of Antony with Cleopatra in the barge. His Roman friends have asked Enobarbus to tell them exactly what kind of a woman Cleopatra is. Aware of the hopes of distracting Antony from Cleopatra by a marriage to Octavia, Enobarbus concentrates on making clear to the Romans the powerful influence which the Egyptian queen exerts. To do this he recalls that first meeting, and how he felt at the time, as well as what he has thought and felt since. He intends to leave them with no illusions about Cleopatra, whose wit, beauty, intelligence, humor, self-possession, confidence in herself and her power over men, all make her a strong threat to the stability of the Roman world.

In these cases, and others like them, there is no reason for the actor to aim at making his audiences imagine that they can see what he describes or narrates. He must use the image to achieve the objective wanted by the role which he is playing; and when this happens the audience will imagine what he describes or narrates. For instance, when Edgar in *King Lear* describes Dover, his intention is to persuade his blind father that they are actually all these feet above the sea. The actor who plays this intention will make the audiences imagine the scene described as if they were Gloucester. The aim is not to convince them, but Gloucester, that the speaker is standing on the cliff.

If an actor is to imagine Shakespeare's images accurately, he must understand the exact sense of each word. When Macbeth is terrified that he has taught *bloody instruction* to Banquo, who will kill him, he longs for the moment of nightfall when this enemy and his son will be destroyed. Macbeth longs for night to come swiftly:

> Come, seeling night,
> Scarf up the tender eye of pitiful day.

Seeling is the use of a falconer's technique to train a hawk to sit at rest on a hunter's wrist with a small hood, or cap, over its head, in complete darkness. Seeling involved inserting a piece of thread horizontally through the hard lower eyelid of one eye (with no pain, owing to the insensibility of this hard tissue). The thread is passed over the top of the bird's head, brought down and put through the lower eyelid of the other eye. By twisting the thread on top of the head, thus tightening it, the falconer forces the eyes to close to some extent. In the image this is the equivalent of twilight. Complete darkness comes when the falconer winds a bandage *(scarf)* round the bird's head, blindfolding it.

When we imagine the image accurately we can relate it to a Renaissance emblematic conceit of the mercy and justice of Heaven at the Last Judgment as an eye with the wings of a hawk in the sky. The predatory bird thus has the qualities of tenderness and pity, virtues which are necessarily at war with Macbeth. His need is to avoid exposure to his subjects and to divine mercy and justice. He believes that to keep himself and his sins hidden he must destroy Banquo and his heirs. Macbeth needs night; Banquo and Fleance will be killed at nightfall; their deaths will enable him to evade the eye of the watchful bird hovering above him in the sky.

Shakespeare uses language precisely; that is why no actor

can afford to neglect the exact sense of every word when preparing to play an emotion, especially when that is related to Shakespeare's imagery. If the actor uses the technique of "private image" or "emotion recall," it is very important that he does not inadvertently substitute his own image for Shakespeare's. For instance, Lear's *Blow winds, and crack your cheeks* is a clear visual image of cherubic faces with cheeks bulging to burst and destroy themselves (with appropriate accompanying auditory and tactile images). And *Strike flat the thick rotundity of the world* involves a clear image of the thunderstone hitting the "thick" bulge of the globe with a violence which knocks it into a vast flatness at one blow. In his preparation the actor might well use another image which allows him to evoke in himself the emotion he needs. But once that image has produced the desired result, he must dissociate it from the emotion, which must be transferred to Shakespeare's. This is because each of Shakespeare's words will become part of the action of the role only when it is thought precisely in the actor's wanting the flatness, in his detestation of the *rotundity* which is so tenaciously surviving the worst that the storm can do. Lear's discontent with things as they are is so intense that he now wills the destruction of the world and all its creatures to punish his daughters for ingratitude.

We have noted above that in the meeting of Romeo and Juliet Shakespeare simultaneously creates a sonnet and a relationship of intention between the two characters in action. The interchange conforms to a structure of ideas which is appropriate to a sonnet, a piece of writing with a definite rhyme scheme. Rhyme itself has been described as "the agreement or consonance of the final sounds of metrical lines." It is one of the many patterns of sound which the Elizabethans called "figures of words," all of which can be involved in the communicating of an imagined dramatic action.

Elsewhere I have dealt more fully with these figures in Shakespeare, for which reason I am limiting myself here to some few patterns which communicate a clear relationship of idea to idea, and which therefore demand that the actor must think the relationship with equal clarity. In the pattern called antithesis, the related ideas are in opposition to one another, as in Gratiano's:

> And let my liver rather *heat* with wine
> Than my heart *cool* with mortifying groans.
> (*Merchant of Venice*, I, i, 81–82)

Heat and *cool* are obviously in antithesis. Almost as clearly, *wine* (a source of heat) is the opposite of *mortifying groans* (a source of coldness).

Troilus has a slightly more complicated example of antithesis:

> Why should I war *without the walls of Troy*
> That find such cruel battle *here within?*
> (*Troilus and Cressida*, I, i, 2–3)

Gratiano knows that he is going to say *cool,* even as he is about to say *heat,* and that *wine* is related in his mind to *mortifying groans.* The actor must therefore relate the ideas in his mind, and their relationship will be apparent in his voice and in the rest of his action. These two lines contain another relationship, which is not necessarily of conflicting ideas:

> And let my *liver* . . . Than my *heart* . . .

Similarly, Troilus has two more sets of ideas, neither of which is in antithesis to its companion:

> Why should *I*(i) *war* (ii) . . . *That*(i) *find such cruel battle*(ii)

Here, too, the actor has to play a character who knows that *I* will have *That* as a counterpart, who speaks *war* knowing it is related to the idea of *find such cruel battle.*

A line spoken by the Player King in *Hamlet* has two sets of ideas which are not in antithesis:

> For who *not needs* shall *never lack* a friend.

This line's bitter wit depends on the King (and the actor) knowing that *not* will be followed by *never,* and *needs* by *shall . . . lack.*

But Shakespeare does not always give us a simple relationship of adjective to adjective or noun to noun:

> Speaking in deeds and deedless in his tongue.
> (*Troilus and Cressida*, IV, v, 98.)

Here, *speaking* is related to *in his tongue, in deeds* to *deedless;* and as a result *Speaking in deeds* and *deedless in his tongue* are in antithesis as more complex units.

There is an even more subtle antithetical statement at the end of Henry V's threat to the Dauphin:

> His jest will savour but of shallow wit,
> When thousands weep more than did laugh at it.

The more obvious level of contrast is that of *weep—did laugh.* But the weeping of tears will provide a deeper flood than there was depth in the shallow wit which is going to lead to them. In fact, the depth of the consequences will emphasize how shallow was the wit.

"Cross-couple" was an Elizabethan term for another patterned relationship of ideas (synoeciosis), as in Pisanio's:

> Wherein I am *false* I am *honest; not true* to be *true.*
> (*Cymbeline*, IV, iii, 42)

There is no need to treat such matters more fully here; attention will be called to patterns of sound and of related ideas wherever they occur in the individual scenes chosen for detailed study. For the actor it is enough at the moment to know that such figures exist in Shakespeare, that it is possible to proceed from mechanical recognition of one to a richer recognition of the relationship of ideas and, inseparable from these, the objective of the character speaking.

Whenever we express meaning in English we stress some

syllables of the words we speak, leaving others unstressed. It should be made clear at this point that by a stressed syllable is meant one spoken with a percussion or beat, resulting from an explosion of air going through the larynx from the windpipe. The fact that we place stress on a syllable is the result of a desire to express meaning, with some part being played by custom. Custom is involved, for instance, in the English pronunciation *ádvertíze* and *advértizement* in England, while in the United States the words are pronounced *ádvertize, advertízement.* In England the noun *cóntract* has the stress on its first syllable; but the verb *contráct* takes the stress on the second. In each of these cases, however, meaning is involved as well as custom.

Meter in English verse consists of a recurring pattern of stressed and unstressed syllables. As it is impossible to speak English without a juxtaposition of stressed and unstressed syllables, they form a pattern in prose, too. But where verse differs from prose is in the fact that meter consists of a recurring pattern. The pattern does not recur in prose.

Most of Shakespeare's verse is in lines of ten syllables, organized in recurring patterns of iambic feet, that is, of pairs of syllables, the first having no stress, the second bearing stress:

> The tongues of mocking wenches are as keen
> As is the razor's edge invisible
>
> (*Love's Labour's Lost*, V, ii, 256–57)

The next line has a variation, the stress falling on the first (not the second) syllable of the first foot:

> Cutting a smaller hair than may be seen

Here the second foot returns to the original pattern, which recurs unchanged in the next line:

> Above the sense of sense; so sensible

But the variation comes again in the first foot of the next line:

Seemeth their conference; their conceits have wings

The iambic pattern returns in the rest of this line, but there is another shift of stress at the beginning of the next (which has twelve syllables) with stress then going back to the second syllable of each pair:

Fleeter than arrows, bullets, wind, thought, swifter things.

And the next line (spoken by Rosaline) consists wholly of the dominant pattern in which each unstressed syllable is followed by one with stress:

Not one word more, my maids, break off, break off.

The performer who reads or acts these lines responds mentally and physically to the recurring pattern, setting up an expectation of its recurrence. Whenever it fails to recur, the sensitive actor will miss it. In the lines just considered the variation is at least as pleasant, or even more pleasant. But in these lines of Romeo's, the failure of the pattern to recur is rhythmically unpleasant:

Where ís she? ańd how dóth she? ańd what sáys
My concéal'd lády tó our cáncell'd lóve?
(*Romeo and Juliet*, III, iii, 97–98)

When an actor experiences an unpleasant jolt such as this, he needs to find out why it has occurred. The cause here is the juxtaposition of two unstressed syllables and two stressed:

My concéal'd lády

In this case we learn that when Shakespeare wrote, *conceal* was pronounced with a stress on the first syllable *cónceal*. If we preserve or repeat the Elizabethan stress we have a pleasant rhythm based on the repeated succession of an unstressed by a stressed syllable:

My cónceal'd lády tó our cáncell'd lóve?

The actor is advised not to give too much conscious attention to the metrical pattern before speaking his lines. For instance, he should not prepare by counting out the syllables to himself. If he is sufficiently sensitive to the succession of stressed and unstressed syllables, he will notice variations. If any of these are unpleasant, or if he is not sure that the variation ought to be there, he can then count the syllables, and if he finds he has erred he can put the matter right.

In Shakespeare's day the vowel of a final syllable printed "ed" was always pronounced. Whenever a vowel is to be elided, the Elizabethan text has "'d"; but, unfortunately, modern printing practice is not so consistent. Some modern editions of Shakespeare print "ed" when the vowel is not to be pronounced, thus adding to the difficulties of the actor. Nevertheless, if he is sensitive to the metrical pattern he will notice that he has an extra syllable. If necessary, the whole line can be counted out as a guide to ignoring the printed vowel and eliding it in speaking. For instance, Romeo's line might well be printed thus in a modern edition:

My concealed lady to our cancelled love.

It would be wrong to speak *concealed* and *cancelled* each as having three syllables:

My cóncealéd lády tó our cáncelléd lóve.

Meter is only one element of rhythm; this itself develops as the actor communicates more of the meaning of his lines as actions of the role. Another element of rhythm, almost as powerful as the basic metrical pattern, comes from patterned language expressing interrelated ideas such as we have treated above. In these patterns of sound the verbal organization evokes from the speaker a pattern of changes of pitch and length, which counterpoints with the metrical pattern of stressed and unstressed syllables:

Wherefore do you so ill translate yourself
Out of the speech of peace that bears such grace,
Into the harsh and boist'rous tongue of war;
Turning your books to graves, your ink to blood,
Your pens to lances, and your tongue divine
To a loud trumpet and a point of war?
(*II Henry IV*, IV, i, 47–52)

Here Westmoreland is speaking to the Archbishop of York, one of the leaders of rebellion against Henry IV. In preparing to act these lines we need to know the precise meanings of a number of words which could be misleading because they look familiar and are still used, but in slightly different senses:

translate: literally, convert from one language into another. But there is also a sense of moving from one ecclesiastical office to another (usually a promotion). Here the first sense is developed, while the second stays in the background. *Translate* also means to change or convert, a sense which is picked up and emphasized in the word *turning,* in the fourth line.

bears such grace: has such felicity, charm, elegance; but there is also a sense of exhibiting a spiritually benign quality.

boist'rous: tumultuous.

Notice the patterns *out of—into, the speech of peace—the . . . tongue of war.* Westmoreland also relates to one another the ideas in *that bears such grace—harsh and boist'rous . . . war.*

graves: the normal literal sense is reinforced by suggestion of engraving.

point: spear point, but the word can also mean a period in punctuation.

In the last three lines we not only have antithesis of ideas, but a series of antithetical images, closed books and open graves, ink on the points of pens and blood on the points of lances, the Archbishop in normal ecclesiastical dress speaking theology to a background of bells and organ and the same man in armor exhorting men to battle against a background of trumpets. The whole passage is dominated by Westmoreland's intention of discomfiting the Archbishop by emphasizing his error in abandoning his vocation of peace for a career of war. Westmoreland has known his adversary a long time; he is also speaking for the rest of the rebels to hear and ponder. But chiefly the aim is to put pressure on York in preparation for the trick of persuading him to a virtual surrender.

When an actor plays the character's intention the rhythm arises partly from the verbal patterns. Westmoreland knows that *speech of peace* will be balanced by *tongue of war*, and so on. Intention and emotion affect pace, volume and intensity, while patterns of pitch and vowel length join in counterpointing with the recurring metrical pattern of stressed and unstressed syllables.

For an actor, this sort of familiarity with and sensitivity to the words as part of the action of the role serves as the foundation for style in performance. This is a sensitivity in which the imagining of the lines as actions of a character is combined with a simultaneous response to them as poetic art. At some stages of preparation the actor is most conscious of the verbal techniques, and may enjoy them partly for what they are as verbal art, and partly for the fact that they lead him to a perception of the actions to be played. In performance, however, he is more concerned with the imagining and playing of these actions as if he were the character. Then the rhythm of his performance evolves from what he is as man and actor responding to the playwright's art as a user of language and as an imaginer of character in action.

Style of acting has other elements. First comes our knowledge (usually incomplete) of the behavior of people on and off the stage at the time when the play was written. Second comes what seems right to the actor in the light of that knowledge and of his knowledge of his own contemporaries, again both on the stage and off. And third must be taken into account what is right for the audience in the light of their expectation of behavior both on and off the stage.

An artist's style is his manner of organizing his medium in order to communicate his work of art in it. Shakespeare's style in Westmoreland's lines cannot be described verbally; but it can be apprehended by a mind and body responding to the imagined action of this character communicated in these arrangements of words. The contrast which his intention demands is expressed in these patterns. From the right deep-seated awareness of them in relation to the character's actions comes the acting style. We do not know exactly how a great nobleman carried himself at such a moment off the stage in the 1590s, nor how he was performed by an actor onstage. Enough is known, however, to call for great dignity and elegance which do not inhibit sarcasm and anger. Yet the result must not seem ludicrous or hyperbolic to the actor today and to his audiences. And set firmly amid our uncertainties we have one sure guide, the actual verbal relationships of Shakespeare's text.

The actor's main task is to create character, to play the character's actions "as if he were the very man." Not only style but character demands understanding of the rank and position of the role in the society which has been imagined in the play. This may not always be an exact image of Shakespeare's society, but his England can usually be taken as a guide, provided we are alert to the fact that there may be deviations in some circumstances.

Most of Shakespeare's characters have been imagined by their author as what used to be called in England, "gentlefolk." In the plays, as in the society in which he lived, there is a fundamental distinction between those who are "gentle" and those who are not, those who are "base."

In Shakespeare's England the gentle were in two main groups, the more important of which (though smaller numerically) consisted of people bearing titles bestowed on them or their ancestors by the monarchy; all the titles but that of knight could be inherited. The word "lord" might be used of duke, marquis, earl, viscount and baron. The larger and less exalted group consisted chiefly of simple gentlemen, each with the style of "master"; but this group also contained, slightly higher in rank, those persons entitled "esquire," the younger sons of peers and their heirs male, the heirs male of knights; certain officials and court functionaries were also legally entitled "esquire."

It was difficult, if indeed possible, to assume illegally the title of a knight or of any higher rank, as all were either bestowed on a man by a monarch or had been so bestowed by a monarch on an ancestor, and were therefore a simple matter of record. But a man might more easily contrive to become accepted as a simple gentleman, a standing which derived from no formal public gift by the monarch; similarly a simple gentleman might illegally arrogate to himself the style "esquire."

In a rough and ready way a man who managed to have himself accepted by his neighborhood as a gentleman could assume the privileges and responsibilities of gentility. Whatever the original source of his money, to be accepted as gentle he must own land, now the fount from which his income flowed; he must not engage in trade or manual labor (though he was permitted a learned profession). He could also live on the proceeds of an office under the crown or on gifts from the crown or great nobles without forfeiting gentility. For the very reason that a man could achieve gentility by a sort of "squatter's right," the monarch (Elizabeth I, in particular) instituted a series of drives by the College of Heralds who visited each area of the land in succession, examining claims to gentility and disqualifying those whose claims were adjudged spurious, causing them serious loss of face in public. The only safety lay in the inheritance of a valid coat of arms and a pedigree registered with the Heralds in the past, or in a valid grant of arms registered in the claimant's lifetime. The Heralds were not incorruptible; pedigree and arms could be provided for a suitable incentive.

Anybody holding or having held the office of justice of the peace was regarded as qualified. Shakespeare's father was a justice of the peace for Stratford-on-Avon; this strengthened his claim to the arms of the Arden family inherited through his mother. These are the well-known arms associated with William Shakespeare.

All the gentlefolk in Shakespeare's plays have a sense of superiority to the base, ignoble population beneath them in society. In their world, as in his, the gentles are a small elite, and never forget that fact. In English society any man below the world of gentility, especially a servant or a laborer, could expect to be manhandled if he excited the dissatisfaction or anger of the elite. Once having attained manhood, however, a gentleman could expect to be spared such indignities, resenting any such violently, and finding there grounds for revenge. This distinction between two sections of society lies at the basis of Hamlet's remark to Polonius that if everybody were treated according to his deserts (as distinct from his social rank), *who would 'scape whipping?* The treatment of naval mutineers in 1618 was found shocking because gentlemen suffered the same punishment as the base; they were all hanged in public, hanging being a more shameful death than beheading. In some respects the base were treated almost as subhuman, as when Lord Herbert of Cherbury and Sir Thomas Lucy refused to allow seamen to take refuge in their boat from a ship sinking off Dover in 1609. The two gentlemen resorted to a drawn sword to keep the sailors off and saved themselves. Neither of these paragons nor their contemporaries found anything shameful in such selfishness.

Contempt for the base is the source of Tybalt's outrage when he finds Benvolio, a gentleman, apparently disgracing his sword (and his rank) by having drawn it against *these heartless hinds,* two serving men (*Romeo and Juliet,* I, i, 72).

While all who were gentle were accepted as elite, that large class was itself divided into hierarchical strata, ascending from simple gentlemen up through esquire and knight to the heights of duke and prince, with the monarch at the peak. A great noble kept up what was virtually a minor court. He acted as what was called a patron to lesser noblemen (his clients) who wore his colors on any occasion when these contributed to his prestige. As certain kinds of service at the royal court were not considered base, so similar offices in noble households were regarded as honorable, and thus were held by the gentle. Indeed, a book entitled *A Health to the Honorable Profession of Serving-men* attests to the fact that gentlemen and gentlewomen could act as servants to the household and estate of a nobleman or noblewoman in ways not regarded as menial, without losing gentility and becoming base in any way.

Actors and actresses of *Twelfth Night* need to know that

almost every role in the household of Olivia is that of a gentle person. Only Feste and the priest can be put in the base class with any certainty. "Signior" Fabian is probably gentle, as his title is the equivalent of "Master." Olivia is a countess, a rank high enough for an establishment of gentle servants; her cousin Sir Toby and his companion Sir Andrew obviously belong to the elite. Maria is referred to as a *gentlewoman*. And, as Malvolio addresses his unruly adversaries as *my masters* (II, iii, 92), so he is himself addressed by the Clown as *Master Malvolio* (IV, ii, 90). This is after Malvolio has sworn, *as I am a gentleman, I will live to be thankful to thee for't.*

Although he is a steward and *the fellow of servants*, Malvolio is a gentleman. He is not the fellow of base servants; he is one of the lower members of the elite (like Oswald in *King Lear*), one who serves the great, not their equal. He outrages Sir Toby in aspiring for Olivia's hand, not because he is socially too low ever to possess it, but because she, a great noblewoman, must condescend to him; she must make the first move. Toby is enraged that Malvolio's self-conceit is great enough to accept the forged letter as a matter of course. The prejudice is more personal than social, for any gentleman can be regarded as an honorable husband for any gentlewoman, however exalted her rank. Sebastian, a simple gentleman, is not too base for Olivia; his sister, Viola, a simple gentlewoman, is gentle enough to marry the duke. We should notice, moreover, that disguised as Cesario, she is referred to as *a gentleman*.

In Elizabethan life and in Shakespeare's plays an individual's dress and behavior conform to his rank. There was strict observance of precedence at court and in places of public resort, those inferior in rank expressing their inferiority by permitting superiors to precede them through doorways, and when going in to and sitting down at meals or places of recreation. A great personage was preceded by members of his household or clients wearing his colors; a similar train followed him. Removal of the hat in the presence of a superior signified subordination. This we can reproduce more or less exactly today, but other signs, such as bows, courtesies, going down on one or both knees, cannot be reproduced accurately. Nevertheless, when we know that the play demands them we can substitute modern equivalents which produce for the modern audience and actor the relationship existing in the play.

In the cities the highest ranks of those who were base consisted of burgesses, rich merchants. Their equivalents in rural districts were yeomen. A yeoman was "a freeman born English" owning land worth forty shillings a year in rent. Burgesses and yeomen were on the border between base and gentle. Some easily rose to be gentlemen; many others, not interested in elevation, were content to occupy a position generally accorded respect. Where a gentleman signed himself "master," by which title he was addressed, the legal title of a yeoman was "goodman" (Kent, disguised as Caius in *King Lear*, feigns ignorance of Edmund's identity, calling him, *goodman boy*). Beneath these all Englishmen were regulated in definite categories, either as qualified practitioners of a trade or handicraft, or as apprentices to one such. Anyone not able to justify himself as belonging to one of these categories was liable to penalties as a vagabond, unless he were a soldier or a sailor, infirm or employed in the service of a nobleman or of a member of the royal family. Actors did not fit into this social scheme; theirs was not a recognized trade or handicraft, for which reason they were liable to prosecution as vagabonds. To avoid such proceedings they would enter into the service of some nobleman or of a member of the royal family; as members of such households they held positions recognized by the law. At the same time they developed their own system of training, apprenticeship and ownership as if they were a trade like any other; but they retained the name and status of household servants, as the King's Men, the Queen's Men, the Lord Admiral's Men.

In Shakespeare's plays what holds good for the England of his time is assumed to apply to other European countries. The British past is also imagined as if it were Elizabethan England, with the same hierarchies, with inferiors accepting subordination. This is true not only of the History Plays and *Cymbeline*, but of *King Lear*. In Shakespeare's England the treatment accorded to a nobleman's or monarch's servant (whether base or gentle) was regarded as tantamount to that accorded to the great personage himself. Thus Goneril is outraged that her father has struck her gentleman; but this gentleman was struck *for chiding of* Lear's Fool; and Regan and Cornwall deliberately treat the disguised Kent shamefully because he is Lear's servant. Thus they express their contempt for Lear himself. Similarly, a servant who looked a noble master full in the face, giving stare for stare, and word for word in altercation, could expect punishment. So, in *King Lear* the king is provoked when Oswald deliberately insults him by look and word. In this play Gloucester is escorted with dignity by forerunners, a train following behind him. This is how Edgar has always seen his father move from place to place. And that is why when he sees his blinded father led by a single low-born tenant, he describes him as *poorly led*.

Within certain limits, which will be treated separately where necessary, Shakespeare imagines his Romans much as if they were Elizabethan, gentles, nobles and base menials. He does this not out of uneducated ignorance, for Elizabethan education developed a picture of ancient Rome in which much that was seen as good or bad in contemporary England was assumed to be true of the classical past. The sense of honor or of shame in the noble Roman in Shakespeare is that of his contemporaries. What he sees admirable in Brutus was regarded as equally admirable in an Elizabethan Englishman. Of course the assassination of Caesar is not equated with the killing of an anointed king, but both are felt as threats to order. Shakespeare's Romans are very like the Elizabethans in the characteristics which we have been considering.

We have treated some of the superficial distinctions in dress and behavior, by means of which society expressed the importance of distinctions of rank; but these pale beside the complex formality of what was known as "ceremony." Some indication of the nature of ceremony is given to us by the words of Sir Thomas Smith in 1583:

> And to no prince is done more honour and reverence than to the King and Queen of England, no man speaketh to the prince nor serveth at the table but in adoration and kneeling, all persons

> in the realm be bareheaded before him: insomuch that in the chamber of presence where the cloth of estate is set, no man dare walk, yea though the prince be not there, no man dare tarry there but bareheaded.

What took place in the presence of the monarch is suggested to us by the account written by the German Paul Hentzner of proceedings at Greenwich Palace one Sunday in 1599:

> First went Gentlemen, Barons, Earls, Knights of the Garter, all richly dressed and bareheaded; next came the Lord High Chancellor of England, bearing the seals in a red silk purse, between two, one of whom carried the royal sceptre, the other the sword of state in a red scabbard, studded with golden fleur-de-lis, the point upwards: next came the Queen, in the 65th year of her age (as we were told) very majestic. . . . As she went along in all this state and magnificence, she spoke very graciously, first to one, then to another (whether foreign ministers, or those who attend for different reasons), in English, French, and Italian: for besides being well skilled in Greek, Latin, and the languages I have mentioned, she is mistress of Spanish, Scotch, and Dutch *(Belgicum).* Whoever speaks to her, it is kneeling; now and then she raises some with her hand. . . . Wherever she turned her face as she was going along, everybody fell down on their knees. The ladies of the court followed next to her, very handsome and well-shaped, and for the most part dressed in white. She was guarded on each side by the gentlemen pensioners, fifty in number, with gilt halberds. In the ante-chapel, next the hall where we were, petitions were presented to her, and she received them most graciously, which occasioned the acclamation of *God save the Quene Elizabeth!* She answered it with *I thancke you myn good peupel.* In the chapel was excellent music; as soon as it and the service were over, which scarcely exceeded half-an-hour, the Queen returned in the same state and order, and prepared to go to dinner.

Hentzner also has an account of the "solemnity" with which the monarch's table was "set out." Although the Queen was absent, the ceremonial was as strict as if she had been there:

> A gentleman entered the room bearing a rod, and along with him another who had a table-cloth, which after they had both knelt three times, with the utmost veneration, he spread upon the table, and after kneeling again, they both retired. Then came two others, one with the rod again, the other with a salt-cellar, a plate and bread; when they had knelt as the others had done, and placed what was brought upon the table, they too retired with the same ceremonies performed by the first. At last came an unmarried lady of extraordinary beauty (we were told she was a countess) and along with her a married one, bearing a tasting knife; the former was dressed in white silk, who, when she had prostrated herself three times, in the most graceful manner approached the table and rubbed the plates with bread and salt with as much awe as if the Queen had been present. When they had waited there a little while, the yeomen of the guard entered, bareheaded, clothed in scarlet with a golden rose upon their backs, bringing in at each turn a course of twenty-four dishes, served in silver, most of it gilt; these dishes were received by a gentleman in the same order as they were brought, and placed upon the table, while the lady-taster gave to each of the guards a mouthful to eat of the particular dish he had brought for fear of any poison. During the time that this guard, which consists of the tallest and stoutest men that can be found in all England, 100 in number, being carefully selected for this service, were bringing dinner, twelve trumpets and two kettle-drums made the hall ring for half-an-hour together. At the end of all this ceremonial, a number of unmarried ladies appeared, who with particular solemnity lifted the meat off the table and conveyed it into the Queen's inner and more private chamber, where after she had chosen for herself, the rest goes to the ladies of the court.

The household of a great nobleman, such as Orsino, Macbeth, Gloucester (in *King Lear*), was organized on a similar scale, if slightly less magnificent, with prescribed ceremony and a host of gentle ushers, stewards, chamberlains. Anthony, Viscount Montague, issued a *Book of Orders and Rules* for his household. A later *Breviate touching the Order and Government of a Nobleman's House* of 1605 calls for a steward and a gentleman usher, both gentle, and a number of nongentle lower servants, eleven yeomen of the cellar, pantry, wardrobe, two yeomen ushers, various cooks, a caterer and slaughtermen.

In every ceremony strict precedence was observed in accordance with rank. Even in circumstances which we do not regard as ceremonial today, Shakespeare's contemporaries maintained formality. A great nobleman could expect to be greeted formally by the mayor of any town through which he passed. When the mayor of Chester failed to appear to pay the respects of the city to the Earl of Arundel in 1635, he was vigorously denounced for his tardiness by that nobleman. The Earl snatched the mayor's staff from him with a shout: "I'll teach you to know yourself and attend peers of the realm."

During St. George's Day celebrations in Whitehall Chapel the Queen's empty seat was treated with the same ceremony as if she had been in it; each Lord of the Garter made three obeisances to it. It is therefore obvious that an actor playing Henry V must imagine himself accustomed to being treated by his subjects in the way that Queen Elizabeth was treated by hers when he asks:

> And what have kings that privates have not too,
> Save ceremony—save general ceremony?
> And what art thou, thou idol ceremony?
>
> (*Henry V*, IV, i, 255–57)

And Richard II realizes how far he has been misled by the same sort of "adoration," when he cries bitterly to his followers:

> Cover your heads, and mock not flesh and blood
> With solemn reverence; throw away respect,
> Tradition, form and ceremonious duty.
>
> (*Richard II*, III, ii, 171–73)

All Shakespeare's kings and queens have accepted "ceremony" as their due, as a tribute to a quality in them which distinguishes them from mere flesh and blood. And so to a lesser degree do all his gentle characters. Conversely, the base expect to treat them as if they were not common clay.

Much emphasis is given in this book to the need for actors to understand that Shakespeare was a very precise and competent artist, who knew exactly what he was doing, who has provided his characters with motives for everything which they say and do, who has himself imagined the relationships between them. To appreciate Shakespeare's art at its true value, to grasp his precision, the consistency of his work, is also to realize that an actor does not have quite as much scope to play what might be theatrically effective as is often assumed to be the case. What freedom is an actor justified in claiming in the interpretation of his role? This varies from dramatist to dramatist, but all dramatists write for performance (Shakespeare, too), in which they must give scope for the actor to use his art and add something to what is to be derived from the script. This gives us essentially an imagining of actions to obtain specific objectives in relation to one another. In his text the dramatist, Shakespeare like anybody else, gives us the essential actions which must be played, but rarely tells us how they are to be played. He also leaves it to the actors to add actions which he has not given, without which it is impossible to play those of the text. For instance, in Act Three, Scene Seven, of *King Lear,* when the Servant tries to prevent Cornwall from putting out Gloucester's other eye the text gives us the following actions: Cornwall's *My villain* shows the action of a nobleman about to deal with an insubordinate underling whom he despises. The Servant does not give way:

> Nay, then, come on, and take the chance of anger.

The text now gives the action of Regan only as a demand for a sword and an expression of resentment that a peasant should dare to oppose her husband with a weapon:

> Give me thy sword. A peasant stand up thus!

The next action in the text is that of the Servant:

> O, I am slain!

The text does not tell us anything more about the actions of the characters at this point. In performance, however, it is usual for the Servant to wound Cornwall, who stops fighting. Regan usually goes to support the wounded Cornwall, takes his sword and, either catching the Servant unawares or taking advantage of his reluctance to fight a woman, swiftly dispatches him. The actions added by the actors make it possible for them to play those of the text.

But these actions are not the only ones which can be added. Regan does not have to ask Cornwall for a sword; she can ask any of the armed men present for his. She does not need to move to support her husband. He does not need to move toward her. Indeed, a few lines further on, the text suggests that Cornwall has not realized nor made plain to anyone else how badly he has been hit:

> *Regan:* How is't, my lord? how look you?
> *Cornwall:* I have receiv'd a hurt.

Although in most, if not all, modern performances, Regan kills the servant herself, there is no demand for this particular action in the text. It is appropriate, and it allows the actions of the text to be played (i.e., the Servant receives a mortal wound, *O, I am slain!*). Indeed, there is an indication in Act Four, Scene Two, that it is appropriate for the Servant to be attacked by Cornwall, Regan and their retainers, without her actually touching him. The Messenger tells Albany that Cornwall *flew on* the Servant *and amongst them fell'd him dead* (IV, ii, 75–76).

The points to be noted are, first, that the text gives us certain actions, but does not tell us how they are to be played; the playwright relies on his actors to act appropriately. And, second, he also relies on them to add actions without which those of his text cannot be played. When we keep these two points in mind we realize that careful study of Shakespeare's text provides an actor with very precise guidance without infringing on his right of interpretation to act appropriately in his exercise of his powers as a creative artist.

TROILUS AND CRESSIDA

Act One, Scene One

TROILUS IS ONE OF the sons of Priam, King of Troy, the city besieged by the Greeks in an effort to regain Helen, abducted by Paris, another son. Troilus has fallen in love with Cressida, daughter of Calchas, a Trojan priest who has deserted to the Greeks. Pandarus is her uncle. He knows that she has no moral objection to giving herself to Troilus. Nevertheless, she is putting up a resistance; Pandarus is determined to overcome this for Troilus.

varlet: a person of gentle birth, serving as personal servant to a man of higher rank. This service does not compromise his own gentility.
unarm: take off arms and armor.
none: i.e., no heart.
Will this gear . . . mended: Will this trouble never be put right?
The Greeks are strong, etc.: Notice the structure of these lines, with the repetitions, *strong—strength, skilful—skill, fierce—fierceness*. This is a combination of two rhetorical figures, *climax* and *polyptoton* (see *Acting Shakespeare*, pp. 20–24, 33–35). The actor must concentrate on the intention, on communicating it in the words and in his acting.
tamer: less fierce.
fonder: (1) more foolish, (2) more insipid.
unpractic'd infancy: untrained childhood (i.e., an untrained infant or, possibly, a guileless infant).
make: act, do.
tarry: wait for.
bolting: sieving.

blench at suff'rance: shy from resignation, resigned tolerance of suffering.
thence: not there, elsewhere.
wedged with: split with (i.e., as with a wedge).
rive: split.
light a scorn: shine mockingly (i.e., not lighting up the sky in a sustained way). Some editors print *a storm* instead of *a scorn.*
couch'd: expressed.
mirth: joy, merriment.
wit: intelligence. Cassandra has the gift of prophecy.

Pandarus speaks as if it were necessary to open Troilus' uncomprehending eyes to the beauty and intelligence of Cressida. But he needs no convincing. Either Pandarus is a chatterer, or he thinks that his talk must be acceptable to a man as much in love with her as Troilus is.

indrench'd: immersed, saturated.
spirit of sense: a very subtle and sensitive physical secretion essential to the functioning of the senses (for a full account see Vol. 2 of this book, pp. 102 f., and *Shakespeare's Eden,* pp. 251 ff.).
balm: healing ointment.
the mends: the remedy, or the remedies.
I have had my labour for my travail: I have done my hard work for no reason except that it has meant trouble to me.
on: by.

In this altercation the actor may choose to play Pandarus, either as confused and not realizing how much Troilus values Cressida, or as a shrewd person, resolved to intensify the Prince's longing for her (the latter is the more probable).

make no more: do no more.
clamours: loud noises, noisy voices.
upon this argument: over, concerning this theme.
starv'd: thin, tenuous.
tetchy: peevish, touchy.
suit: appeal.
Daphne: a nymph who evaded the advances of Apollo.
Iliam: This is often used of the city of Troy, but here only of Priam's palace.

flood: sea.
Aeneas: another of Troilus' brothers. Traditionally, the founder of Rome after the fall of Troy.
sorts: fits.
horn: the sign of a cuckold. Paris cuckolded Menelaus in abducting his wife, Helen, the cause of the Trojan war.
would I might: I wish I could.
I may: I can.
(Aeneas and Troilus leave toward the battle.)

Act One, Scene Two

Cressida is an experienced woman with no moral objection to accepting Troilus as her lover, but she values her independence and has not yet made up her mind to give it up. If she decides to accept his love she does not intend to commit herself to him completely, but rather to enjoy her conquest of a splendid and heroic young prince.

commands as subject: dominates.
fix'd: unshakable.
was mov'd: i.e., lost control.
husbandry: economy, thrifty management (which traditionally involves early rising).
he was harness'd light: There are quibbles here on *harness'd*, meaning (1) wearing armor, (2) in traces to pull a vehicle, and on *light*, (1) not heavy, (2) illuminated (not dark). Before the horses of the sun in their harness had started to pull his chariot across the sky, Hector was up in his own light (bright) harness.
his cause of anger: the cause of his anger.
the noise goes: the rumor is.
a very man per se: a unique man, the sole man in his own outstanding class.
additions: titles, attributes.
churlish: rough, sullen, moody.
nature . . . humours: Nature can be read as meaning both an abstract principle of life and concrete physiological processes.

Humours—idiosyncrasies. *Humour* has a basic sense of physiological secretion, corresponding to a particular element (earth, air, fire or water). In the sense of "idiosyncrasy," *humour* derives from the fact that the predominance of one of the four physiological secretions in a human being's metabolism controls him psychologically as well as physically (see *Shakespeare's Eden*, pp. 251 ff.).
sauced: alleviated.
attaint: vice, defect.
against the hair: in conflict with a natural tendency.
Briareus: A monster in Greek myth endowed with one hundred hands and fifty heads.
Argus: A monster in Greek myth endowed with one hundred eyes.
cop'd: met, fought, encountered.
disdain: resentment.
lay about him: fight fiercely, strike hard.
in some: by several.
Condition, etc.: "If Troilus is himself, I have walked barefoot to India."
favour: complexion.
merry Greek: quibble on literal sense and on secondary sense of "harlot."
compass'd: bay, circular.
tapster's arithmetic: weak ability to count, reckon.
lifter: i.e., thief, with quibble on literal sense.
stand to the proof: (1) accept the test, (2) prove himself, (3) have an erection.
rack: torture to extract a confession.
Two and fifty: Priam had fifty legitimate sons and one bastard, Margarelon.
chaf'd: was angry.
against: just before, in time for, in expectation of.
bravely: excellently.
brave: fine, excellent.
anon: in a moment.
give the nod: call a fool, cause to look foolish.
laying on: exchange of blows.

tak't off: denigrate.
by God's lid: i.e., by God's eyelid (an oath).
goes: walks.
to boot: in addition.
chaff and bran: inessentials (removed in milling).
drayman: a carter, who draws the cart himself.
camel: i.e., beast of burden.
minc'd: (1) simpering, affected in manner, (2) mutiliated, deprived of an essential part. Cressida quibbles on (1) and a bawdy extension of (2) (i.e., lacking an essential part, his penis). She also quibbles on a third sense, "finely chopped and highly seasoned food."
date: time (with a quibble on the sense "fruit").
at what ward you lie: what defensive posture you adopt (in fencing).
at a thousand watches: on guard a thousand times.
Say one of your watches: Tell me one of your signals (i.e., challenge and password).
ward, watch: Cressida plays with the commonplace phrase *watch and ward* (i.e., guarding and defending). She says: "If I cannot defend what I do not want to be hit (i.e., pierced), I can superintend you to stop you from telling how I received the blow."
past watching: past guarding against.
unarms him: takes off his armor.
doubt: (1) fear, (2) not think.
than in the glass of Pandar's praise may be: than can be reflected in Pandarus' praise.
wooing: when being wooed.
she belov'd: beloved woman, she who is beloved.
That she, etc.: That woman has never existed who found that love was as sweet when once attained (or granted) as when desire was still begging for it.
Achievement . . . beseech: What has been gained can be commanded, what has not been gained must be begged for.

Here is the key to Cressida's behavior, as we noted above. She will not commit herself, even give herself physically, not wanting Troilus to have any hold over her. Only when she dominates him utterly will she give way to his *beseeching*. At this point she admits to herself that she loves him. But she has no confidence in his committing himself in unselfish love as a return. Her experience assures her that to admit love to a man is to invite his domination.

Act Two, Scene Two

In this scene there is a discussion and argument between Priam and four of his sons.

Nestor: one of the Grecian princes besieging Troy.
cormorant: a seabird with an enormous greed for fish. Controlled by a ring around its neck to stop it swallowing, the bird can be used to catch fish.
as toucheth my particular: as concerns me individually.
bowels: regarded as the seat of compassion and tenderness.
spongy: absorbent.
suck in: absorb.
the wound . . . surety: A sense of security damages peace.
secure: overconfident.
modest doubt: moderate fear, uncertainty.
tent: probe.
every tithe soul: The soul of every tenth man exacted by the war (i.e., the war has cost one out of every ten men, and every one of those ten has been as dear as Helen).
I mean of ours: He emphasizes the fact that their loss has been of their fellow citizens, what belongs to their city.
our name: were it Trojan.

Hector is a great hero, in no way afraid of the Greeks, ready to risk death whenever he is called upon; but he is convinced that Helen is not worth the bloodshed.

Troilus takes a different view, insisting that Helen has become inseparably involved with the honor of Priam and of all Troy, and that an attribute so vast as that honor cannot be measured by the yardstick of danger.

Fie: for shame.
counters: metal discs used in calculating (counting).
past . . . infinitude: his infinitude which outruns all comparison.
fathomless: immeasurable.
span: small measurement (actually the distance from tip of thumb to tip of little finger when the hand is fully extended. This is about nine inches).
bear . . . with reasons: support, conduct the great weight of his affairs with reasons.
sway: weight.

Troilus believes that despite all violence and suffering which ensues, Helen is essential to the honor of Troy and to the city's future fame. He believes that to yield her now is to lose all the prestige gained from withstanding the Greeks until now. While we may deplore these values, we should remember that they have been shared by millions of human beings; moreover, in Shakespeare's day, Troilus and his heroic brothers were a byword for honor and heroism for the very fact that in the story of Troy his attitude prevailed. Troilus is not an immature romantic young man, but a warrior of the stamp of Beowulf and Roland, prepared to take on impossible odds, and honored in consequence.

object of all harm: everything which is perceived as a harm.
Mercury is described and depicted as having small wings on his heels or on his sandals.
chidden: Mercury, Jove's messenger, was often scolded by him.
disorb'd: out of its sphere (i.e., a shooting star).
have hare-hearts: lack courage (be as timid as hares).
cramm'd: fattened, forced to take food.
respect: careful consideration.
lustihood: vigor.
what's aught . . . valu'd?: i.e., nothing has any intrinsic value, but is given one by human beings according to their set of values.

Here Troilus again accepts a rarely contested commonplace,

that honor cannot be evaluated in material terms (see *Conscience and the King*, pp. 38 f.). But Hector insists that human evaluation of deed or person is related to some essential quality in them.

his: its.

dotes: loves foolishly, is infatuated with.

is attribute: pays tribute to.

affects: loves.

without some image, etc.: without some appearance, sign of the merit which is loved.

Troilus insists that once honor has been involved in a decision, it cannot be maintained if the decision is arbitrarily reversed.

election: choice.

my election . . . will and judgement: My choice is guided by my will; my will is excited by my eyes, two experienced pilots who go back and forth between the perilous shores of will and reason.

avoid: evade.

there can be no evasion, etc: It is impossible to stand firm by honor while evading and shrinking from this.

remainder viands: food left over from a meal.

unrespective sieve: garbage pail that swallows everything with equal alacrity.

bellied his sails: i.e., helped to send him on his journey (literally, puffed out his sails, making them swell like bellies).

wranglers: opponents.

An *old aunt:* i.e., Hesione, sister to Priam.

wrinkles: gives wrinkles to.

avouch: admit.

issue: outcome.

rate: condemn, decry.

beggar: make valueless.

estimation: value, price.

warrant: confirm, guarantee.

eld: age.

betimes: early.

moiety: part.

moan: grieving.
strain: flow of impassioned language.
remorse: regret.
qualify: dilute, reduce the intensity of.
justness: validity.
event: outcome, consequence.
deject: depress.
distaste: make distasteful.
several: individual, respective.
touch'd: involved.
offend the weakest spleen: excite the weakest inclination to controversy and resentment.

Troilus is opposing Hector's question concerning *fear of bad success in a bad cause.*

Paris is happy to have Troilus' support; he insists that they all agreed when he carried off Helen, and that he will not give up now if they do not desert him.

convince: prove guilty of, convict.
attest: testify to before.
propension: inclination.
dire: terrible, horrible.
my single arms: my arms alone (unsupported).
propugnation: defense.
protest: insist.
pass: experience.
retract: disavow.
in the pursuit: in continuing to carry out.
rape: abduction.
ransack'd: carried off.
so degenerate a strain: descendant of a common ancestor so lacking in the essential virtue of the rest of the family.
gloz'd: commented, explicated.
allege: urge, plead.
conduce: promote, support, aid.
free: objective, unprejudiced, untied.
affection: passion.
of partial indulgence: in prejudiced (not impartial) indulgence.

benumbed: enthralled, stupefied.
back: again.
spritely: spirited.
propend: incline.
affected: wanted, loved.
magnanimous: great souled.
canonize: enroll among the glorious.
roisting: noisy, blustering.
factious: disunited, split into factions.
amazement: alarm, consternation.
advertis'd: informed.
great general: i.e., Achilles.
emulation: envious rivalry.

Act Three, Scene Two

stalk: walk like a ghost, silently; walk with dignity.
strange: newcome, unfamiliar.
staying: waiting.
waftage: conveyance over the river Styx.
Charon, Styx, etc.: In Greek mythology, the souls of the dead wait on the bank of the river Styx, until Charon ferries them across to the infernal regions.
propos'd: promised.
painted: brightly colored.
expectation: anticipation, experiencing imaginatively in advance.
relish: enjoyment, taste.
wat'ry: watering.
repur'd: purified, refined.
sounding: swooning.
ruder powers: coarser (less sensitive) faculties.
lose distinction in: be unable to keep separate.
battle: army.
be witty: use your wits.
fray'd: frightened.
sprite: spirit.

thicker: faster.
bestowing: function.

To some extent Cressida is sincerely reluctant to meet Troilus because she recognizes that he has fallen sincerely in love with her, will make demands on her to commit herself, which she does not wish to do. In her circumstances to commit herself to genuine love must mean unhappiness and dependence upon another person. She wants to keep her independence, does not want her happiness to be so closely involved with the wishes and fortunes of another person.

i' the fills: between the shafts.
rub on, etc.: take a devious path and hit the target.

The *rub* (i.e., a protuberance on the surface of a bowl) makes it run obliquely or in a curve. The player uses the *rub* to curve the bowl round obstructions to hit the central target (i.e., the master, called here the *mistress*).

tasted: proved, tested, sampled.
allow: acknowledge.
perfection in reversion: perfection promised in the future.
addition: rank, style of address.
play the tyrant: act like a tyrant.
but I might master: that I was not able to master it.

Cressida recalls the stresses of the past weeks, a time when she was unable to suppress her love for Troilus, but was still determined not to commit herself to him unless she was certain that he was equally committed to her, that he would not take advantage of her admission of love to dominate her.

counsel: private thoughts, secrets.
fool: (1) dupe, (2) darling.
roundly: bluntly, openly.
to keep, etc.: to keep her countenance unbroken and fresh.
blood: (1) passion, (2) body.
affronted: confronted.
winnow'd: purified, refined.
simplicity: plainness, lack of artifice. (For the structure of these lines, see *Acting Shakespeare*, p. 33.)

in fee-farm: with a grant of land in perpetuity.
falcon as the tercel: female hawk in conflict with the male.

Pandarus wagers all the ducks in the river on Cressida as a match for Troilus.

have interchangeably: i.e., have exchanged. This is the end of a formula which was applied to bonds and agreements. Pandarus declares that these kisses stand for deep commitments to one another by Troilus and Cressida, as if they had signed legal documents containing the formula.
abruption: breaking off.
curious dreg: minute residue (*curious* has the sense of overfastidious. Thus the statement means "What dreg does your overfastidiousness perceive?").

The image here is of a clear spring welling up copiously from the ground, but in which Cressida fearfully imagines dregs or pollution.

Cupid's pageant, etc.: i.e., the cast of Cupid's play contains no monsters.
confin'd: limited.
hares: These animals are traditionally associated with cowardice, as are lions with courage.
swains: lovers.
approve: confirm.
protest: assertion, insistence.
want: lack, are short of.
iteration: repetition.
plantage: vegetation (i.e., to the phases of the moon).
adamant: magnetic stone (loadstone).
to th' centre: to its immovable position at the center of the Ptolemaic universe.
authentic author: reliable writer, trustworthy expresser.
crown up: be the final statement, the highest point of.
sanctify: make holy.
the numbers: the verse.
characterless are grated: are ground to nothing without record (pronounced *char-ác-ter-less*).
stick: pierce.
Press it to death: Pressing to death was a torture which might

legally be applied to a prisoner charged with treason; weights were placed on his chest with additions made periodically until he was forced to answer or death ensued.
gear: equipment, something needed to accomplish a purpose.

Act Four, Scene Four

Cressida entered into a liaison with Troilus thinking she would be able to evade committing herself to him completely, that she would be able to retain her liberty of action. But she has found that her love makes her utterly dependent on him. Suddenly her father, Calchas, who has deserted Troy for the Greeks, has arranged for her to be exchanged for Antenor, a captured Trojan. The time has come for Cressida to leave Troy and Troilus, and to be escorted by Diomedes to her father in the Grecian camp. She is sincerely in love with Troilus and is overwhelmed with grief at having to leave him. The fact that she knows her own instability does not make her grieve any less at the parting.

fine: extreme.
violenteth in a sense: affects the sense as violently.
temporize with: compromise, negotiate with.
allayment: dilution.
dross: impurity, thrown off in the smelting of a metal.
qualifying dross: dross which modifies the strength.
In this image she imagines her love having been refined to utter purity, unweakened by any extraneous emotion.
spectacles: sights (with quibble on *pair of spectacles*).
strain'd: filtered (i.e., through a strainer).
fancy: love.
injury of chance: Fortune's injury.
puts back: obstructs.
beguiles: robs.
rejoindure: reunion.
embrasures: embraces.
rude: discourteous.

brevity: briefness, brief space.
discharge: unburdening, getting rid of.
distinct: individual.
consign'd: devoted, allocated to.
fumbles up: mumbles incoherently.
scant us: reduce our share, give us no more than a niggardly.
distasted: made distasteful, made bitter.
Genius: the attendant spirit which is, according to ancient lore, allocated to every person at birth and remains with that person until death.
anon: at once, in a moment.
merry Greeks: see above, p. 40.
see: i.e., see one another.

At this moment Cressida intends to be true to Troilus and would like to keep faith for the rest of her life. But she knows her own weakness and hates to admit it to herself. As a result she is wounded by his *be thou but true,* because it seems that he must doubt her.

deem: thought, assumption.
expostulation: opportunity for talk.
throw my glove: i.e., challenge.
maculation: impurity, stain.
fashion in: serve as an introduction to.
protestation: insistence.
imminent: impending, close at hand.
corrupt: bribe.

Troilus is afraid that she might not be able to withstand one or other of the Greeks, who throughout this play are regarded as setting the standards of elegance, sophistication and courtliness in conversation and bearing. He considers himself their inferior in these attributes.

well compos'd: with great natural gifts, excellently developed physically.
arts and exercise: skills and proficiencies.
parts with person: talents with physical attractiveness.
godly jealousy: godly—benevolent, *jealousy*—easily awakened fear of future loss. Troilus insists that his uncertainty comes from his own humility, which leads him to fear that she will find others really superior to him.

villain: dishonorable person.
lavolt: the dance called *lavolta* involved jumping in the air.
prompt and pregnant: disposed and ready.
dumb-discursive: silently eloquent.
may: can.
will not: do not want.
changeful potency: power which fluctuates.
opinion: false opinion.
moral: maxim.
all the reach of it: as far as it extends.
port: gate.
entreat her fair: behave well to her.

Diomedes recognizes Cressida for what she is. He plans to supplant Troilus and loses no time in attempting to ingratiate himself with her. Troilus is provoked by Diomedes' attitude.

charge: command.
bulk: lump, huge body, torso.
mov'd: provoked, excited.
answer my lust: do as I wish.
on charge: on command.
brave: boast, bravado.
bend: aim, direct.
spent: wasted.
remiss: negligent, slack.
address: make ready.

OTHELLO

Act Three, Scene Three

AT THIS POINT Desdemona still regards Iago as a plain, straightforward, rough diamond. An honest, loyal friend, tactless, but reliable: this is the image of himself that Iago has succeeded in impressing on all his superiors. In fact, he is treacherous, proud, full of resentment against Othello for having passed him over for promotion in favor of Cassio, a theoretician with far less practical experience of campaigning. Iago also resents the fact that Othello, a Moor, has married Desdemona. On top of all, Iago's exaggerated sense of personal honor resents the name of his wife, Emilia, being coupled by rumor with that of his commander, Othello. Even if the rumor has no foundation, its existence adds fuel to Iago's hatred. He intends to erode Othello's trust in Desdemona and Cassio, taking advantage of his own reputation for blunt, tactless, simple honesty. He will take advantage of two facts: first, Othello is old and black; second, he trusted Cassio (a young, elegant Venetian with superb manners) to woo Desdemona on his behalf.

The fact that Othello could do this shows his essentially trusting character. He has an assured confidence in his Venetian allies and masters. He does not suspect them of yielding to his wish to marry Desdemona only out of their great need of his services. He assumes that they respect him for what he is, and that they sincerely welcome him as a member of their state. Othello is not a jealous man by nature. He is far too trusting, and his trust exposes him to Iago. By jealousy, Shakespeare means a state of distrust, of fear of being caught unawares, of suffering a great loss as a result. With his intense suspicion, the jealous man combines an alert preparedness to anticipate and prevent in advance whatever loss he fears. Iago is determined to awaken this jealousy in Othello, to which end he has trapped Cassio into seeming to be the drunken cause of a riot the night before. Now Othello sees Cassio as irresponsible. Iago has also set his wife to make sure that Desdemona intercedes with Othello on Cassio's behalf. Iago has, in addition, advised Cassio to ask Desdemona's help. This scene opens with Desdemona assuring Cassio that she will do what she can for him.

strangeness: alienation, unfriendliness.
a politic distance: distance demanded by a policy of not offending the inhabitants of Cyprus.
supplied: filled by a substitute.
doubt: fear.
watch: stay awake.
shrift: confessional (on empty stomach).
suit: request.
solicitor: one who pleads on behalf of another.
his present reconciliation take: be reconciled to him now.
incur a private check: result even in a private reprimand (i.e., not public).
mamm'ring on: hesitating, stammering about.
bring him in: give attention to him.
boon: granting of a favor.
poise: weight.
wretch: affectionate nickname (ironic understatement of endearment).
conceit: idea.
close delations: secret, unintentional expressions of accusation.
ruminate: consider over and over.
apprehensions: suspicions, fears.
keep leets and law-days: take control of making judgments.
leet: court.
law-days: sessions, court days.
spy into deceptions: scrutinize in search of possible deceptions.
jealousy: alert suspicion to detect harm in advance and circumvent it.

conceits: has ideas.
immediate: essential, integral, inseparable.
filch: steal.
green-ey'd: alert, sharp-eyed. The epithet is derived from the fact that jealousy is perpetually alert. The eye of a jealous man is sharp and fresh with the vigor of youth. In *Romeo and Juliet* (Act Three, Scene Five), the Nurse tells Juliet that an eagle *Hath not so green* an eye as Paris. In other words, jealousy is eagle-eyed.

Othello's *O, misery* does not necessarily come from his feeling the misery already. He may be imagining it in others, with an imaginative awareness of what it can be.

Note how Iago plays with the sounds of *dotes, doubts.*
fineless: illimitable, endless.
still: ever.
exsufflicate: puffed out.
blown: puffed up.
revolt: rebellion, turning away.
Away at once with love or jealousy: Othello insists that he will not tolerate a state of jealousy. Grounds for suspicion must be supported by absolute proof; without it he will abandon suspicion. If it is confirmed it will mean the end of his love. Without absolute proof there will be an end to his jealousy. He will not love and suspect; he will not suspect and love.
look to: watch.
secure: secure without justification, oversecure (this is the Elizabethan sense of the word).
self-bounty: natural generosity of mind.
abus'd: deceived.
seel: hoodwink (see the account of seeling in the section on *Macbeth*, p. 213).
oak: mentioned because it is a tough, dense wood.
grosser issues: more substantial importance (or results).
larger reach: wider scope.
affect: have desire for.
in position: in assertion, in argument.
recoiling to: returning to.
match you with her country forms: may regard you as equal to what she is accustomed to from her own country.

scan: examine.
strain: urge, exert pressure for.
entertainment: being maintained in place.
free: guiltless.
government: self-control.
haggard: untamed female hawk which flies where it pleases.
jesses: straps fastened round the legs of a trained hawk.
at fortune: at random.
Haply: perhaps.
chamberers: gallants (i.e., frequenters of ladies' chambers).
vapour: damp fumes.
keep a corner: reserve a small space.
prerogativ'd: privileged.
unshunnable: inevitable, not to be evaded.
forked: i.e., with the horns of a cuckold.
quicken: conceive, acquire life.
watching: staying awake.
generous: noble.
napkin: pocket handkerchief.
conjur'd: impressed on her earnestly.
reserves: keeps.
work: embroidery.
common thing: something shared with others (i.e., her vagina).
earnest: determined.
Be not . . . on't: admit to no knowledge of it.
proofs: confirming evidence.
conceits: ideas, fantasies.
act: working, action, application.
mandragora: soporific.
drowsy syrups: soporifics.
medicine: act as a medicine to procure.
What sense, etc.: In which way could I experience?
I found not Cassio's kisses, etc.: There was no physical evidence of any intimacy with Cassio. This shows that Desdemona is a virgin when she marries Othello. He may well be thinking that whatever has happened must have been since the wedding.
pioneers: laborers (the basest of the camp).
big wars: heroic campaigns.

make ambition virtue: Normally, ambition is regarded as a vice. It may be regarded as a virtue, however, when it leads men to strive to outdo one another in skill and valor in great campaigns. Then it provokes heroism.
quality: attribute, attainment.
circumstance: formal display.
mortal engines: death-dealing instruments.
counterfeit: imitate, copy.

Iago must *prove,* or Othello wants to hear nothing.
probation: proof.
bear no hinge or loop: cannot be pushed aside and has no loophole in it.
remorse: pangs of conscience.
On horrors, etc.: i.e., accumulate horrors on top of horror.
satisfied: convinced.
supervisor: onlooker.
grossly gape on: coarsely stare at.
behold her topp'd: look at her covered.
prospect: open view.
bolster: share a bolster (i.e., lie together).
prime: sexually vigorous.
in pride: in sexual desire.
imputation: charge, accusation.
a foregone conclusion: a termination which has happened before.
shrewd doubt: sharp fear.

Notice how Iago relates *thicken* to *thinly.* "This may help to give substance to other fears which were tenuous before."

Notice the image of *black vengeance* and *hollow hell.*
tyrannous: remorseless.

Othello subdues his love for Desdemona, subordinating it to the resentment which comes from his outraged pride.
fraught: burden (freight).
aspics': asps'.

Othello's image involves the bosom swelling with rage; it is charged with asps' tongues, the poison of which also induces swelling. His answer to Iago's cunning suggestion that his mind might change is to insist that no such thing will ever happen. Othello is convinced of Desdemona's treachery; from now on his mind will be completely devoid of every thought of love, of memories of humility and tenderness toward his wife. Instead he will be dominated by unchanging thoughts of bloodshed, which will never leave him until he has satisfied himself with a comprehensive and extensive (*wide*) revenge.

At this moment Othello is consumed chiefly by rage against those Venetians whom he believes to have conspired to make a fool of him while binding him in gratitude for Desdemona to serve the Venetian state. From the complete trust which lets him ask Cassio to woo on his behalf, from the assurance with which he congratulated himself on having been accepted by the Venetians, valuing him at his true worth as man and nobleman, he has swung in suspicious revulsion. As great as his trust was is his present distrust; he has convinced himself that they have all joined to make use of him and laugh at him, all except Iago. He alone is to be trusted; the rest are enemies; they must be destroyed, whoever they might be and however many. His revenge is not restricted to Desdemona and Cassio. Othello expresses his cold rage in the image of the *Pontic Sea* (the Black Sea), from which the water flows unchanged, icy and swift, into the *Propontic* (the Sea of Marmora) and the *Hellespont* (the Dardanelles). Like the water, his rage will not change its nature or its course. And as the water flows on relentlessly, maintaining its *Pontic* quality in all three names (*Pontic*, Pro*pontic*, Helles*pont*), so his thoughts will be only of blood, he will not think back to days and nights of love, but only forward to the moment when his vengeance will destroy everyone who has derided, plotted against him, hurting his honor and his pride. (For a fuller treatment of this *Pontic Sea* speech, see *Acting Shakespeare*, pp. 112–14.)

marble: unchanging.
elements: i.e., the four elements of which the world and its inhabitants are made. In the Elizabethan view, each of the elements occupies a part of the space within the sphere of the moon.

clip: embrace, surround, enfold.
execution: exercise.
wit: reason.
to obey shall be in me remorse: My pity shall function as obedience to him, however horrifying the business may be.
put thee to't: employ you, set you to work.
lewd minx: lascivious, wanton woman.

KING LEAR

Act One, Scene Four

If but as well . . . call hither my fool.

IN PREPARING TO PLAY this scene, the actor of Kent has to note that he must imagine himself to be a man who has lived for many years as a great nobleman, one of the highest in the realm, one of the King's most powerful counselors, one to whom the King has been consistently most gracious, showing him great trust. Kent has been inured to the deference and respect of all the King's subjects of inferior rank to him. Very recently all this has been lost when the King banished Kent, who now goes in danger of being killed on sight if recognized. In returning to serve (and possibly save) his king, Kent risks his life. To achieve his end of serving the King, Kent is prepared to undergo vicissitudes regarded by men of his rank and breeding as worse than death. He has adopted the disguise of a very menial servant, not primarily to evade death, but to preserve himself to serve his master. Kent has swallowed his pride and is ready to accept innumerable humiliations; he is dominated by love for and loyalty to Lear, the man, as well as Lear, the King. He genuinely regards himself as expendable, as continuing to breathe for no other purpose than to serve the King. And he must suppress every trace of the elegance and self-assurance of the great nobleman in manner of speech and bearing, exposing himself to the hard realities of life for a man at the other end of the social scale; he must behave so consistently as this man, the menial servant, that his disguise is never penetrated.

At the end of the play Kent is described by Edgar as one who:

> Follow'd his enemy king, and did him service
> Improper for a slave.

In this scene Kent is ready to follow the King and do this service, but note that he never regards Lear as his enemy.

As the scene begins Kent is satisfied to have made his way to Lear without his disguise having been penetrated. He is happy to know that he will soon be with Lear, in Lear's presence, if not yet in his service. But he knows that his greatest test may come with this meeting; for Lear will recognize him if his disguise is not perfect in speech as well as in appearance; he must therefore *other accents borrow.* As a result, he feels a certain tension, a resolution to try, with no absolute certainty that he will alter his voice well enough to deceive the man who knows him so well.

diffuse: disorder, make indistinct.
intent: determination.
issue: outcome.
raz'd: obliterated.
full of labours: capable of and ready to undertake all kinds of work.
stay a jot: wait the least bit.
"Let me have dinner with no delay at all."

At this moment Lear speaks as if he were in his own household, not his daughter's. If he causes inconvenience, it is not intentionally. He is not deliberately encroaching on Goneril's authority. As he has ungrudgingly given her half of his kingdom, he has the right to presume on her yielding him a minor establishment inside her household. A bargain was struck in the first scene of the play. He has given her a lot; she owes him some indulgence. He does not want too much; he knows he must not take offense easily or find slights where they may not be intended by his daughter and her husband and their servants (noble and base), but he expects the bargain to be kept. He does not expect love from Goneril, nor even a gratitude which softens her toward him, but recognition of a bargain to be kept.

When Lear addresses Kent, the latter must reply with some deference, which he has to combine with the right kind of self-confidence to engage the King's interest. He knows Lear very well from years of service.

What dost thou profess?: (1) What is your occupation?, (2) What do you claim to be capable of?
put in trust: have confidence in.
converse with: associate with.
fear judgement: i.e., the Last Judgment, listen to my conscience.
cannot choose: have no alternative.
eat no fish: eat better food than fish (this may be a way of saying I am not a Papist).
What wouldst thou?: What dost thou want?
Dost thou know me?: Kent's very confident *you* makes Lear wonder if this newcomer knows who he is.
countenance: facial expression and general bearing.
Kent's answer, *Authority*, interests Lear.
keep honest counsel: (1) keep an honest matter secret, (2) keep a secret honestly.
qualified in: suitable for.
diligence: (1) speed, (2) assiduousness.
yet: still.

Act Three, Scene One

As Kent is disguised as a servant, he cannot exercise any authority in searching for Lear. When he recognizes the Gentleman as one of the King's personal attendants, he hopes that Lear will not be too far away. He expects the Gentleman to be able to tell him where to find the King. The Gentleman does not know where Lear is, but tells Kent what was happening when he last saw him. The actor must imagine himself to have just seen the incident he describes, just before he became separated from Lear.

fretful: angry.

elements: (1) the weather, (2) the four elements (earth, air, fire and water).
main: land.
things: the world.
make nothing of: (1) annihilate, (2) show no respect for.
little world of man: i.e., his body and mind (himself). (For a fuller account of the microcosm, see Bamborough, *The Little World of Man*, pp. 20–26, 78; and *Shakespeare's Eden*, pp. 256 f.)

The Gentleman stresses the horror he feels at realizing that Lear has a greater storm within him than that which is raging outside him, which is raging around them all.
cub-drawn: suckled dry (and therefore fierce with discomfort and hunger).

Kent is anxious to learn if Lear is alone, or, if not, who is with him. But the Gentleman knows only that the Fool is with Lear, and is afraid that the Fool's insistence on reproaching the King for his folly will hurt, not help, him.

Realizing the urgency of the situation Kent makes a decision to confide in the Gentleman. Kent has returned in disguise to try to protect Lear and to act as a link with Cordelia, whom he left in France. He knows now that he must bring her father to her at Dover; in addition, however, he must send word to her of the latest developments, of the new dangers which will threaten Lear once it is known that she has landed at Dover.

Kent analyzes the situation between Albany and Cornwall as far as he knows it.

warrant: guarantee.
note: observation.
commend . . . to you: ask you to be responsible for a matter of great consequence.
seem no less: seem nothing else.
snuffs: quarrels.
packings: intrigues.

Kent detests both the dukes for their treatment of Lear (in fact, he is mistaken about Albany, but he shares his mistake with the Gentleman).

furnishings: trimmings.
power: army.
scatter'd: divided.
wise in our negligence: (1) wise where we are negligent, (2) well-informed of our negligence.
at point: ready, about.
their open banner: (1) their unfurled banner, (2) their banner openly.
Now to you: Kent has been giving the Gentleman confidential information, information which a servant might not be expected to possess. He now has to convince his listener that he really knows what he is talking about, then to persuade him to do as asked.
on my credit: on your belief in me, on my good faith.
so far To: so far as to.
making: for making.
just: accurate.
plain: complain.

Kent sees that the Gentleman has not yet been persuaded, and therefore adds that he, too, is of gentle rank.

assurance: reliable information, conviction.
office: function, service.
I will talk further: i.e., the Gentleman is still not convinced.

Kent now makes his final effort, knowing the importance of sending the message to Cordelia.

out-wall: outside, exterior.

In this dialogue Kent has been speaking with his old authority as a great nobleman (see pp. 60 f. regarding his transformation), not in accordance with his menial disguise.

fellow: companion, servant, person of low rank.
to effect: i.e., in their practical importance.
in which your pain . . . this: You exert yourself in that direction, I'll take this.

Act Four, Scene One

Edgar, the elder and legitimate son of the Earl of Gloucester, was rejected by his father and proclaimed an outlaw as the result of false testimony by the younger son, the bastard, Edmund. After one lucky escape from pursuers, Edgar has disguised himself as a madman by the expedient of stripping away his rich clothing. Unable to risk searching for a disguise, he has remained almost naked, like a vagrant madman, darkening his skin, piercing his flesh with wooden skewers, feigning insanity, erasing all trace of his noble appearance and behavior. Despite all that has happened to him, however, Edgar has maintained his determination to survive. In addition, he has wasted no time or energy on resentment and brooding over the wrongs done him by a father. At this point in the play he thinks he has nothing more to lose, his fortunes cannot deteriorate further.

Yet better thus . . . flatter'd to be worst: It is yet better to be like this and acknowledged as despised, than always to be the worst while being openly flattered, but secretly despised.
dejected: debased, cast down.
stands still: endures, is stable.
the lamentable . . . to laughter: The change which brings grief is the change from the best (which must be to something worse); the change from the worst brings rejoicing (it must be to something better).
The wretch . . . blasts: The wretch whom thou hast blown to the lowest state of fortune has nothing that thy blasts can claim from him (i.e., has been stripped by them of all he had).

But when Edgar sees his blinded father, led wretchedly by one poor tenant, he suffers more than he thought possible. Fortune can still hurt him through the miseries of his father. Edgar uses the words *poorly led,* because he has been accustomed to seeing Gloucester proceeding about his private and public affairs splendidly accompanied by lesser noblemen preceding him in procession, with clients and servants wearing his colors or livery, with heralds and pursuivants, and armed escorts. Now Gloucester's splendor has been reduced to one simple aged tenant.

But that . . . to age: Only because of such changes as this are people ever willing to die.

Edgar knows from experience of the impulses to despair which afflict men in misfortune. He has overcome his temptation, is confident that he will never yield to it, but he knows what misfortune is, and so he understands just what his father is going through and feels compassion for him.

At this point in physical agony and shock, tormented by the shattering realization of the truth about his treatment of Edgar, aware of the miseries of the King, his master, Gloucester wants death, but even more he wants to feel the beloved features of his wronged son, Edgar.

stumbled: went astray, tripped up.
means: wealth, possessions.
mere: utter, sheer.
defects: (1) things we lack, (2) organs of which we are deprived.
commodities: assets, advantages, benefits: i.e., our possessions give us the illusion of security, and the things that we lack (and the organs we lose) turn out to be assets.
the food . . . wrath: i.e., on whom your deluded father fed his anger.
Might . . . touch: Gloucester is referring to the fact that a blind person can form a mental image of shape and surface by means of the sense of touch. He remembers the beloved features and wants to renew his image of them, tracing them in a caress. He can never see Edgar again, but his love will be satisfied in touching his son.
The worst . . . the worst: i.e., we have not experienced the worst so long as it is not possible to look back on it when things have improved (Edgar's logic is based on the fact that what seems to us the worst may be followed by even worse. Only after improvement can we see what was worst).
has some reason: is not devoid of reason.
I have heard more since: I am better informed now.

Gloucester actually saw Edgar on the heath in the storm with Lear but did not recognize him. Since then he has heard the truth, when betrayed to torture by Edmund. And since then, Edgar has overcome his impulse to reveal himself and try to help Lear. He has determined once more to survive in obscurity until circumstances beyond his control give him an opportunity to rise once more, just as circumstances beyond his control were responsible for the calamity which has overtaken him. When he sees that the time has come, however, Edgar is determined to act. That time has not yet come.

wanton: irresponsible.
How should this be?: i.e., what is happening here?
Bad is the trade: It is a bad occupation.
the times' plague: the time's destruction.
Do as I . . . thy pleasure: Do as I ask you—or rather do what you wish—but above all leave me.
'parel: apparel.
Come on't what will: whatever the consequences.

The Bedlam reminded Gloucester, in a way which is not clear to him, of Edgar last night. The same thing is happening now; as he thinks of what he was deceived into doing, the wish never to have done this, never to have put himself as well as Edgar into Edmund's power, prompts the agonized declaration that we are to the gods *as flies to wanton boys.* And from this agony comes the determination to kill himself, making use of the Bedlam to put him in a position to do so.

For Edgar, the difficulty is to keep his composure enough to continue to play the madman consistently and disguise his voice from his blind father. He must not let Gloucester touch his face, for fear that will lead to recognition. His genuine compassion is transmuted into the crazed *Bless thee, master.* Edgar says *master* deliberately, as if he thought Gloucester no more than a simple gentleman, giving no hint that he knows him for an earl.

Gloucester asks the Old Man to get the clothes for Edgar as a way of being alone with the Bedlam long enough to direct him to lead the way to the top of the cliff. There is also a genuine wish to give the poor naked fellow some clothes for protection and warmth.

daub it: dissemble (literally, paint it white).

When Edgar approaches Gloucester, he sees for the first time that his father has just been blinded, that he is still bleeding from the ill-treatment.

horse-way: bridle path.

mopping: grimacing.

mowing: making faces (Fr. *moué*).

who since . . . waiting-women: i.e., who therefore takes possession of.

Gloucester feels glad that at least he can do some good in his misfortune. Of course, there is bitterness in his remark.

strokes: blows (of Fortune).

heavens deal so still: (1) May the heavens always share things like this, (2) *heavens, deal so still* (an invocation).

superfluous: too well-provided, pampered.

dieted: fed, fostered, cherished.

lust-dieted: whose lusts are fostered and satisfied.

slaves your ordinance: tramples on your commandment (makes subservient to him whatever you ordain).

quickly: (1) swiftly, (2) in a lively manner, (3) in a way which affects the senses of the living body (i.e., not after death merely).

distribution . . . excess: The appointing of his own portion to each should destroy anyone's having too much (in law *distribute* meant handing over a case to special investigators to conduct a reliable investigation).

bending: beetling.

fearfully: terrifyingly.

confined deep: bordering sea.

repair the misery thou dost bear: transform, alleviate the misery you endure.

Act Four, Scene Two

This scene takes place in the courtyard of Albany's castle. Goneril and Edmund have been riding to her home after the blinding of Gloucester, his father. On their journey they have come to an arrangement to displace Albany as her husband, and probably as ruler of half of the country. In any case, Goneril despises Albany for sentimentality because he does not approve of her treatment of her father.

They are met by Oswald, Goneril's steward. A steward in the household of a great noble or royal person is in no way a menial. He is a man of gentle birth who acts much the same way as an agent to a great landed estate, and who also organizes the household without performing any service himself that is unfit for a gentleman. Oswald is a confidential servant to his mistress, who entrusts him with matters of great importance and even leaves a certain amount of scope for his independent judgment. He is in no way too obsequious or too subservient. He shares Goneril's view of Albany and is her loyal supporter to the end.

mild: merciful.
Our wishes on the way, etc: On the way they have both expressed wishes that Albany could be removed. Now she sees a way of turning the wishes into realities—*effects.*
musters: levying and parading of troops.
conduct his powers: lead his forces (Cornwall, badly wounded, is not fit to do this himself).
change arms: (1) exchange weapons, (2) exchange insignia. The distaff in heraldry stands for the female side of a family. Goneril has decided to exchange it for the emblem of the male, the sword.

Notice that Goneril regards Oswald as *this trusty servant.*
decline: put lower.
stretch thy spirits, etc.: (1) inspire you to aspire higher, (2) give you an erection.
usurps: has no right to possess.
I have been worth the whistle: There was a time when you thought me worth some little attention.

Goneril takes the offensive. She is surprised by his intensity, but does not yield an inch, secure in her secret arrangement with Edmund.
I fear: I have misgivings about.
disposition: (1) character, (2) intentions.

it: its.

Albany is overcome with disgust and foreboding for what she has done and what may be expected to happen to her if she continues in her actions.

That nature . . . certain in itself: That nature which despises its origin cannot be contained securely within its own limits.

sliver: tear, slice away.

disbranch: sever herself like a lopped branch (like a branch which lops itself off).

From her material sap: from the sap which has given her life and nourished her.

material: essential, forming the substance of.

deadly use: destruction.

A well-known Renaissance emblem likens the criminal being executed by the sword to a withered branch being cut from the tree by the gardener's pruning hook. Albany imagines Goneril not waiting for the gardener to do this. She cuts herself off while superficially healthy; she will come to the end appropriate to the diseased by her own hand, not the executioner's.

savour: stink, smell of. *Savour* also means to perceive a smell with a sense of relish.

Filths, etc.: Filths can smell nothing but their own stench, which is all they can emit and all that they enjoy.

perform'd: actually carried out.

head-lugg'd: dragged by the head.

visible: in the sight of men and women.

tame: chasten, check, quell ("chasten these vile criminals").

milk-liver'd: white livered, i.e., cowardly.

an eye . . . suffering: an eye capable of distinguishing between what honor demands from you and what you endure shamefully.

Where's thy drum?: Where's thy call to arms?

noiseless: not ringing with a call to arms.

moral: priggish.

proper: appropriate.

deformity: ugliness, unseemliness. Albany plays on the senses *seemly, unseemliness.*

self-cover'd: deceitful, sham.
Were't ... blood: were it fit for me to let my hands do the bidding of my strong emotion and wish.
apt: capable of, itching to.
howe'er ... shield thee: However much you may be a devil essentially, the fact that you have the appearance of a woman protects you.
shape: counterfeit likeness.
Marry: i.e., by the Virgin Mary!
your manhood: Albany has talked of her false-seeming womanliness. She sneers back at his alleged manliness in threatening her, a threat that does not in the least frighten her.
bred: brought up.
thrill'd: quivering with.
remorse: the prick of conscience.
bending: aiming, turning his sword on.
amongst ... dead: They felled him dead between them.
justicers: judges.
nether crimes: crimes committed here below.
May all . . . hateful life: may pluck down all that has been built in my imagination upon my life which will be hateful as a result.

In the image of a vast and splendid edifice collapsing and ruining the site on which it is built, Goneril expresses her wry awareness of the fact that her life may become loathsome precisely because she has indulged herself with fantasies which may never become fact, now that Edmund has gone back without her to the widowed Regan.
tart: piquant.
back: returning.

Albany's question can be played as suspicion or as a genuine wish to know what will happen if Edmund does not know about his father.

Albany's apostrophe of the absent Gloucester is a determination to punish all who are responsible for the loss of his eyes; that includes Goneril and Edmund as well as Regan.

Act Four, Scene Five

In preparing this scene, refer to what is said about Oswald as a steward in Goneril's household in the last scene (see Introduction, pp. 27 ff., and *Shakespeare's Eden*, pp. 93 f.). One thing is certain; Oswald, a gentleman, is immovably loyal to Goneril. He will not betray her trust.

By this time, Goneril and Regan, who have always been rivals and have never trusted each other, are competing for Edmund. Regan has the advantage of being a widow. (Goneril is still encumbered with her husband, Albany. Nevertheless, whatever commitments Edmund may have made to Regan while in her household, he has certainly committed himself to Goneril in the event of her getting rid of Albany.) The arrangement took place on the way to Albany's castle, and is mentioned in the dialogue of Act Four, Scene Two, with Goneril planning for Oswald to carry their messages to one another:

> This trusty servant
> Shall pass between us.

Since realizing clearly that the daughters are ill-treating Lear, Albany has shown his dislike for them and for Edmund, and has sworn to avenge Gloucester's lost eyesight. The Duke's reluctance to join the other British leaders against Cordelia and the French is interpreted by them as a dislike of fighting, a sort of cowardice. That is why Regan asks if Albany's army has taken the field.

my brother: i.e., my brother-in-law.
powers: forces.

The actress might ask this question in surprise, as if she has just heard that Albany is in the field. She might prefer a straight question, simply because she wants to know what is happening.

with much ado: not very easily, with a lot of unnecessary fuss.

Regan distrusts Edmund and Goneril, and wants to find out

if there is anything between them. There is also the possibility that he might be plotting with her sister against her.

import: mean.

The actor can choose whether he will play Oswald as really ignorant of the letter's contents, or as pretending to be. But it is certain that he will not betray Goneril.

Faith: i.e., by my faith. This is not a light oath, but a very determined assertion of conviction.

posted: dashed away at top speed. The fastest means of conveying messages in Shakespeare's day was by a succession of post-horses, each ridden at top speed until it began to flag, then exchanged for a fresh animal.

serious matter: important business.

ignorance: error, folly. It also has the sense of blind ignorance (i.e., it was a blindness of wit to let the blinded Gloucester live).

nighted: darkened.

moreover: on top of that, in addition.

I must needs, etc.: The moment Oswald hears that Edmund has left, he determines to follow, to deliver the letter as instructed. A loyal servant of Goneril, he is uncomfortable in such close contact with Regan, every second of which might expose him to new pressures to betray his mistress or to subtle attempts to worm confidences out of him. When Oswald makes it clear that he wants to leave, Regan decides to try to detain him and to learn the contents of the letter to Edmund.

transport . . . word: carry her orders, wishes, intentions, by word of mouth.

Belike: probably.

Madam, I had rather: The actor must provide himself with a complete statement which she interrupts. The difficulty can be overcome by giving himself the intention of wanting to leave as quickly as possible.

at her late being here: when she was here recently.

oeillades: amorous looks (the glad eye).

of her bosom: in her confidence.

I speak in understanding: I know what I'm talking about.

take this note: pay careful attention to this.

convenient: suitable.

have talked: have come to an understanding.
you may gather more: You may put two and two together for yourself.

In this dialogue Regan is formidable. The actress can choose between cold determination and a silky manner under which the steel is sensed if not seen.
thus much: what I have told you.

Regan realizes that she cannot prevail on Oswald and she gives in to her hatred of Gloucester. She knows that she can rely on Goneril's servant against a common enemy. Oswald is only too happy to leave, and to assure Regan that he is committed in his loyalty to her sister, but that he is no enemy to her as such.
what party I do follow: what side I'm on (i.e., hers and Goneril's, not Albany's).

Act Four, Scene Six

When shall I come . . . and patient thoughts.

When Edgar found himself an outlaw by his father's proclamation (Act Two, Scene Three), he made up his mind to survive. Unable to risk discovery while trying to get clothes for a disguise, he then adopted the disguise of stripping off his clothes and pretending to be an almost naked, insane beggar, with mutilated flesh and raving speech, his accent changed from that of a nobleman to a madman's at the bottom of society. In this scene, however, he is wearing a decent suit of clothes, suitable to a yeoman, and he need no longer behave as if he were mad. He still does not speak or behave like the nobleman which he is, but as a yeoman. He has decided not to let his father commit suicide, but to trick him into believing that he has been miraculously preserved by the gods, that they have not abandoned him.

In playing Gloucester the actor must imagine himself weak with pain, confused by the sudden plunge into darkness so short a time ago, completely disoriented. His confusion is increased by mental and emotional stress. His confused state of mind combines with his blindness to let him be tricked by Edgar's benevolent deception.

In the first part of the scene, Edgar's aim is to convince Gloucester that they are making their way up a steep slope near the sea.

By your eyes' anguish: as a result of the mental and physical pain caused by the loss of your eyes.

Gloucester is still too alert to be easily deceived as to the change in Edgar's voice. He has also been skeptical about the steep slope. Edgar, therefore, decides to wait no longer, for fear Gloucester might refuse to believe him. His intention now is to convince his father that they are actually standing at the top of a high and steep cliff just overlooking the sea, which is hundreds of feet below. The actor must avoid the mistake of trying to convince the audience instead of Gloucester. The whole effort must be directed at the frail, aching, tormented, old blind man. Edgar must behave as if they were where he says they are. It must be remembered that his aim is to restore to his father some true faith in the gods as not wholly given over to hostility or indifference to humanity.

Stand still: This is an intense warning not to move for fear of falling over the edge.
chough: large black bird of the crow family with red legs.
gross: large.
sampire: samphire, an aromatic plant used for pickling which grows at Dover.
cock: cockboat (a small ship's boat, the equivalent of a dinghy).
unnumbred: innumerable.
idle: barren.
chafes: rubs against one another.
deficient: weak, clouded.
extreme verge: very edge.

Gloucester must be made to imagine that to move forward a few inches is to go over the edge. To this end, Edgar says that he would not dare to jump straight up in the air for fear that he might not land back on the top of the cliff. As he sets Gloucester beside him Edgar moves with great caution as if really perched precariously so high above the water. The actor must imagine himself there, imagine that he sees everything described, using the images to communicate his shock at being so high, shock which becomes fear of being dizzy and of falling over. All this to achieve Edgar's intention of deceiving Gloucester.

The actor can concentrate on the fear which comes from looking down when up so high. He can concentrate on imagining the distance to the water, in part by imagining what is seen, and in part what is heard. As Edgar says he dare not look longer, the actor turns toward Gloucester who hears the change in the direction from which the voice comes. And in placing Gloucester as if on the *extreme verge*, the actor takes great care to stop him going too near the imaginary edge.

prosper it with thee: give thee a prosperous life.

Seeing his father standing there pitiably, deceived into thinking death is a few seconds away, many hundreds of feet beneath him, Edgar starts to reproach himself in his love and compassion, but reminds himself that what he is doing is to put an end to Gloucester's despair.

The actor of Gloucester might decide to follow the example of those who commit suicide on one of the high cliffs of Southern England. To throw themselves over they merely kneel on the edge and lean forward. So, standing or kneeling, Gloucester needs only to lean forward in his darkness. If he is on his feet, his knees give and he collapses. Standing or kneeling, Gloucester loses consciousness from the moment that he feels himself moving forward and down. He imagines himself dropping hundreds of feet to the distant beach below. He is unconscious before he touches the ground so few feet away.

fall to quarrel: start quarreling with.

snuff and loathed part of nature: The snuff is the last half inch (or less) of a candle, which gives intermittent, flickering light and a strong and unpleasant smell. By *nature* is meant natural life in the flesh. With this metaphor Gloucester says that the last very unpleasant part of his life on this earth would be permitted to end from natural causes, instead of by suicide (like the light of a candle which is not put out but is left to burn itself out).

When Gloucester thinks he is dropping to certain death and collapses, Edgar has a moment of intense fear that the strain on his father might have proved fatal.

conceit: imagination.

may rob . . . theft: can be regarded as stealing life from the repository in which it is hoarded, when life itself submits willingly to being taken.

Edgar is happy to think that his father was not really on a cliff edge, for by now he would be dead. This happiness is followed by fear, almost terror, that the old man may have died of shock. The fear gives place to intense relief when Gloucester begins to regain consciousness.

Now Edgar takes on another *persona*, behaving as if he were a man on the beach below, who has witnessed Gloucester's terrifying fall and miraculous survival.

pass: die.

precipitating: dashing straight down.

Hast heavy substance: are composed of substance with weight (i.e., not insubstantial air with no weight). It was believed that spirits (whether good or evil) could manifest themselves to human sight by taking on a shape of air, which seemed substantial, but was not. Edgar pretends to have assumed that what he saw falling must have been an insubstantial apparition, not a substantial human being with weight.

at each: on top of one another, end to end.

perpendicularly: straight down.

fell: fallen.

bourn: shore, limit, edge.

a-height: on high, at the top.

Earlier Edgar worked successfully to convince Gloucester that they were standing on the top of a cliff; he now works as hard to convince him that they are on the beach at its base.

shrill-gorg'd: shrill-throated, shrill-voiced.

whelk'd: twisted.
enridged: furrowed.
father: old man.

Here the actor of Edgar imagines that he saw the fiend, that he was afraid for Gloucester, that he felt horror at seeing him drop so far, and that, as a result, he is delighted at the happy outcome of the incident, and that the gods should have chosen to show such favor to this particular man.

clearest: most righteous, most free from sin.
who make . . . impossibilities: who inspire adoration and reverence for themselves by performing what is impossible for men.

As Gloucester listens to Edgar he gradually believes the story and feels awe mingled with relief and exaltation for the fact that the gods should have troubled themselves about his welfare so soon after his miseries had reduced him to such deep despair.

free: at ease, unconstrained.

Gloucester is now reconciled to his troubles.

Act Five, Scene One

The scene takes place in the camp of those Britons who are led by Regan and Edmund; these two are waiting to hear if Albany is on his way to join them, or if the constraint of moral scruples prevents him opposing Cordelia and Lear, even if he does not aid them.

Edmund may be played as the acknowledged equal of Regan, or as one who simulates subservience to her as his sovereign and as the woman he loves. To everybody else Edmund is the army commander among subordinates. He has utter contempt for Albany, whose mildness and moral integrity he miscontrues as weak cowardice.

the duke: i.e., Albany.

Edmund commands the officer: "Find out from the duke if his last intention has not been changed."

advis'd: counseled.
aught: anything, something or other.
full of alteration . . . reproving: i.e., he keeps changing his mind and reproves himself one moment for a decision of the moment before.
constant pleasure: unchanging wish (i.e., if he wants something long enough for his mind not to have changed a second later).

Regan wants to find out if Edmund has received the message from Goneril. She hopes to pick up something from his reaction to her statement, but he gives nothing away.

miscarried: come to harm, been destroyed.
doubted: feared.

Each simulates concern for Oswald to deceive the other.

the goodness I intend upon you: The plans I have for your benefit.

This is an attempt to remind him that he can trust her, that she has kindly intentions toward him, that he ought to think twice before offending her. Edmund responds by playing the strictly honorable knight.

abuses: (1) deceives, (2) denigrates.
doubtful: fearful.
conjunct: closely joined.
bosom'd: confidential, familiar.
I never shall endure her: With the memories of a thousand jealous tussles with Goneril, and further incensed by her sister's attempt to steal Edmund, Regan expresses all her loathing for her. Regan argues that she is a widow with a legal right to marry Edmund, while Goneril wants to thwart her despite the fact that her husband, Albany, is alive.
familiar: confidential, overfriendly.
Fear me not: Have no fears about me, don't worry on my behalf.

The appearance of Albany at the head of his army is unexpected. Now the sisters reveal their mutual dislike. Goneril's word play on *lose, loosen* emphasizes her hatred of Regan. The two sisters are overwhelmed by what seems insuperable hatred for each other.

Albany has not decided what to do. Cordelia has come with a French army. Albany must prevent the hereditary enemy from taking over the country, much as he dislikes opposing Lear and Cordelia. Her justification for the invasion can be found in Lear's need and her own right to a share of the kingdom. Legally, Cordelia can claim one third of the country or a dowry instead, for until 1926 English law did not recognize primogeniture in the case of heiresses. Legally, she can argue that her disinheriting was invalid.

Nevertheless, Albany realizes these valid reasons for Cordelia's return with an army might well be used by the French as a pretext for conquest. He broods uncertainly, not knowing whether to support Lear and Cordelia and accept the presence of a strong French force at a time when his countrymen are weakened by disunity, or to join the other British leaders in repelling the invaders. Admitting to himself how much right there is on the side of Lear, Cordelia and their British supporters, Albany hopes that he will be able to defeat the French, and then to restore Lear to his throne and set Cordelia free. But he has still not made up his mind.

Albany greets Regan as his *ever-loving sister* with some politeness. But his *Sir, this I heard* to Edmund is abrupt. He is implying that Edmund and the two daughters have behaved with such barbarity that they have unintentionally contrived the present dangerous situation in which not only has the King joined the invaders, but he is accompanied by other Britons outraged by their rulers.

it touches us as France . . . oppose: It concerns us in that France invades our land, not because he supports the King, with others, who, I fear, are led to oppose us by just and weighty motives.
Sir: This mode of address used by Edmund and Albany to each other is insulting. Edmund should be addressed as "my lord" and Albany as either "my lord" or "your grace."
you speak nobly: It is hardly possible for Edmund to mean these words. They appear to provoke Albany to the edge of violence. His impulse to turn on them is strengthened by Regan's *Why is this reason'd?* (What are you splitting hairs for?)

The threat of blows between Edmund and Albany prompts Goneril's plea not to fight each other, but to combine against the French.
particular: i.e., individual instead of common.

There is a moment when Albany almost succumbs to the temptation to fight his uncomfortable allies. But he manages to restrain himself and adhere to his plan. This is to fight the French. If he has the victory he will then deal with Edmund, Goneril and Regan while setting Cordelia free and restoring the crown to Lear.
ancient of war: advisers experienced in war.
presently: immediately.

Edmund has his own plans for Albany, Goneril, Regan, Lear and Cordelia. He therefore simulates docile and subordinate obedience to a commander. When Regan asks Goneril to accompany her and Albany, Goneril answers *no,* in the hope of a quick word with Edmund, ignorant of the fact that he has not received her letter with the plan to murder Albany. When Regan persists, Goneril realizes that there will be no opportunity of speaking privately with Edmund. She acquiesces, saying to herself, *I know the answer* (i.e., I know the answer to my problem).

To both these sisters, etc.: This speech must not be misunderstood as intended to provoke the laughter of the audience. Edmund is deadly serious. He thinks over the situation, considers the choices open to him and calmly and deliberately decides on what seems to him most advantageous. He is concerned entirely with his own advantage. The soliloquy has three sections. In the first he considers the situation.
jealous: alert and determined not to be caught napping (as a person once bitten by an adder is not easily caught a second time, but is alert and kills the reptile before it has a chance to attack him).

In the second stage of the soliloquy Edmund considers how to deal with his problem. Goneril will never be reconciled to his taking Regan. It will therefore be simplest for Regan to die as well as Albany, clearing the way for his marriage to the newly made widow, Goneril.

In the third phase of this speech Edmund decides how his aim can be achieved. Once Albany has been used to defeat the French, he and Regan can be murdered by Goneril. All that remains is to dispose of Lear and Cordelia.

exasperates: madly enrages.
carry out my side: win my game.
countenance: authority.
taking off: assassination.
state: position in society.
stands on: depends on (i.e., my position in society depends on my defending it, not arguing about it).

Act Five, Scene Three

Some officers take them . . . convey her to my tent.

Edmund now has control of Lear and Cordelia. But the troops under his command owe no allegiance to him; he cannot rely on them to show or even allow any kind of force toward Lear and his daughter, for they are both surrounded by the aura of royalty. Indeed, their very presence evokes pity and respect (mixed with love) from the King's former subjects.

To succeed, Edmund must act before Albany arrives. The Duke intends to free the prisoners and place Lear back on his throne. The captives must therefore be removed to prison before Albany comes on the scene. But Edmund must not betray the slightest hint of his intention. On the surface he must behave impeccably so that, later, when the murder of the captives is discovered no witness to his present activity will be able to recall anything suspicious. He behaves now as if he were nothing but a dutiful subordinate who makes no decision himself and who does not let his personal attitude to the royal prisoners influence his behavior. He is careful to give them objective respect, equally devoid of hostility and cordialness. His main need is to have them removed to prison while seeming to insist on their being carefully guarded, as much for their own safety as to prevent their escape. (For more on the attitude toward royal personages, even in captivity, see *Shakespeare's Eden*, pp. 96 ff.)

Good guard . . . censure them: Guard them carefully until the time that we know the wishes of the greater personages whose place it is to give judgment on them.

Cordelia wishes to wait for her sisters and brother-in-law. She does not intend to let herself be led away until she has confronted them and made a fight for her father out in the open in front of his former subjects, whose feelings can count in restraining the victors.

meaning: intention.
incurr'd: rendered themselves liable to.
cast down: downcast, dejected.
oppressed: subjected to injustice, burdened with wrongs.
outfrown, etc.: i.e., stand my ground and fight back at Fortune.

Cordelia's question comes from her determination to stay and confront her sisters. But Lear does not want her to fight for him. He no longer wants worldly rank and wealth. He thinks he will be quite happy living with Cordelia in prison, even happier there than anywhere else. His memories of Goneril and Regan are so painful that he does not want Cordelia to expose herself to them in order to fight for something which no longer has any meaning in his life. He therefore sets himself to persuade her to go to prison, to convince her that once there they will avoid everything unpleasant. There they can have undiluted happiness in each other's love. He speaks almost as if she were still the little girl whose fears he has calmed in the past with kindly promises and reassurances. For the whole of this speech his objective is to persuade her to come with him to prison. Cordelia is as determined to withstand him and to stay. So long as she refuses to move nobody will try to force her away.

alone: by ourselves.
cage: (1) cage, (2) prison.
gilded butterflies: gaudy courtiers who flit hither and thither and do not last long.
poor rogues talk of court news: Lear refers to the habit of *poor rogues* of gossiping about the court, despite their ignorance of what goes on there. In prison he and Cordelia will amuse themselves, he says, by indulging such people and gossiping with them.
take upon's . . . spies: claim to have the inside story on most obscure matters as if we had been endowed with supernatural vision and were spying out the land for God (i.e., as if we saw everything with the clarity and knowledge of angels).
that ebb and flow by the moon: i.e., that are in and out again as swiftly as the tide.

Lear stops speaking and Cordelia remains silent. But when Edmund once more gives an order for them to be led away, it is clear that the King has not persuaded his daughter. Until she decides to go of her own accord they will not leave. Nobody will touch them. Edmund must wait, apparently polite and not involved, until Cordelia yields to her father. Once more Lear tries to persuade her not to stay, but to accompany him to prison.
Upon such sacrifices . . . incense: The gods themselves sweeten the bitterness of sacrifices such as these. When an animal was sacrificed, the unpleasant smell of burning flesh was sweetened by incense. This practice was associated with the notion that incense sweetened sacrifice for the nostrils of the gods. From this notion developed another, that the bitterness of sacrifice is sweetened by the fact that it does service to the gods, or, later, to God. Lear insists that to give up the world for life in prison will not be bitter, the gods will make life sweet for them (i.e., he says that they are making a renunciation of what is not worth keeping, as a result of which it will not be bitter).

Cordelia's sense of reality tells her that he is wrong, that they will not be permitted to live on happily in prison; their presence there alive will be a perpetual danger to the winning side, an incitement to disaffection and rebellion. Nevertheless, she can withstand his pleading no longer. Once she refused his request in the past when he had so much to offer her. She cannot continue to deny him his wish now when he has nothing to offer her but his sincere love for her as his daughter. She gives way, letting him take her in his arms.

Have I caught thee?: This is as if Lear is recalling to her a game which they played in her childhood, when he played something like hide and seek with her and when they were both delighted each time he caught her.
He that parts us, etc.: i.e., no human agency will be able to part us now my arms are round you; it will take fire from heaven to do that.

He sets himself to console her as if she were once more the little girl whose tears he had always been able to dry long ago in her childhood.
The good years, etc.: They shall be eaten up by time (i.e., it will take longer than they have left to live).

This time, when Lear says, *Come*, Cordelia does not resist. She goes with him. They are accompanied by the guard with the normal respect for majesty.

While Cordelia has been refusing to leave, Edmund has had no alternative but to wait, apparently in no way personally involved, but knowing that the minutes were ticking away and that at any moment Albany might arrive and release the royal captives. Now that they are on their way to prison Edmund must act very swiftly. He needs an assassin, and he has already marked his man, selecting a person without scruple who can easily be tempted with the promise of promotion. There is no time for persuasion or discussion.

Take thou this note: listen carefully to this.
advanc'd: promoted.

Edmund reminds the man that he has been promoted to captain. This is proof of Edmund's ability to promote him further, but only if he does what is asked of him without question or hesitation. From a common soldier he has been advanced to noble rank; in return for willing service his patron will promote him from the lowest rank of simple nobility to that of a great magnate.

The captain does not answer; he has doubts, perhaps whether Edmund has the power to fulfill his promises, or whether he intends to once his goal is achieved. The silence leads Edmund to declare that in turbulent times a man who wants advancement cannot afford scruples. With the captain still silent, Edmund points out with some tinge of sarcasm that to show compassion is not suited to a fighter. It ought not to make the captain hesitate.

But this time the captain is near agreeing to do what is asked of him, but first wants to know what it is. Edmund prevents him asking what is on the tip of his tongue with the brusque insistence, *Thy great employment will not bear question.* As it is now clear that the captain is not going to refuse, Edmund clinches the matter by telling him to say yes immediately or look for some other patron for advancement.

Edmund knows his man and is given the assurance he requires. In this swift interview, although the captain stays silent, his doubts, uncertainties, hesitations can be inferred from his manner. Edmund reacts to his responses until it can be seen that his man will obey. Edmund's dialogue is elicited by the interplay between them. Once the captain has consented, Edmund, always conscious of time passing swiftly, insists on the need for great haste.

write happy: style yourself, let yourself be known as happy.
carry it so: arrange it in such a way, carry it out in such a way.

No sooner has the captain left than Edmund hears the approach of Albany and his troops, and he prepares to fool his enemy. To succeed now Edmund has merely to take care not to arouse the slightest suspicion of what he has done. The captain must be given time to kill the two captives; Albany must be deceived into not sending for them immediately.

Although Albany intends to set Lear and Cordelia free, he knows that his murder has been plotted by Edmund and Goneril, and that they must both be dealt with. His hatred of Edmund is increased by detestation for what has been done to Gloucester.

Nevertheless, just as Edmund dissembles his feelings toward Albany, so Albany, too, starts by hiding his toward Edmund, whom he praises for valor in the battle just won.

strain: race, descent, lineage.

Albany says virtually that Edmund has been dominated by that part of him inherited from his valiant ancestry (i.e., from his father), but suggests that he has been lucky *(Fortune led you well).*

opposites: opponents, those opposed.

Notice that Albany says *I* when he demands the captives, but changes to the royal *we* for *we shall find.* It might be argued that here he is speaking for himself and the two sisters, but this is unlikely, as he knows they do not share his intentions for Lear and Cordelia.

merits: deserts, qualities.

Edmund needs to delay Albany long enough for the captives to be murdered, if not longer. To this end he adopts the manner of a scrupulously fair and loyal subordinate, anxious to prevent his superior from doing injustice in the heat of the moment, which he will deeply regret when his anger has cooled.

retention: detention.

appointed: (1) equipped, adequate; (2) picked and organized.

common bosom: (1) loves of the common people, (2) general love.

our impress'd lances: our spears (i.e., spearmen) who have been forced into service.

in our eyes/Which: in the eyes of us, who.

hold your session: hold your court (i.e., to sentence them).

As Albany has not interrupted him, Edmund is emboldened to go even further in his imitation of a reliable, levelheaded subject doing his best to restrain his ruler as a good counselor should.

quarrels in the heat: motives for quarrel in the heat of passion.
a fitter place: a more appropriate place than the field where victory has just been won.

Albany is not surprised or deceived by Edmund's dissembling, but may well be outraged by this exhibition of hypocritical audacity, in itself a masterpiece. His reply puts Edmund in his place with a reprimand for assuming equality while pretending to be a subordinate.

subject of this war: only as a subordinate in the fighting (not a leader).

Not unnaturally, Regan is nettled by Albany's treatment of Edmund.

list: wish.
immediacy: direct connection (without intervening superiors).

Regan's assurance that Edmund is hers annoys Goneril, who is so certain of the imminent destruction of her husband and sister that she has no qualms about declaring her own love.

your addition: title of honor which you have granted (i.e., nothing you can give can add to his natural nobility).
compeers: equals.
That eye . . . a-squint: the eye that told you that was squinting with jealousy and did not see clearly.
full-flowing stomach: unrestrained anger.
patrimony: what is inherited from a father.
The walls are thine: i.e., I yield to you completely.

Albany lets the altercation continue until he reminds Goneril that she is his wife. But he is diverted from sending for the captives by it and by the fact that Regan incites Edmund to challenge him *(Let the drum strike, and prove my title thine)*, with her troops rather than in single combat. Edmund must be dealt with before Albany can send for Lear and Cordelia. The only way to avoid a serious clash between the two British forces is to denounce Edmund and await the unknown champion in accordance with the arrangement made with the disguised Edgar before the battle.

let-alone: prohibition (leave alone).

half-blooded: bastard.
Let the drum strike: strike up the drum (i.e., call the troops to arms).
hear reason: These words are to Regan who is ignorant of the plot between her sister and Edmund to kill her as well as Albany.
in thy attaint: (1) convicted in your guilt, (2) infected by you.
sub-contracted: additionally contracted (i.e., in addition to her marriage contract to Albany).
banns: announcement of intended marriage (the occasion which gives opportunity for cause to be shown in public why marriage should not take place).
bespoke: sold, ordered, reserved for sale (i.e., she is no longer merchandise offered for sale).
interlude: comedy.
trumpet: trumpeter.
manifest: exposed and obvious.
exchange: reciprocal pledge. The word also means "substitute." If he is aware of this, Edmund is sneering that, unlike Albany, he does not need a champion, but does his fighting in his own person.
What in the world . . . he lies: Whatever may be the rank of the man who calls me traitor, he lies like a low fellow of no nobility.
On him . . . maintain: preserve against him.
virtue: valor.

Edmund seems to be looking for supporters, not realizing that the troops he has led in the battle are no longer ready to follow him.

What you have charg'd me with . . . nor live so long.

When the trumpet has sounded for the third time, Edgar appears disguised by unmarked armor to give Edmund a mortal wound in fair fight. Then, confronted by the evidence of her treachery, Goneril leaves the scene hurriedly. Still ignorant of the identity of his opponent, Edmund admits that he has committed crimes, but with no hint of remorse for them. He is more interested in knowing who has vanquished him. For all his scorn of conventional assumptions about worth and honor, Edmund subscribes to them enough to want the opponent to be of noble rank, despite the fact that he himself is illegitimate. Edgar realizes that by these standards Edmund would not receive forgiveness, not being noble himself, and proposes instead an exchange of *charity* (i.e., love with no conditions attached).

As Edgar comments on the justice of the gods, he regrets what has happened to his father; wishing it had been otherwise, he realizes that when Gloucester indulged himself he unwittingly created the instrument of his own destruction. But Edgar understands that his father lost his eyes, not only because he begot Edmund, but because he was immovably loyal to Lear.

The dark and vicious place where thee he got: the dark bed of vice where he begot thee.
The wheel: i.e., Fortune's wheel.

Edmund recognizes that his endeavor to rise in the world to the top has failed, and at the last moment. Taking advantage of Fortune's favor, he rose, almost to the throne. But, as ever, Fortune turned her smiles to frowns and he lies in the dust where he began. He cannot avoid some bitterness in admitting to himself that like so many others he was misled into thinking himself Fortune's immutable darling. Now, at the very moment when he seemed to have won, Fortune has turned her wheel and disaster follows disaster. He does not know how Goneril's letter reached Albany, and he does not know how his brother managed to survive. Too confidently he fought the unknown champion, and now he lies dying at Edgar's feet.

I am here: i.e., I am back at the bottom, where I began.
thy very gait: Edgar now walks with the majestic bearing of a great noble man, a way in which he could not walk when disguised as the Bedlam and as the peasant when he accompanied Gloucester.
worthy: noble.
shift: make a change of clothing.
rings: eye sockets.

jewels: literally, gems; figuratively, eyes.

The sudden change in Edmund's fortunes has weakened his self-assurance. He is no longer so confident that his standards are right. His cynical scorn for such qualities as loyalty and unselfishness is beginning to be shaken. He is struck in particular by the fact Edgar not only tells how he cared for the father who wronged him, but obviously loves their father, bearing no resentment against him. Edgar has also offered Edmund an exchange of *charity*. For as long as he can remember, Edmund has been guided by the certainty that every human being cares for nobody but himself and that talk of morality, love, self-sacrifice, unselfishness is nothing more than a trick by which those who are clever make fools of those who allow themselves to be deceived. Edmund's assumption has been that nobody of consequence ever puts such principles into action. His father spoke of loving him as much as Edgar, but in fact kept him *out* nine years and intended to send him away again. Edgar is received at court with honor and will inherit his father's title and property. Edmund is sent away and will inherit nothing. Such unequal treatment does not suggest equal love. But now Edmund finds that Gloucester did not suffer because he made a political miscalculation in taking the King's part, but because he loved Lear; and Edgar is succeeding without selfish treachery. But Edmund is not yet quite ready to ignore the conditioning of a lifetime (and in many ways up to now a very successful lifetime). He is still uncertain; to confess to what he has done against Lear and Cordelia might be to expose himself to the ridicule of his enemies as a man unable to maintain his constancy in the face of misfortune; he is afraid of being scorned for the very traits which he has found so contemptible in Albany.

dissolve: melt into tears.
This would have . . . sorrow: This would have seemed the end of the story for those who like to avoid sorrow.
amplify too much: (1) expand it too much, (2) repeat it too often in different words.
top extremity: outdo the utmost.

clamour: noisy grief.
puissant: powerful.
strings of life: The phrase tends to be used in Elizabethan anatomy to denote fibrous tissue, ligaments or nerve fiber at any point which is crucial for the continuance of life. Edgar is recalling how Kent began to lose consciousness, suffering a stroke or a heart attack.
tranc'd: senseless, unconscious.
his enemy king: the king who was hostile to him (was his enemy).

Edgar has the greatest admiration for Kent.

smokes: steams.
compliment: formal greeting.
very manners urges: manners themselves insist on.

Kent has been unconscious a few moments earlier. He is weak and moves with difficulty. He knows he is dying and has come to reveal himself to Lear and say farewell in the few hours he has left to live (if so long).

object: spectacle.
Yet Edmund was belov'd: Edmund's life has been dominated by resentment for what he has regarded as the withdrawal of his father's love. He has believed that, whatever Goneril and Regan might have said about loving him, they have really been dominated by their own selfishness; he has given them gratification, but they have not loved him as an essential element of life. Now he finds that he has been *belov'd:* one woman has killed another out of love for him, and, rather than face life without him, has killed herself. One human being can matter that much to another; he has been loved. This realization completes the work started by Edgar's account of his life and his looking after Gloucester. Edmund finally decides to overcome the tendency to do evil which he believes to be a part of his physiological and psychological inheritance *(my own nature).*
after: subsequently.
mean: intend, have made up my mind to.
my writ is on: i.e., I have given written order for the execution of my sentence on.
fordid: destroyed.

When Lear enters he is greeted with silent horror and pity. In his grief he misinterprets the silence as outrageous indifference to Cordelia's body. He calls on the onlookers to howl their grief. He is too old and weak to mourn her adequately, he lacks the energy. Their horrified silence provokes him to call them *men of stones*, to explain to them that she is really dead, as if in their silence they were suggesting that he has nothing to grieve for. Then he is struck by the hope that she may not be dead and that they are right to be silent, although he knows she is dead.

stone: looking glass (made of polished crystal).
promis'd end: last judgment.
I might have sav'd her: It is possible that he reproaches himself for not having been quicker and more alert. But it is also possible that he feels crushed by the knowledge that if he had not persuaded her to go to prison she would be alive now.
I have seen the day: there was a time when I.

Lear regrets the fact that age has made him too weak to save Cordelia. There was a time when the captain would not have stood a chance against him.

falchion: broad curved sword.
crosses: misfortunes.
spoil me: impair my faculties.
If Fortune, etc.: If Fortune boasts of having treated two people with such intense changes of love and hate, we are looking at one of them here.

Kent considers what has happened to Lear. For years Fortune gave him happiness, treating him lovingly; then she changed, hating him and giving him misery. But she changed again, this time in his favor, letting him be reconciled with Cordelia. Fortune has allowed herself yet another change toward Lear; again she frowns on him. His friends are defeated and Cordelia is dead. He has suffered two complete revolutions of Fortune's wheel, from happiness to misery, back to short-lived happiness, and finally to overwhelming misery from which there will be no relief.

a dull sight: (1) a dismal sight, (2) I do not see clearly.

see that straight: have that put straight.
That from . . . sad steps: who have followed your sad steps from the very first that you have taken into vicissitudes and declining fortunes.
boot: i.e., with a bonus.
addition: titles of rank.
poor fool: (1) the Fool, (2) Cordelia. The choice can be left to the actor.

Lear dies, overcome with the excitement of thinking that Cordelia is just barely breathing.

ghost: spirit.
usurp'd: held without legal right. Lear has lived longer than the "statutory" three score years and ten.
I have a journey, etc.: Kent knows he is dying. He has no alternative but to follow his master into death.

If Edgar is given the last four lines of the play, he speaks as the man about to be crowned King. He insists that this is no time for a conventional speech of consolation in which benevolent intentions would be pronounced toward his new subjects. Instead, he will say what he feels, his grief for Lear, his certainty that in Lear they have lost a man who can never be replaced.

ANTONY AND CLEOPATRA

Act One, Scene One

ALTHOUGH SUBORDINATE TO Antony as a soldier, Philo is a friend of his. Demetrius has just arrived from Rome. Both he and Philo are noble; they have not only the nobleman's sense of superiority to all who are not of gentle birth, but the freeborn Roman patrician's certainty of the inferiority of all other cities and nations to Rome. They are unhappy because their friend is debasing his own nobility, and his and their Roman citizenship. They resent Cleopatra as the cause of Antony's delinquency; to them she is an inferior, addicted to luxury and soft immorality, with which she would destroy the sterner morality of Rome.

dotage: irrational infatuation.
o'erflows the measure: is beyond all measure (the image is of a liquid overflowing the vessel used to measure it).
files and musters: ranks and parades.
glow'd: shone.
like plated Mars: like Mars in silver armor.
office: function.
devotion: exclusive attention.
view: gaze, look, glance.
tawny: dark brown.
front: forehead.
reneges all temper: renounces (denies, repudiates) all moderation.

Temper in smelting of sword blades also means conditioning to a high degree of hardness and flexibility.

The image of *bellows* and *fan* derives from the use of bellows to pump air into the fire of a forge to make it burn with more heat. The pumping of Antony's heart makes Cleopatra's passion burn more fiercely. His efforts to satisfy it cool her *lust.*

gipsy: Egyptian whore (i.e., Cleopatra).
take . . . good note: just look carefully.
triple pillar: one of three pillars.

The other two are Lepidus and Octavius Caesar. Having divided the Roman Empire into three parts, they each rule one.

As they approach, before they speak a line, Antony and Cleopatra behave to one another as lovers. Antony's appearance and actions clearly express an overwhelming love for Cleopatra.

reckon'd: calculated (i.e., "If love can be measured it cannot be great").
bourn: limit.
find out: discover.
grates: vexes, annoys (grates upon).
the sum: i.e., give the gist of it, be brief.

Cleopatra expresses her contempt for Octavius and for Fulvia, Antony's wife in Rome.

mandate: order, command.
take in: absorb, conquer.
enfranchise: set free.
damn: condemn, sentence.
How, my love?: What's the matter, what do you mean, my love?
dismission: dismissal.
process: summons, writ.
homager: vassal, one who pays homage.
rang'd: (1) ordered, organized, (2) extended.
my space: all the space I need.
mutual: exchanging equally, sharing equally.
to weet: to know.
peerless: unequaled.

Cleopatra speaks of Antony in the third person, but addresses him mentally in the second.

stirr'd: moved, excited.
confound: destroy, reduce to chaos.
conference: conversation, exchange of words.

wrangling: arguing, quarreling.
becomes: suits.
admir'd: wondered at.
priz'd: valued.
property: essential quality.
approves: confirms.

Act One, Scene Three

In the previous scene Antony decided to return to Rome after receiving the news of the death of Fulvia, his wife, and of the revolt of the son of Pompey the Great against Octavius Caesar.

He has not told Cleopatra of his decision; nevertheless, in the beginning of this scene she suspects him of having made it, either as a result of her jealousy of Fulvia (whose death is not known to her), or because she has been given some inkling by courtiers.

sad: serious.
hold the method: adhere to the method.
the like: the same.
I do not: that I do not do.
cross: obstruct, deny.
sick and sullen: ill and in bad humor.
give breathing to: (1) express, (2) give a pause to.

Sense (1) applies if Antony is imagined as referring to his intention of leaving. If he means his wish to spend his life making love to Cleopatra, sense (2) applies.

sides of nature: her anatomy.
the married woman: i.e., Fulvia.
planted: hidden where they could thrive.
you . . . who: you, who have been false.
riotous: dissolute.
entangled: caught by.
color: pretext.
none . . . so poor: not the poorest of our attributes, features.

a race of heaven: a race of heavenly origin.
in use: (1) for use, (2) earning interest, i.e., increasing while not being used.
civil swords: swords used in civil war.
scrupulous: carefully balanced.
creeps: moves stealthily (not necessarily slowly).
apace: swiftly.
would purge: wants to regain health by expelling the cause of illness.
my more particular: what concerns me more specifically.

Cleopatra does not really feel what she says. She wants him to stay and thinks that her behavior will disturb him, so that his love for her will not let him depart with her believing him guilty of her accusations. She also hopes that her apparent distress will make him afraid of her doing harm to herself, as the result of the despair into which his departure will cast her.

safe: make safe.
from childishness: i.e., age makes her free of childish credulity.
garboils: disturbances.
sacred vials: This is a reference to the Elizabethan belief that the Romans deposited bottles filled with tears in tombs.
are, or cease, as you shall give the advice: which exist or end in accordance with your counsel.
the fire: the sun.
quickens Nilus slime: brings to life the wet mud of the Nile.

After the spring floods, the Nile deposited alluvial mud on its banks and the adjoining land, in which seed was quickly germinated by the sun's heat. This happened until the recent construction of dams in Egypt. The Elizabethans believed that creatures were engendered by the sun out of the mud.

lace: cord fastening the bodice.
so: if only, so long as.
evidence: testimony, proof.
Egypt: i.e., Queen of Egypt.
meetly: tolerably good, appropriately.
target: shield.
still he mends: He continues to improve.

this is not the best: There is yet better to come.
Herculean: Antony was credited with descent from an ancestor, Anton, son of Hercules.
How . . . of his chafe: How his angry bearing suits this Herculean Roman.
my oblivion . . . Antony: My forgetfulness is just like an Antony, i.e., forgets all knowledge of me.
idleness: trivial humor.

"Were it not for the fact that you make use of (control) trivial humor, I would take you for trivial humor itself."

sweating labour to bear: She says that far from being trivial, the cause of her "humor" is heavy enough to give her great trouble to bear it.
my becomings: things that look well on me.
eye well to you: look well to your eye.
abides: remains, stays here.
flies: goes swiftly away.

Act Two, Scene Two

Lepidus is the third of the triumvirate, the three rulers of Rome. He is a friend of Caesar's but not hostile to Antony. He wants reconciliation between Octavius and Antony.

Enobarbus is a close friend of Antony's, who has been with him in Egypt. He wants what is best for Antony, thinking that the latter ought not to lose face by being too conciliatory.

the wearer of Antony's beard: To pluck by the beard was a traditional way of provoking a fight. Enobarbus says that in Antony's place he would not try to avoid a necessary conflict.
private stomaching: satisfying personal resentment.
passion: strong emotion.
compose: come to an agreement.
rend: tear apart.
curstness: bad temper.
grow to: add itself to.
being: i.e., being, in fact, ill.
derogately: disparagingly.

Caesar has regretted receiving bad reports of Antony, partly lamenting the shaming of a noble Roman, partly from a need to combine with him to hold the Roman world together; it is now threatened by Pompey's son. Antony agrees for the most part with Caesar about the political problem, but sees him as a younger, less experienced man, by whom he is underestimated.

Both Antony and Caesar would like to combine, but each regards the other as his inferior, and, conscious of the gaze of the whole world upon them, each is afraid of losing face. Antony suspects Caesar of disparaging him. Caesar suspects that Antony has plotted against him from Egypt. To some extent Antony's dead wife, Fulvia, is responsible for their discord, but it also derives from their fundamental differences of character. Caesar is much more circumspect, less generous of disposition. Antony exposes himself to hostility by assuming that nobody is petty enough to deny his essential worth, whatever superficial faults may exist in him.

practise on: plotted against.
how intend you?: What do you mean?
you may be pleas'd to catch at: You can guess at my meaning if you care to.
was theme for you: concerned you.
the word: the subject, topic.
urge me in his act: put me forward (1) as justification for his action, (2) by means of his action.
having alike your cause: having the same reason for resentment as you.
if you'll patch . . . make it with: If you want to piece together a quarrel as you do not have a complete justification for one.

Notice that Caesar deliberately uses Antony's word *patch.*

with graceful eyes attend: regard with favor.

"I know you could not avoid being conscious of this essential thought."

he: i.e., Antony's brother.
fronted: opposed, threatened.
pace: walk through its paces.

Enobarbus means that then, instead of being stirred up to

fight one another by individual wives, all the men would unite against the troublemaking women.

garboils: brawls, riots.

rioting: living dissolutely.

missive: messenger.

out of audience: from your audience (from his interview with you).

question: difference.

Lepidus is frightened by Caesar's charge that Antony has broken his word. But Antony knows that unintentionally his behavior has given grounds for Caesar's complaint, and that an explanation is owing, to salve his own honor, quite apart from giving satisfaction to the younger man.

but mine honesty, etc.: Although Antony will admit himself in the wrong, he will not admit that he has broken his oath of friendship. Such a breach of faith would really blot his honor. "My honesty in admitting what happened shall not destroy my honor, neither shall I use my power dishonestly" (i.e., If I have to fight, it will be as a result of my honesty).

Antony scorns to lie; on the other hand, if his honesty provokes a fight, he can now fight back with a good conscience.

ignorant motive: ignorant subject of dispute.

Mecaenas (Maecenas) is a friend of Caesar's. He is the man whose generosity to artists will make his name for all time synonymous with generous patronage.

atone: unite (pronounced *at one*).

Antony wants reconciliation and rebukes Enobarbus, whose realistic attitude (which could be called cynicism) may imperil the object of the meeting.

considerate stone: a stone unable to act but capable of reflection.

Enobarbus' manner has shown no consideration for the rank of the triumvirs. He has blurted out his opinions as if to equals, in contrast to the cautious and courteous manner of all the others.

conditions: physical and psychological temperaments.

stanch: immovably.

admir'd: wondered at.

unslipping: firm.
jealousies: suspicions leading to counteraction in anticipation of what is feared and suspected.
import: signify.
tale: half-told story.

Agrippa is a friend of Caesar's, but values Antony and wants to avoid conflict. At the beginning of his speech he emphasizes his intention. Notice that he himself declares that his suggestion comes from careful thought about the problem and its solution.

The actor of Antony can choose whether to be genuinely enthusiastic at the thought of marriage to Octavia in itself, or at the thought that the marriage solves the problem. He can also play Antony as one who does not intend to abandon Cleopatra, but hypocritically shows an enthusiasm which he does not feel.

fly off: desert, abandon.
strange: unusual.
at heel of: immediately after.
presently: immediately.
Mount Mesena: i.e., Mount Misenum. Misenum is an Italian port.
absolute master: in complete control.
fame: report.
dispatch: complete swiftly.
to my sister's view: to see my sister.
Half the heart of: very dear to.
light: (1) lit, illuminated, (2) giddy, frivolous.
noting: commenting on, remarking on.
most triumphant: all conquering.
square: just, accurate.

While he has been listening to the schemes for allying Antony and Caesar permanently, with Antony's protestations of enthusiasm for marriage to Octavia, Enobarbus has been remembering Cleopatra, contrasting her with Octavia, considering the chances of the latter dominating Antony to the exclusion of the Queen of Egypt. Enobarbus does not expect the plan to succeed. Now he sets himself to try to convey to his companions the quality of Cleopatra as he understands it. He re-experiences his own thoughts and feelings when he saw Cleopatra's first meeting with Antony. In all that follows, Enobarbus tries to make his listeners understand what kind of a person she is, how formidable as a rival to Octavia for Antony's love.

devis'd: invented, imagined.
cloth-of-gold of tissue: cloth made of gold thread woven with silk.
o'erpicturing: making a better picture than.
glow: make glow.
Nereides: the daughters of Nereus; they lived at the bottom of the Aegean Sea and had golden hair.
tended her i' th' eyes: they waited in her sight.
bends: courteous bowings.
adornings: additions to the beauty of the sight.
yarely: nimbly.
frame the office: perform the work.
strange: unusual.
wharfs: banks.
but for the vacancy: except for creating a vacuum.
had gone: would have gone.
ordinary: meal.
Caesar: i.e., Julius Caesar, uncle of Octavius.
cropp'd: bore fruit (Julius Caesar and Cleopatra had a son, Caesarion).

Mecaenas seems to be realizing for the first time just how powerful an attraction Cleopatra exerts, her full quality as a human being, and that Antony has apparently made up his mind to give her up.

become themselves: make themselves appropriate, good-looking.
riggish: wanton, sexually aroused.

Mecaenas hopes for something, of which he is not himself convinced, that Octavia's qualities will hold Antony away from Cleopatra. Enobarbus does not think this possible. His certainty discomforts Mecaenas and Agrippa.

Act Two, Scene Five

The scene takes place in Cleopatra's palace in Alexandria. Since he left her, Antony has met Caesar in Rome and agreed to marry Octavia, Caesar's sister.

moody: exerting an effect upon moods.
billiards: The game existed in Shakespeare's time (but not in Cleopatra's).
play: The word has a secondary bawdy meaning.
come too short: (1) be inadequate, (2) literally, be too short.
angle: rod and line.
betray: trick, lead to disaster.
wager: bet.
fervency: eagerness.
tires: (1) headdress, (2) clothes.
Philippan: the name given to the sword which Antony used in his victory in the battle of Philippi against Brutus and Cassius.
Ram: Notice the quality of the image with the use of *fruitful* and *barren*. The Messenger's *Madam, madam,* expresses the disastrous nature of his message.
tart: bitter, sour.
trumpet: announce.
formal: (1) ordinary, (2) in the form of.
allay: dilute.
good precedence: the good that came before.

Notice the foreboding expressed in the image of a gaoler who releases a criminal guilty of monstrous crimes. The image communicates what Cleopatra feels about the appearance of the Messenger, the disconcerting tone of his voice, his reluctance to "bring forth." She wants the bad news not to be told. As Antony is in good health and friends with Caesar, the Messsenger's demeanor can mean only that she has been deserted. Cleopatra uses the word *free* deliberately.
to what good turn: (1) to do what kind of good, (2) to do whom good.

Cleopatra is reluctant to be told what she fears she will hear.
turn: act, performance of an act.

spurn: kick.
ling'ring: persisting, long-lasting.
boot thee: give thee in addition.
thy modesty can beg: Anything you can ask for without being immodest. (This may mean sexual modesty or merely moderate wants.)
given myself the cause: i.e., by being so much in love with Antony.
hold thee still: refuse to change that.
so: even though.
scal'd: with scales.
Narcissus: He was punished by the gods for rejecting Echo. He was made to fall in love with the reflection of his own face in the water of springs, pools and streams. Cleopatra asserts that if the Messenger's face were as beautiful as that of Narcissus in his own eyes, she would now find him repulsive.
Take no offence, etc.: Do not be offended by my reluctance to offend you (i.e., in his silence).
unequal: unfair, unjust.
That art, etc.: The Messenger is certain of his innocence, that she has no cause to punish him. But she insists that merely to bear the message is to deserve her hatred. If he were a *knave* (i.e., dishonest), she could punish him without compunction.

At this moment Cleopatra admits that he is not personally guilty of an offense against her, but she still hates him as the bearer of such news.

undone: destroyed.
lie they: let them stay unsold.
inclination: general character, disposition.
him: i.e., Antony.
Painted one way, etc.: A perspective was painted this way, to show a Gorgon from one angle, which changes into the god Mars, when seen from another.

Act Three, Scene Six

Agrippa is a friend of Caesar's, who has suggested that in the interests of unity Antony should marry Octavia, Caesar's sister. But the marriage has failed, and Antony has returned to Cleopatra in Egypt. Caesar has crushed Lepidus, the third of the triumvirs who rule the Roman world. This has left Antony and Caesar political rivals as well as personal enemies. Mecaenas is another of Caesar's friends. Caesar is giving an account of Antony's shocking behavior.

contemning: decrying, denouncing, slighting.
tribunal: raised seat of honor, dais.
stablishment: settled possession.
exercise: drill, performance of gymnastic or martial feats.
Ptolemy: Cleopatra's brother.
habiliments: dress and trappings.
Isis: Egyptian goddess, associated with the fertility of the Nile valley.
queasy: disgusted, nauseous.
spoil'd: plundered.
unrestor'd: not given back.
frets: grumbles.
and being, etc.: Antony objects both to the deposing of Lepidus and to the fact that after the deposition Caesar has retained his revenue.
castaway: rejected.
stol'n upon: come unannounced.
usher: one who precedes, one who leads to a place.
populous: numerous.
ostentation: public display.
supplying every stage: giving fresh horses at every stage, providing all necessities.

Octavia, not knowing that Antony has returned to Cleopatra, has come quietly and modestly to try to prevent war between her brother and her husband.

levying: summoning to the armed forces, drafting.

withhold: restrain.
in negligent danger: in danger thanks to negligence.
o'er your content: over (to the detriment of) your happiness.
determin'd: not to be changed.
ministers: servants; "uses us and those that love you as instruments."
abominations: disgusting and degrading vices.
potent regiment: powerful rule.
trull: prostitute.
noises: boasts, makes public.

Caesar, combines affection and a wish to comfort his sister with the assurance of his determination to crush Antony as a consolation.

Act Four, Scene Fifteen

Cleopatra has taken refuge in the monument from the victorious troops of Caesar. To evade Antony's anger at her responsibility for his defeat, she has sent him a false report of her suicide. When he received the news he fell on his sword, giving himself a mortal wound. He now learns that Cleopatra is alive and orders his guard to take him to her. In this scene he is hoisted up to Cleopatra in the monument.

strange: terrifying.
upon him: near him.
great sphere thou mov'st in: See pp. 229 f. for a fuller account of the spheres.

The sun is moved in the sky by the rotation of a great crystalline circle (sphere) on which it is mounted. Cleopatra wants the sun to burn its sphere. The consequent devastation and chaos communicate the intensity of her wish not to have caused Antony's death.

darkling: in darkness.
varying shore: changing division, dividing line.
woe 'tis so: alas that it is so.
imperious show: imperial triumph. According to custom,

Cleopatra would be preserved alive to be exhibited as a captive as part of Caesar's triumphal procession in Rome.
brooch'd: adorned.
still conclusion: silent determination.
demuring upon: deploring.
heaviness: (1) sadness, (2) weight.
quicken: acquire life.
huswife: (1) literally, housewife, (2) figuratively, hussy, wanton.

Fortune is painted and described as turning a wheel on the rim of which human beings are fixed. With each turn of the wheel, some descend, others move up.
miserable change: change into misery.
pole: (1) banner, (2) lode star (i.e., immovable guide).
level with: equal to.
odds: differences, distinctions.
remarkable: worth taking notice of.
chares: chores.
it were for me: It would have been possible for me.
sottish: stupid.
does become: fits, is appropriate to.
sirs: i.e., to the women who are going to behave like men.

Act Five, Scene Two

Once Antony is dead, and with Caesar the victor, Cleopatra is determined to kill herself. When this scene begins, she has already decided to use the venomous asp as her way out. Yet her mood is not one of despair. She has two reasons for feeling a sort of triumph and exaltation. She believes that after the short agony of death, however painful, her reward will be immediate reunion with Antony on the other side. She can also congratulate herself on her ability to elude the Romans in a noble death. And once that is over she and Antony will no longer be subject to Fortune. In life after death their love will be invulnerable to time and chance. In this they will be superior to Caesar, who still alive will continue vulnerable to the fickle goddess.

The actress will find that Cleopatra has resolved to die, but that she expects some agony, some great unpleasantness and must steel herself to go through with it. Her love for Antony and her need for him give her the determination to submit to whatever agony may come, but it is difficult not to shrink from it, nevertheless.

Her realization that suicide can lead to a new and better beginning rather than to a mere end to desolation is expressed in her opening speech.

knave: menial servant.
minister: servant.
that thing: i.e., dying, which puts all to sleep.
accidents: chance happenings.
bolts up: imprisons, deprives of liberty.
palates: tastes.

Proculeius comes in with the intention of preventing Cleopatra's suicide, knowing that while he absorbs her attention, the Guard will be climbing the monument to take her prisoner.

study on: consider carefully.
care: trouble about, worry about.

This is true as she knows she is about to end her life.

make . . . reference to: apply to.
pray in aid: ask for help from outside (i.e., pray, beg, aid in).
doctrine: lesson.

When the soldiers reveal themselves, Cleopatra, not sure that she will have an opportunity to use the asp, attempts to use her dagger.

languish: lengthy incurable disease.
undoing: destruction.
acted: put into effect, figuratively, performed.
let . . . come forth: permit to take the stage.
temperance: moderation.
mortal house: i.e., body.
pinion'd: ignobly bound.
varletry: common, base people, rabble, canaille.
censuring: critical, finding fault.

blow: lay its eggs to make swell.
abhorring: being abhorrent.
pyramids: (1) obelisks, (2) pyramids.
would die: want to die.
trick: habit.

When Dolabella is left with her, Cleopatra tells him ironically that she cannot remember having heard of him, all she can remember is the reality of Antony as she knew him, as she remembers him, a reality which has gone as if it had never existed, which exists now only in her power to recall and imagine him. She is intent on letting Dolabella know what the world has lost in Antony and in consoling herself privately with the knowledge that she will soon rejoin him.

crested: formed a crest for, projected from the top of.
propertied: had the qualities.
tuned spheres: See pp. 229 f. for an account of the spheres and their music.
quail: make quail.

She concentrates on trying to let Dolabella grasp the enormous generosity and creativity of Antony.

dolphin-like: The dolphin was regarded as the natural monarch of fish, a creature full of generosity and capable of life in air as in water.
livery: uniform, colors (i.e., as his dependents).
plates: pieces of money.
past the size of dreaming: No dream can contain or equal such a person.
vie strange forms with fancy: compete with imagination in creating unusual forms.
piece: masterpiece.

To imagine an Antony would be to realize a living reality which overshadows and eclipses any image that fancy could create out of itself.

shadow: image, figment of the imagination.
Sole sir: only master.

Cleopatra aims at deceiving Caesar into believing her to be

reconciled to her situation and to have given up all hope of suicide.

project: imagine, conceive.
clear: spotless, innocent.
extenuate: undervalue, weaken, dilute.
enforce: reinforce, emphasize.
apply . . . to our intents: yield to our intentions, conform to our intentions.
lay on me: burden me with.
Antony's course: i.e., suicide.
bereave: deprive.
purpose: plan, intention.
And may: And you are able to come and go as you please.
scutcheon: shield of honor displaying symbols of victory, conquest; i.e., those whom Caesar has vanquished exist to attest to his glory to the world; in this they are like scutcheons.
sign of conquest: trophy.
brief: list.

Cleopatra's procedure with the *brief* is aimed (successfully) at deceiving Caesar into thinking that she has given up all intention of suicide. No would-be suicide bothers to try to cheat her adversary out of booty. She feigns confusion and shame and deceives him utterly.

not petty things admitted: petty things excluded (*petty things:* small details).
parcel: give individual details of.
lady trifles: worthless things dear to women.
reserv'd: kept back.
immoment: of no moment.
modern: ordinary (i.e., ornaments, jewelry appropriate for relaxed occasions, not fit for those of state formality).

Livia is Caesar's wife; Octavia, his sister and Antony's widow.

unfolded with: exposed by.
bred: brought up in my household.
cinders: still glowing remnants of fire.
chance: ill fortune.
Forbear: leave.
misthought: misjudged, misunderstood, thought ill of.

answer in our name: we are held accountable for.
merits: qualities (good or bad).

Caesar now aims at reassuring Cleopatra that she will be treated with dignity. He wants her for his triumph in Rome, does not want to lose that pleasure by driving her to despair and suicide.
put i' th' roll of conquest: included in the list of what has been obtained by victory.
make prize: haggle.

As Caesar departs, Cleopatra makes so convincing a show of believing him that he is completely lulled into relaxing the strictest security. As he treats her so graciously, his soldiers are deceived into carelessness and allow the peasant access to her with his seemingly innocuous figs.

During the preceding dialogue Cleopatra has been waiting for the moment when she will be free to kill herself in the high Roman fashion. As soon as Caesar has left she acts swiftly.

words: lies to.

She whispers to Charmian to send for or admit the peasant who is waiting to provide the asps. Charmian immediately leaves.
finish: end it, die.

Dolabella may be played as an honest man who really believes Caesar, or as one who dissembles in order to convince Cleopatra that she still has much to live for. He goes on his knee and treats Cleopatra as a queen, one much higher than him in rank.
religion: sacred duty.
puppet: like a puppet in a puppet show.
mechanic slaves: ignoble manual workers, artisans.
rank of gross diet: thick and stinking from coarse food.
lictor: minor official, like the Elizabethan beadle.
scald: mean, scurvy.

Cleopatra is both testing Iras and trying to inspire her to commit suicide as well, to help and not hinder what now has to be done.
I am again, etc.: Once more she is about to undertake a journey

to meet Antony and she wants to be made once more as splendid and entrancing as on the earlier occasion.

chare: task (there is a possibility that Cleopatra knows that a *chare* or *chore* is a task which has to be repeated from day to day, and is playing with the idea that this is one that will never be repeated).

Cleopatra is fully committed to suicide as the swift way to reunion with Antony; nevertheless, there is a reluctance to feel the pain which she thinks inescapable from dying. There is a shrinking from the sharp bite of the asp and whatever cramps and distortions its poison will bring. Even so her resolution is not shaken.

plac'd: set, firmly fixed.

marble-constant: as unchangeable as marble.

fleeting: changeable, inconstant.

worm: snake.

pains not: gives no pain.

In her short dialogue with the Clown her wish is to be reassured that the *worm* is indeed painless. He cannot give her the certainty which she wants, but she is not deterred and wants him to leave so that she can do what she has to.

immortal: This is what has been known as a malapropism since Sheridan, but in one sense Cleopatra will be made immortal in eternal reunion with Antony after death.

falliable: almost certainly a comic blunder for "infallible."

do his kind: (1) act according to his nature, (2) possibly, act with kindness.

mar: spoil.

Still determined to die, to meet Antony beyond death, Cleopatra has not abandoned fear of the pain involved.

luck of Caesar . . . afterwrath: i.e., Antony mocks the luck of Caesar, saying that the gods give men good fortune as a kind of compensation which justifies their change to hostility later.

prove my title: (1) confirm my ownership, confirm my right to the name, (2) confirm my appellation.

fire and air: the two nobler elements, both higher than earth and water.

It was believed that all created things, including men and

women, consist of the four elements in varying proportions. Cleopatra declares that she is freeing herself of the two elements which would be out of place in the heavens where she is to meet Antony.

aspic: asp.

When Iras falls, Cleopatra marvels that death can come so swiftly and painlessly. She still thinks of it as hurting, even if desirable, however.

nature: life in the mortal flesh.

Dost thou lie still: She is amazed that there is no sign of struggle or of life in Iras' body. This death seems without a pang. Nevertheless, Cleopatra expects a stab of pain from the asp in the way that we know that a hypodermic syringe in dentistry can be very unpleasant before the anaesthetic works.

mortal wretch: insignificant, but deadly, creature.

She expects to feel the sharp teeth, but is now ready for them.

intrinsicate: intricate.

poor venomous fool,/ Be angry and dispatch: Cleopatra expected to feel the asp's teeth bite her. The absence of discomfort, of pain and swelling, convinces her it has not done so. She scolds it as a ridiculous, poisonous creature without the wit to bite her. She wants it to bite her quickly and get the matter over.

Unpolicied: overreached in policy (i.e., cheated and deceived by the very person he intends to cheat and deceive).

She still expects to feel the asp's teeth, and as a result to die, and she can gloat at the thought of Caesar when he finds himself so easily outwitted by one whom he despises.

Charmian's outcry brings a sleepy protest from her mistress. The poison has begun to work without her realizing it as she slides quietly and luxuriously into a contented drowsiness from which she does not want to be roused by Charmian's lament. For Cleopatra the experience is like what she remembers from nursing her children, a completely relaxed and satisfied losing of consciousness.

Suddenly the thought of Antony makes her remember that

she ought to be doing something to kill herself to join him after death. And still not realizing that this delicious languor is the descent into death of which she has been so terrified, she tries to rouse herself to take another asp, as she thinks the first has failed her. She tries to pick up another asp; it is slippery and wriggles, and weakened by approaching death, her fingers are unable to grasp it. Still not knowing that she is dying, Cleopatra is determined to use this asp as well as the other, adjuring it, *Nay, I will take thee too;* but before she can complete her question: *What should I stay—*, she is dead, without ever having realized what has been happening to her. And the question is ended for her by Charmian.

What should I stay: Why should I stay here longer?
Of eyes: by eyes.
mend: put right.
play: make a move.
beguil'd: outwitted.
touch their effects: meet reality.
perform'd: having been performed.
augurer: one who foretells the future.
levell'd at: aimed at, saw clearly.
trimming up: setting straight.
toil: net, trap.
vent: erupt.
blown: swollen.
conclusions: experiments.
clip in: hold, embrace.
in solemn show: in ceremonial array.
See/High, etc.: Caesar had intended to expose Cleopatra to dishonor as part of his own triumph in Rome. Instead, he gives orders for the army to honor her with the most respectful ceremonial accorded only to the glorious. He has lost his contempt for her, recognizing a grandeur in her death which demands honor from the sternest of Romans.

JULIUS CAESAR

Introduction

ALTHOUGH SHAKESPEARE WAS aware of many differences between Caesar's Rome and Elizabeth's England, he has still imagined Roman society as if it conformed to many assumptions held in his own time. The Roman Republic is not imagined as the rule of mob; Shakespeare does not look on Brutus and his supporters as republicans of the order of the English commoners who would like to overturn all good rule and civilization in various English History Plays. The Roman republicans are recognized as aristocrats, men of dignity and nobility, proud of their race, their city, their civilization, as jealous of honor as any Elizabethan nobleman. Brutus' fellow conspirators are imagined much as if they were the self-seeking, unruly aristocrats of the Wars of the Roses, resenting any authority which might restrain them, but still aristocrats.

Assumptions about the relationship of wife and husband, of king to subject, and of friends, which hold good for Shakespeare's England also apply to Caesar's Rome; there, too, the state is organized as a hierarchy. And, while Shakespeare is well aware that Rome is pagan, this does not mean for him that Roman thinking on portents, fortune, the stars and the exercise of free will is different from that of his own age. Where a Roman might ultimately see the world ruled by his gods or by necessity, Shakespeare seems to believe in the Christian God who works through an interaction of Fortune and human free will. He ascribes to his Romans no belief in Christ, of course; but their understanding of the mechanism is the same as that of an Elizabethan: humans are influenced by the stars, but they can exert free will, they are "at some time masters of their fate," even if their decisions and actions still conform to the intentions of "the mighty gods." Similarly, portents and prodigies warn the Romans, as they warn the Elizabethans of divine anger, in one case, that of the gods, in the other, God's.

Act One, Scene Two

Will you go see . . . to other men.

Cassius hates Caesar for a combination of political and personal reasons which are inseparable. As an individual who can thrive in the republic, rather than for republican principle, he wants to stop Caesar turning Rome into his personal monarchy or empire. He despises Caesar, sees only his physical weaknesses and cannot admit to himself any admirable qualities in Caesar which have led him to power. The contrast between Caesar's power and his own contempt for the man is a perpetual goad to Cassius' resentment. As he is convinced that Caesar will soon have the crown, Cassius has decided to plot against him. Failure means death, but so does inaction, sooner or later.

Any attempt to stop Caesar depends on Brutus' help for success. Cassius has been close to Brutus; but recently Brutus has been behaving strangely, almost in a hostile manner, certainly aloof, as if in deep disapproval of one from whom he has become estranged, possibly in suspicion of some kind of conspiracy against Caesar.

Cassius has decided to risk declaring himself to Brutus; but first he must try to repair their friendship. And so he wants Brutus to accompany him to watch the race.

gamesome: inclined to indulge in light entertainment.

Cassius now openly reproaches Brutus with being unfriendly. Until this coldness is overcome there will be no possibility of winning him over against Caesar.

gentleness: tolerant flexibility.

you bear too stubborn, etc.: You are too intolerant and too unfriendly in your treatment of your friend.

Brutus now makes clear to Cassius that his manner has not

derived from animosity to others, but from an inability to be satisfied with himself.
veil'd my look: not been frank and open in the expression on my face.
passions of some difference: conflicting wishes and emotions.
conceptions only proper to myself: ideas which concern nobody but myself.
construe: interpret, read a meaning into.
shows of love: outward expressions of friendship.

Then, Brutus . . . had his eyes.

Still a little cautious, Cassius remarks that his misinterpretation of Brutus' behavior has prompted him to keep to himself what he has been thinking, his careful appraisal and reappraisal of possibilities of action of great importance. Had he realized that Brutus so underestimated himself, Cassius would not have felt inhibited from speaking out, but rather would have done so all the more readily in order to make his friend realize that so far from being inadequate he is generally considered a man of great integrity and ability.

Cassius maneuvers for position by reminding Brutus that no human being can see himself with his own eyes; he depends upon an image reflected back, either in a mirror or in the opinion of other people.

your passion: your emotion and the intention from which it arises.
worthy cogitations: not negligible appraisal of plans.
worthiness: heroic quality, dignity, worth.
shadow: reflection, image.
respect: honor, reputation.
had his eyes: had the use of his eyes (to see himself and others clearly).

In other words, a man's opinion of himself must be faulty if he ignores the high estimate made by fellow men who observe him closely. Cassius wants to make Brutus realize his own importance. There may well be a certain flattery involved here. Cassius values Brutus deeply as a friend, recognizes his integrity, knows that his support is essential, and rightly realizes that his influence comes from selfless moral integrity. Cassius also knows that Brutus may be a leader of men morally, but is not a man of action of the caliber required of a leader who acts against Caesar.

It is impossible for a man of the stamp of Cassius to understand that Brutus is invulnerable to flattery and to every attempt to stir up personal resentment against Caesar. Cassius therefore tries both to flatter Brutus into the illusion that he is as great a leader as Caesar and to goad him into personal resentment of Caesar's preeminence.

Brutus is accurate in his appraisal of himself; he cannot be flattered into seeing himself as a man of action of Caesar's caliber. Nor does he harbor personal animosity against Caesar. The troubles which have made Brutus *veil* his *look* from his friends derive from two conflicting commitments: he is committed to the Roman republic, by tradition, by upbringing, by principle and by deep love; he is also committed in friendship to Caesar, a man whom he loves, who inspires him with admiration and respect. He is fundamentally modest, knows he does not have the qualities of a leader in action like Caesar. He does not see himself as an alternative to his friend. If anything he harbors an illusion that he can inspire his fellow Romans with his own noble, disinterested motives.

To play Brutus it is essential to understand that he really has a deep love for Caesar, that he does not see in himself those qualities which shine so splendidly in Caesar. But Brutus cannot conceive of Rome, as he loves and honors it, becoming a monarchy or empire. To him Rome is not Rome if it is not the republic in which he was born, of which he has read, in which he has gloried, which he has been brought up to serve and which he has served and intends to serve so long as there is life in him. He is disturbed because the service of the republic may demand conflict with his friend Caesar. Brutus is ready to kill Caesar if it ever becomes clear without any possible doubt that Caesar will destroy the republic, will accept the crown. Until that becomes clear, however, Brutus will not act. His friendship for Caesar divides Brutus from Cassius; Brutus' determination to save the republic can give them a common aim, the destruction of Caesar; but where Cassius hates Caesar and wants to destroy him, Brutus loves him, does not want his destruction, but fears it may be unavoidable.

When he asks his question of Cassius, whatever he may suspect, Brutus has no certainty as to his friend's *cogitations.* They have not been in one another's confidence. Brutus is the last person in whom Cassius can be expected to confide plots against Caesar. Only an extremity of envy, resentment, hatred and fear that the crown is Caesar's for the accepting, not even the asking, leads Cassius to committing himself so far. If Caesar has the crown Cassius expects death; so it seems to him worth the risk to try to sound Brutus in the hope of finding an ally.

When Brutus insists on his own knowledge of himself with the question *Into what dangers?*, Cassius concentrates on making clear a conspiracy's real need of Brutus. First he reminds Brutus that a man needs a *glass* in which to see his own reflection. What would be a breach of modesty for Brutus to recognize in himself, Cassius can show him modestly.

jealous: suspicious, alert, not to be taken at a disadvantage or lulled into negligence.
new protester: every person who asserts his love for the first time.
scandal: talk against; spread slander about.
profess myself: make a declaration of my friendship.

Hearing the trumpets and shouting, Brutus now declares his fear.

What means this shouting? . . . than I fear death.

Cassius pounces on this to make Brutus admit that he does not want Caesar to be king.

Brutus, who knows his Cassius, tries to make clear the motive for his *fear.* His opposition to Caesar's political intention in no way affects his love for the man. He tries to establish once

and for all that he is not afraid to move if it is in the public good; nothing but the public good can prevail on him, not animosity or ambition; and in pursuit of the public good no threat or danger of death can deter him.
I would not: I do not want.
so speed me: give me success (or failure).

I know that . . . As easily as a king.

Cassius, having obtained this declaration, couches his argument in terms which he hopes will make it seem relevant to and in tune with Brutus' principles. What he has to say is a matter of honor. To let one man rule is dishonor, especially when that man has no clear outstanding quality over others to justify his preeminence.

Cassius starts by insisting that he is as certain of the heroic quality within Brutus as he is of recognizing his outward appearance.
I would as lief, etc: I would be as content to die as to live.

Notice the sound play *lief not be–live to be.* Cassius knows it is there and is using it to express his feelings. He argues that they were all born with the same freedom as Caesar, have the same abilities to endure physical hardship. Then the memory of his rescue of Caesar from the Tiber overcomes his control and he lets his resentment and hatred of one whom he considers a lesser man express itself in the rest of the account.
gusty: windy.
chafing: angry with; attacking.
accoutred: laden with arms and equipment.
lusty sinews: robust muscles.

Aeneas, who left Troy after its fall and founded Rome, carried his father, Anchises, to safety out of the burning city. The sting of this statement comes in the fact that Anchises was old and infirm and needed to be carried to safety by one with more strength: Caesar, the mighty soldier, needed help in the midst of his glory as much as the aged, decrepit Trojan father.
hearts of controversy: hearts full of will to fight back.
bend: the direction of whose penetrating look.

feeble temper: weak physical condition (inability to endure, like badly tempered metal).
bear the palm: win the race on his own; be ahead of all competitors at the finishing point.

Whatever goes through Brutus' mind during this recital, he definitely does not agree with Cassius about Caesar. Brutus is concerned chiefly with his fear that his love of Rome, the republic, may force him into an alliance with such as Cassius, who hate Caesar, against his best friend, for whom he has no spark of hatred.

The new shout and burst of trumpets lead him to express his fear. Cassius seizes on Brutus' words *new honours,* as if they in themselves are grounds for resentment (while Brutus regrets only that they must be such as to destroy the republic). Cassius remembers to emphasize the fact that Caesar's triumph will mean *dishonourable graves* to all who submit (death in opposing will preserve honor). Cassius insists that although men are subject to the influence of the stars and to other vagaries of Fortune, yet there are times in each man's life when he can exercise free will to determine what happens to him. Cassius now makes his strongest effort to persuade Brutus to make the decision to act. He insists there is no intrinsic quality in Caesar's name to give it such awesome strength. As no agreement comes from Brutus, he tries another tack, deploring the absence of heroic spirits in modern Rome, which has space within it for only one man.

Having tried to stir a sense of shame in Brutus as involved in a general decline of quality, Cassius now turns on him as an individual, reminding him of the republican tradition of his family, reproaching him with falling below the standard of his heroic ancestor whose name he bears.

sound: speak.
becomes the mouth: sounds as well when spoken.
conjure: use as a magical spell to invoke a spirit.
start: raise up.
soon: quickly.

age: the time in which we live.
but it was fam'd, etc.: that it did not have more than one man in it to make it famous.

Cassius deliberately plays on the similarity of the sounds of *Rome* and *room.* It was both Rome enough and room enough, i.e., there was little room and not much Rome.
brook'd: tolerated.
eternal devil: immortal spirit of implacable evil.

That you do love me . . . Caesar is returning.

I am nothing jealous: I am not in the least suspicious of your love for me. Brutus tries to make the situation clear. He has no misgivings over Cassius' declaration of friendship and admiration for him. To some extent he has the same aim as Cassius. But he will not yet say what he has been thinking. He asks Cassius not to be a nuisance by making more efforts to win him over (after all, Brutus knows that if Caesar decides to destroy the republic, he will be ready to kill him). Finally Brutus makes a declaration, which in his mind ought to end all doubts as to his intentions, should there be a certainty that Caesar will be king unless something drastic is done to stop him. When Brutus is saying he had rather be a villager it is as if a high-ranking nobleman in Shakespeare's England insisted he would rather be a mean servant performing the most menial and dishonorable of tasks, as if a southern planter in the last century, proud of his aristocracy, insisted he would prefer to be a black slave. For Brutus, to be a citizen of free Rome is the highest of all honors; to deny that birthright in favor of sharing the dishonor of any undistinguished village is unthinkable.

Cassius recognizes how great a commitment he has received and the impossibility of getting more so long as Caesar has not made it clear that his next move will be to secure the crown.

The image is of striking one stone against another to produce a spark.

In studying this scene we should not forget to consider the nature of the admiration of Cassius for Brutus. Some of the terms used here, and even more those of the quarrel scene, suggest that Cassius has a homosexual love for Brutus, though there seems to be no indication that it is returned or even recognized. If Shakespeare has imagined Cassius feeling sexual love for Brutus there is not the slightest suggestion that it is either reprehensible or admirable. It merely exists and must be taken into account as one more motive for Cassius' envy of Caesar who has the loyalty and affection of Brutus which Cassius wants and values.

Act Two, Scene Two

In this scene Caesar refuses to be deterred by the alleged "portents" of the night and by the report of the augurs of a beast without a heart. He is not moved by the pleas of Calpurnia (Calphurnia) to stay at home at first, then suddenly accedes to her request. But when Decius Brutus interprets her dream as an auspicious portent, Caesar changes his mind once more and decides to go.

The actor playing Caesar is faced with some questions to which differing answers may all be valid, but in providing his answers the individual actor can rely on two certainties. One is that Caesar definitely wants the crown, and the second, that he is convinced that he has the support of Brutus. Like his opponents, Caesar knows that no conspiracy against him has any chance of success so long as Brutus is with him. That Brutus is against him does not occur to him until the truth is revealed by a hostile dagger; then with the words *Et tu, Brute,* he admits to himself that this is the end, he has no chance: *Then fall, Caesar.*

Nor heaven nor earth . . . Who's within?

Remembering the certainty that Caesar wants to go to receive the crown there are three possibilities for the actor:
(1) Caesar is genuinely indifferent to the events of the night. (If we choose this, we have to account for his decision to send to the priests.)

(2) He scoffs at both the storms, etc., in the heavens and Calpurnia's lack of peace on earth.
(3) He does not dismiss the possibility of trouble portended by the previous night, but, secure in his confidence in Brutus, is ready to face trouble and overcome it. He has spent a lifetime successfully taking calculated risks and continues to do so today.

What mean you . . . when it will come.

mean: intend, want to do.

She and her husband both know that his only danger can come from discontented Roman noblemen, determined to preserve the republic or their own selfish interests or both. For Calpurnia, her dreaming and the sounds and sights of the night amount to warnings of disaster if he carries out his intention of going to be acclaimed as king. She may not know which individuals will kill him, but she knows they exist.

Caesar may actually know of some kind of conspiracy, may suspect or be certain of the involvement of various individuals. He may expect an attack which will fail, lacking the support of Brutus. With Brutus to guard his back and discourage enemies he cannot fail to receive the crown. With that in his possession, it will be time to deal with such enemies as are not prepared to reconcile themselves to a *fait accompli.*

So he declares his intention of going; such dangers as may exist do so only until he confronts them. Conspirators who have to face him openly will be easily overcome; the battle may be fierce, much blood may be shed, but he will emerge as king.
are vanished: have disappeared.

the things that threaten'd me
Ne'er look'd but on my back; when they shall see
The face of Caesar, they are vanished.

This is not a vainglorious boast, but a confident assertion of what his experience has shown him. Dangers may well have gathered in the security of planning when he is not present. Danger can threaten only until the moment comes to act in his presence. Then he has always triumphed, and he expects to once more.

Calpurnia is appalled because, although she has never taken any notice of ceremonial predictions, this time she cannot ignore them.

watch: civil night patrol of one or more persons.

"There is somebody inside the house, who gives an account not only of the things that we ourselves have seen and heard, but adds that most horrifying sights have been seen by the watch."

in ranks and squadrons and right form of war: This is of immense importance for Calpurnia. This clash of armed men in the heavens was not simply a confused conflict. The *fierce warriors of fire* were drawn up in their battle array, rank upon rank, in their centuries, their larger divisions, deployed in the exact orderly manner prescribed for Roman soldiers engaged in battle. Whoever told Calpurnia this made her imagine it clearly, and her image conveys her intention of making Caesar admit that he is faced with a danger which he must avoid.

A few moments earlier, Calpurnia imagines graves opening, the dead emerging in various stages of decomposition, with and without shrouds; the terror which she feels is for Caesar, her only intention is to prevail on him to save himself by staying home.

beyond all use: outside all normal experience.

Listening, the actor may refuse to admit that the events portend his death. It is more likely that Caesar admits to himself that great danger lies in wait for him, but he is convinced he will survive it with Brutus to help him. He concentrates on calming Calpurnia. Instead of admitting the danger and insisting that he will survive it, he says no human being can avoid his *end when it is purpos'd by the mighty gods.* This adds to Calpurnia's desolation, at which he tries to calm her by insisting that whatever may be predicted does not apply only to him, but to the world as a whole (it was a point made by those who believed in astrology in Shakespeare's day that predictions are "general" not "particular").

Calpurnia fights back with the assertion that prodigies do not precede the death of beggars, only that of people of importance.

blaze forth: (1) burn with, (2) announce, advertise.

Now Caesar tells her to learn from his experience, that to be terrified of the possibility of death is to suffer every time there is such a possibility. He wants her not to torment herself with what may not happen. So far in his life, despite his many risks and dangers, he has never suffered death in his imagination. It will happen to him only once, when it really comes. And she should reserve her fear and grief for that sole occasion.

What say the augurers? . . . I will stay at home.

offering: sacrifice.

The absence of a heart in the sacrificial animal is a prodigious event, such as those reported during the night, and suggests failure of any enterprise about to be undertaken. This is the message of the priests, whose vocation is to interpret portents and presage the future. But Caesar is determined to have the crown today. He knows the risk and is convinced he can overcome whatever dangers face him. The statement about *danger* knowing *full well* comes from his knowledge of enemies who are about to attempt to stop him, even by assassination. Still confident of the support of Brutus, he believes that his assailants will find him more terrible than they expect. He has faced danger since before his birth, which needed the celebrated Caesarean operation; having faced and overcome danger since before drawing his first breath, he is correct in seeing himself the more terrible inasmuch as he acts in accordance with his own will and has always triumphed over danger.

confidence: overconfidence.

There are two possible motives for Caesar's change in response to Calpurnia's pleading; as she says she *never stood on ceremonies*, which means that her intense fear now cannot be ignored. Either it moves him to compassion for her; really loving her he cannot inflict such mental torment on her, seeing that she really is in torment. Or the alternative is that the intensity of her fear makes him wonder if the risk might not be too great this time, if it might not be better to wait until another day; the senate will not dare to change its mind; to stay at home now will confuse his enemies, upset their plans. If the actor chooses this motive, he can play a man who nevertheless disguises it as compassion for his wife.

I have left it for the individual actor to make his own decision as to Caesar's tendency to believe that the portents mean danger in conflict with his confidence that the risk is worth taking, and with the strength of his determination to have the crown today.

for thy humour: to indulge your caprice.

Here's Decius Brutus . . . Give me my robe, for I will go.

When Decius Brutus enters he sees that Caesar is not dressed to go to the senate house; instead of an air of preparation before leaving for some event of overriding importance, there is an atmosphere of relaxation, of domesticity. Calpurnia does not look like one who is about to bid farewell to the man who is to be offered the crown; nor does she seem perturbed by the prodigies of the night. On the contrary, she is content, as if she does not expect to be deprived of his company, and Caesar has no air of immediate activity. Decius Brutus decides to ignore these signs and to behave as if there is no doubt that Caesar will accompany him to the senate as arranged. He has assured his fellow conspirators during the night that he is intimate enough with Caesar to be able to overcome any change of intention as a result of the portents. He has managed to present himself to Caesar as one who wishes him well, and Caesar's statement in a few moments betokens a relaxed familiarity which leads the great man to make remarks which, made to any other listener, would seem like indiscretions:

> But for your private satisfaction
> Because I love you, I will let you know.

Caesar can let himself talk about the senate in a way which would offend the strict principles of Marcus Brutus; to Decius Brutus he can speak almost as confidentially as to Mark Antony, lightly expressing his disrespect for the graybeards. Caesar's response to Calpurnia's suggestion can now be equally light; there is no need to bother to lie to the senate; powerless and to some extent ludicrous as he sees them, there is no reason why they should not be told the truth, that he *will not come*.

But it is important for Decius Brutus to know the reason. Only when he knows, can he try to change Caesar's mind. Moreover, Decius Brutus suspects that both the portents and Calpurnia have much to do with the decision to stay at home. He points out, reasonably and ruefully, that the message as it stands will expose him to ridicule. Caesar's feeling for him becomes clear in the two lines quoted above; he makes an exception for Decius Brutus.

statua: statue.
stays me: keeps me.
lusty: happy; sturdy.
does apply for: interprets (applies to the present circumstances).
press: crowd, throng.
stains: colors of heraldry.
cognizance: heraldic emblems.

Knowing how strongly Caesar wants the crown, Decius Brutus adroitly offers a more acceptable interpretation of the dream. Caesar's approval of the interpretation encourages him to continue with his news of the senate's intention. Throughout he presents himself as one who wishes Caesar well, who rejoices that his great moment has come, who regrets deeply the possibility that in his indulgence of Calpurnia's fear, Caesar might well lose the crown.

mock apt to be render'd: gives ground for a derisory remark which would be made quite fittingly.

Decius Brutus relies on his intimacy with Caesar to laugh at the whole thing as a mistake which Caesar is not going to make simply to allay his wife's fears in his unselfish kindness to her. As he meets with no rebuff he dares a slightly more dangerous ploy, which he knows will sting Caesar into action, even if at the risk of drawing his anger. So after the warning against appearing to be afraid, he swiftly propitiates Caesar with the apology and explanation that his offensive remark comes from wishing well to Caesar's undertakings.

reason to my love is liable: Reason yields to my love.

While persuading Caesar to change his mind, Decius Brutus contrives to exclude Calpurnia from the discussion; both men are aware of her; neither is prepared to involve her.

Wanting the crown strongly and hearing for certain that it will be offered to him if he goes to the senate, Caesar accepts the more propitious interpretation of Calpurnia's dream and does what he wants to most. He prepares to leave at once.

Act Four, Scene One

Lepidus, Mark Antony and Octavius are each ruthless, prepared to sacrifice anyone to gain their ends. Antony is not concerned only with his own power, but to avenge Caesar by destroying Cassius and Brutus; for this latter he has the deepest hatred and contempt as one who betrayed a friend. Antony has no compunction, however, about destroying Publius, his nephew, in return for Lepidus' consent to his own brother's death. Octavius, dead Caesar's nephew and heir, is in no position to repudiate his allies.

prick'd: checked, marked off. It was Elizabethan practice to prick a hole against a name in a list on paper as the equivalent of the modern habit of making a mark beside it in pen or ink.

with a spot . . . I damn him: (1) literally, "with a mark I condemn him," (2) "with a sin or flaw, I send him to damnation."

cut off some charge: reduce some expenditure called for.

Antony despises Lepidus and confides in Octavius his intention of merely using their ally and then of getting rid of him.
meet: fit.
the threefold world divided: with the Roman Empire divided into three between them.
proscription: denunciation and sentence to death.

Octavius is not overawed by Antony and has no hesitation in expressing his disagreement with him. Antony regards himself not only as the senior to Octavius, with more experience of the world, but as a mentor to the younger man, to whom he will be a guide out of friendship to his dear friend, Caesar.

Antony's intention is to explain political realities so that Octavius will not hamper him, but will benefit from his ability.
divers sland'rous loads: various activities, which will burden us with scandal, make us be regarded as dishonorable.
graze in commons: (1) literally, "graze on the common land," (2) satisfy himself with ordinary sustenance.
store of provender: right amount of fodder.
wind: twist, turn.

Elizabethan psychology and physiology taught that bodily motion is possible as the result of the energy imparted by a substance secreted in the heart and carried in the bloodstream, in virtue of which the senses operate. The substance is called "spirit." Antony uses *spirit* in two senses; (1) the secretion which gives effect to the senses, (2) soul in the normal sense. Lepidus would have no soul to govern him, but for Antony taking charge of his body.
abjects: refuse; food rejected by others.
orts: scraps not wanted by others.
imitations: things now out of fashion.
property: something to be owned, to be made use of.

As Octavius does not demur, Antony addresses himself to the task of organizing opposition to Brutus and Cassius.
levying powers: raising forces by conscription.
make head: (1) raise our army, (2) take to the field against.
presently: at once.
covert: hidden, secret.
at the stake: The image is of a bear which cannot retreat nor

advance far in attack; it is tied to a stake on a fairly short rope. It must fight defensively. The bear "at bay" is surrounded by barking dogs. So is the triumvirate by enemies.
mischiefs: planned attacks, evils.

Act Four, Scene Three

That you have wrong'd me . . . Chastisement!

In preparation for this scene, remember that Brutus has just had news of the death of his wife, Portia. What he has regarded as the service of Rome has led him to kill his friend, Caesar, to leave his wife when she needed him, to be absent on her death. The news of Cassius' involvement in corruption has made Brutus desperate at the thought that all that he has done and sacrificed may have been in vain; it may have led to a Rome exposed to such as Antony and Cassius instead of the ideal republic for which he has been striving. Perhaps it would have been better to have accepted Caesar than to exchange him for these rulers; then Caesar would not have been murdered, Portia would still be alive, he, Brutus, would not be plagued with his own reproaches for having betrayed a friend only to make bad worse.

Cassius is also full of bitter anger. The unworldly, priggish Brutus has humiliated him publicly, as if corruption could possibly be eradicated from politics. The affection which Cassius has for Brutus embitters him further; he has been humiliated by one whom he loves, and who has no consideration for him, who treats him on the contrary with hostility. In addition, Cassius is certain that Brutus threw away their victory by letting Antony speak and has continued to indulge his sense of moral pride in the same kind of futile behavior, ignoring advice, overruling all other plans.

Each actor has the choice of trying to control his indignation at the beginning, or of letting fly immediately the two are alone.

Cassius tries to prove his case first, reproaching Brutus. The argument is basically one of the triviality of the offense which true friendship would ignore. But Brutus tries to get him to see that any corruption, however small, betrays their conspiracy. If anyone but Cassius had done this, Brutus would not have been restrained by friendship and honor for the name involved; he would have punished the criminal. Cassius' response is in the word *Chastisement!* The actor can choose between incredulous outrage, violent repudiation, quiet, dangerous amusement, etc.

To avoid physical violence or some irrevocable decision which will negate all that these two have achieved, Brutus tries to remind Cassius of the high ideals which (he still thinks) were the inspiration for the conspirators.

Remember March, the ides . . . tempt me no farther.

In his love for Brutus, Cassius is vulnerable; he believes that friendship should temper judgment. Brutus is strengthened by his determination not to sacrifice the principle for which he thinks he killed Caesar and left his wife to kill herself. Each man is bitter in the belief that the other has outraged a fundamental principle.

villain: Brutus deliberately uses this word for its ignobility, its lack of honor.

Cassius responds with an attempt to make Brutus see that practice must demand a relaxation of ideal standards. As a soldier he knows how far one may go and where to stop. Brutus is driven to abandon his self-control by this failure to understand what he cherishes. He shows Cassius what rage and contempt really are. This may be to awaken him in the only manner he understands; or Brutus may simply have lost control and does not worry in his despair what the consequences might be. Cassius is restrained by his genuine love of Brutus and his amazement at such behavior from him.

budge: retreat in terror.

spleen: used both figuratively and literally. It was believed that the spleen was the source of secretions active in anger; these literally are "the venom" of the spleen. Figuratively, the statement can be read as "poison of your uncontrolled temper."

You wrong me . . . as huge as high Olympus.

Cassius remonstrates that in fact he did not boast. In fact he said "older" and "abler to make conditions," but now he is appalled at the thought of fighting Brutus and tries to insist that *better* was no part of his meaning. He tries to make Brutus understand that only personal affection, not fear, has restrained him from reacting to the insults violently.

But Brutus passes to the offensive, accusing Cassius of having treated him as no friend should treat another.

vile: Brutus considers it shameful for a nobleman to force dishonorable peasants to give him their worthless property.
indirection: subterfuge.
rascal counters: shameful tokens of wealth (coins).

Finally Brutus insists that his rebuke to Cassius is the action of a friend as distinct from a flatterer.

Come, Antony, and young Octavius . . . leave you so.

Two conceptions of honor and friendship have clashed. Brutus is, as ever, putting principle above persons. One's value of a friend must show itself in such concern for his honor as to tell him when he risks it; no friendship must come before the public good. With him now these considerations are sharpened by his grief for Portia, his fear that Cassius has made, or might make, the whole enterprise worthless. Brutus must restrain Cassius, must make him see his conduct clearly.

For Cassius, friendship lies in putting the friend first, in overlooking small faults; it does not lie in perpetual evaluation of conduct and in criticism. Cassius could not imagine having Brutus' affection for Caesar and still killing him for the public good. To join the conspiracy is interpreted as showing a preference for Cassius. And Brutus' recent and present behavior means personal hostility to one who thought himself a friend.

brav'd: provoked, challenged.
check'd: observed and criticized.
bondman: serf, slave.

Cassius does not understand and cannot understand that when Brutus struck at Caesar there was no hatred in the blow. He feels that Brutus' behavior shows less love for him than he had for Caesar when striking him down.

Brutus realizes what he has done to Cassius; he realizes that Cassius cannot work except in terms of personalities, that Cassius has been hurt too much, reduced to despair. Liking for Cassius, understanding of him and an awareness of the reasons for his own outburst, not all of which are the fault of his companion, move Brutus to regret and conciliation.

rash humour: temperamental hastiness (deriving from physical makeup).

HAMLET

Introductory Note

THE GENERAL CONCEPTION of this play which underlies the treatment of the following scenes has been developed in *Conscience and the King* (1953). Nothing fundamental in my reading of this play has changed since writing that study. Such points as need reemphasis or were not given due weight in that book are treated here.

Act One, Scene Two

Though yet of Hamlet . . . heartily farewell.

Claudius starts with a reference to his dead brother, admitting that to emerge from mourning so swiftly might seem a breach of decorum. He is not afraid to mention that he has married his *sometime sister*, despite the fact that to have done so has been to commit the grave sin of incest.

Claudius obviously must feel secure. He has no fear of his murder of his brother ever being discovered. (In the event, it takes a ghost to reveal what has happened, so that the King has every justification to assume his guilt will never be known.)

Before we consider one of his main intentions in this scene, we need to examine closely one particular statement made by Claudius immediately after Hamlet's assurance to his mother: *I shall in all my best obey you, madam.* The King then says to Hamlet: *Be as ourself in Denmark. Ourself* is the royal equivalent of "myself." Claudius is telling the Prince to be as Claudius is in Denmark. This can mean either: "Consider yourself exactly the same as me in Denmark"; or "When the time comes you be what I am now in Denmark."

To understand the second reading of the statement we must consider that in this play Denmark is an elective monarchy. The ruling monarch has the right to name his successor, who is then elected by the electoral college. Hamlet's father died unexpectedly without naming a successor. In the subsequent crisis, with Norway threatening and with the Prince absent in Wittenberg, Claudius was named and elected; thus, as Hamlet says later, popping in between *th' election and my hopes.* In the normal course of events he would have waited for his father to name him, and after his father's death the throne would have come to him. Superficially, therefore, his position has not changed. He merely has to wait for his uncle to vacate the throne. To the Danes (who have no reason to suspect Claudius of fratricide, which is also regicide), it seems that Hamlet has lost nothing. He stands in the same relation to his affectionate uncle, his mother's second husband, as he stood to her first, his dead father.

If Claudius is to be imagined telling Hamlet (in our first reading) to be henceforth what the King is in Denmark, an enormous amount of power is being put into the Prince's hands, for the statement is made in public in the presence chamber. This suggests that Claudius has no qualms about his nephew, is confident that the younger man harbors no resentment, no thwarted ambition or thoughts of revenge for any reason whatsoever.

On the other hand if we read the statement as the formal naming of Hamlet as the successor to Claudius, again the logical inference must be that the latter has no fear of, but complete confidence in, his nephew. To name the next monarch (unless the reigning one is near death) is to risk the establishment of a second court, a focus for malcontents, for greedy courtiers anxious to show their loyalty to the rising sun, to the man who will be king. Again, Hamlet is being given great power and an opportunity to intrigue (and with success) against his uncle.

Claudius cannot risk danger in either of these ways. We can explain his statement only as coming from a man who is utterly secure in his new position, who expects no hostility from his nephew.

With this made clear, we can now ask why Claudius needed to kill his elder brother. He did it to inherit all that he envied in the elder Hamlet—his conquests, his subjects, his wife, his son. Claudius wants to enjoy with Gertrude and Hamlet the happy family life which he observed and envied. With the King once dead, it has been easy: Denmark needed a strong leader; while not trying to diminish the stature of his predecessor, Claudius has asked to be allowed to do his poor best as a substitute; he manages not to have to pretend that he has not married his sister-in-law, he admits it and procures general consent; he substitutes himself as a husband, and when the scene begins he intends to substitute himself as a father. For Claudius cherishes a genuine affection for his nephew, whom he welcomes dearly as a son.

When the scene opens, Claudius is serene; since the murder his whole life has changed; he has overcome every difficulty and has inherited everything of his brother's except his son. Today he is sure that he will manage to win Hamlet over as well. That is his main intention. From playing second fiddle to his elder brother all his life, Claudius has become the center of attention. He enjoys it; it gives him superb confidence; he is relaxed and at ease.

First Claudius has to transact public business; in this case, foreign policy. He is confident enough to run over recent events, even to mention the fact that the court is not keeping the deepest mourning for the dead king, which convention demands. Claudius even reminds his listeners that he has gone through a form of marriage with his sister-in-law.

The actor has a choice of playing a man who realizes clearly that he is involving his subjects and clouding their awareness of right and wrong; or he might be a man whose success has deadened him to reality, who no longer sees anything wrong in lack of mourning and in the "marriage." In each case the King makes no secret of what he has done and is doing, apart from the fact that it all started with the murder of his brother. (Does he even manage to hide that from himself?)

green: fresh (with a sense of an unhealed wound).

it us befitted: It would be suitable.

"Our whole kingdom to give way to its grief."

discretion: awareness of what is prudent.

nature: demands made by the natural feeling of family members.

Skillfully Claudius relates how his *wisest* sorrow has led him, in the interests of the country, to commit incest, which is transformed in his presentation into a healthy and admirable union.

sometime sister: If we play the man who has deadened himself to his incest, then Claudius ignores the fact that Gertrude cannot be his *sometime sister.* Once married to his brother, she is always Claudius' sister, and is so still.

jointress: partner.

warlike: armed and dangerous.

auspicious: happy.

dropping: tearful.

dole: grief, suffering, dolor.

Claudius delays until the end the delicate statement *taken to wife.* This might be deliberate or might derive from his refusal to admit to himself that he is committing incest, with a rationalized excuse for all that he is doing.

barr'd: excluded.

Claudius has now expressed his satisfaction at the way things have gone, including the fact that his counselors have associated themselves with his actions and decisions. He now proceeds to the first matter on his agenda, the embassy to Norway. Their instructions are now backed up by the strength which comes from his speedy preparations for war. In his knowledge of these and of the physical condition of the King of Norway, Claudius' confidence is all the greater.

supposal: estimate.

disjoint: dislocated.

out of frame: disorganized (literally, out of joint).

colleagued: combined.

dream: fantasy.

bonds: binding terms.

his further gait therein: his taking further steps in this.

full proportions: total extent.
out of his subject: from what is subject to him.
dilated: detailed.

And now, Laertes . . . spend it at thy will!

Claudius now shows a gracious interest in Polonius and Laertes.
suit: petition.
native to: physically, anatomically and physiologically related to.
instrumental to: the servant of.
Dread my lord: my awe-inspiring lord.

Laertes speaks like a courtier who must have royal permission to withdraw from court, apart from wanting to leave the country. He points out that he came to the coronation *willingly* (of his own wish) to perform a pleasant duty.
bend: turn, aim.
bow: submit to.
will . . . hard consent: Polonius indulges himself in a play on words in his imagery. He says he has placed the imprint of his consent sharply on his son's will; *will* and *seal* are used in two senses. Claudius and others appreciate the easy wit of Polonius' speech.
and thy best graces spend it at thy will: And may you spend it as you wish, and in the inspiration of your best attributes.

Claudius genially extends Polonius' word play with another use of *will:* we should not overlook the easy and friendly sense of being on very good terms with one another which pervades these three.

But now, my cousin Hamlet . . . Come away.

Claudius turns at last to his most important and most pleasant task, to assure himself of, and enjoy himself in, the conquest of Hamlet's grief. The uncle wants to console his nephew, to treat him as a dear son and be treated by him as a beloved father. Claudius' main intention is to dissipate Hamlet's grief, communicate with him as a consolation for a dead father; he is genuinely trying to win Hamlet (not as a stepson whose hostility must be overcome, but as one loved as a son whose unhappiness must be conquered).

Hamlet's silent response depends in part on the Elizabethan pronunciation of *kind* as "kinn'd." It says virtually a little more than "kin" (i.e., blood relation), and less than natural *(kind),* less than benevolent *(kind),* less than akin to (kinn'd).

clouds hang on: metaphorically, depressed, literally, in darkness.

Hamlet answers Claudius' words in their literal sense, but he does so metaphorically: *too much i' the sun:* too exposed to the center of the life of Denmark to be in the clouds. This is a compliment to his uncle, on the face of it; and there is no evidence that anyone sees it as anything else. Gertrude takes the compliment as an amiable refusal to admit the depth of his inability to enjoy life, coming from a determination to continue to grieve for his father; this will lead nowhere but to Hamlet's own unhappiness. It would be better for him as a human being to come to terms with his grief and allow himself to respond to her love and his uncle's; they can both do much to make him happier if he will only let them.

through nature: through life in the flesh (what is called natural life).

Hamlet's reply that death is common leads her to ask him why he makes it seem so special, so uncommon *(particular).* Her intention is not to hurt him but to reason with him, get him to see that he is making himself unnecessarily unhappy.

Hamlet insists that it is not a matter of seeming, of appearance. He tries to make her understand that his behavior is normal and comes from a real emotion which cannot be completely expressed.

shows: tokens, appearances.
windy suspiration of forc'd breath: deep sighs.
denote me truly: express me accurately and completely.

passes show: cannot be expressed in outward appearance or behavior.
trappings: dresses, costumes.
suits: appropriate garments, uniform, dress.
woe: grief.

His outward signs of grief are in no way equal to the sincere emotion within; they are, nevertheless, the appropriate and usual token of mourning; in manifesting them he is in no way unusual, *particular*.

Claudius now makes a great effort to make Hamlet see that he is prolonging his grief unnecessarily and making himself unnaturally unhappy, depriving himself of consolation that nobody could blame him for accepting, a mother's love and the sincere affection of an uncle who feels to him as a father toward a beloved and unhappy son. Claudius is genuinely kindly; he is doing all he can to win his nephew to him, relying on all those similarities between brothers which can console the bereaved, which have consoled Gertrude.

in filial obligation: obliged as son or daughter.
for some term: for a definite period. Claudius insists that there is no obligation to continue mourning indefinitely.
do obsequious sorrow: express the grief of mourning the dead dutifully.
condolement: grief, mourning.
impious stubbornness: irreligious willfulness.
incorrect to: unreconciled to.
unfortified: weak, without fortitude for what must be.
unschool'd: ignorant.
as common . . . thing to sense: the most obvious thing to which our senses can respond.
absurd: irrational.
still: always.
corse: corpse. The first corpse, the body of the first human being to die, according to the Bible, was that of Abel, killed by his brother, Cain. It is a matter for each individual actor to

decide how conscious Claudius is that he is guilty of the same sin as Cain when he makes this allusion.
unprevailing: impotent, hopeless.

Claudius pleads with Hamlet sincerely; once the Prince can overcome his unhappiness, he, his mother and uncle can have a substitute for the family relationship which existed with the dead King.
Let the world take note, etc.: This is a state occasion; Claudius is making what is tantamount to a royal proclamation that Hamlet is *most immediate* to the throne. This means he is next in noble rank, in the order of precedence, and that he has direct access to the monarch without going through intermediaries. During this speech an actor who imagines himself Hamlet cut off from his mother, grieving for his father, will find in himself a temptation to accept what is offered; after all, it is what he needs, the love of a father, the warmth and sense of belonging to a close family circle. The more Claudius reminds him of his dead father the harder it is for Hamlet to resist; Claudius senses the Prince's need and quite naturally, from no malevolent motive, increases his pressure. The King can even permit himself a slight joke, saying that to go back to Wittenberg is going back on his wish, *In going back . . . is most retrograde.*
cousin: kinsman.
bend you: make it your intention.

Gertrude, sensing that Claudius is prevailing, adds her pleas. Hamlet feels outmaneuvered. He cannot disobey the royal request not to leave court (nobody may withdraw from court without permission). His uncle speaks with such tact and kindness that the onlookers would be alienated by the discourtesy of a refusal toward so kind a plea made by an uncle who obviously wants his nephew with him as a person dear to him.

Hamlet takes an easier way out; he can produce a semblance of polite affection toward Gertrude. That Claudius accepts Hamlet's reply as *loving and . . . fair* has already been argued. He would not reward anything which he finds an insult or boorish with a public announcement of Hamlet as his successor. And this, as we have seen, is the meaning of *Be as ourself in Denmark.*

unforc'd accord: unconstrained acquiescence, agreement.
in grace whereof: (1) in thanks for which, (2) to enhance which.
bruit: resound.

Hail to your lordship . . . to men's eyes.

Notice that Hamlet returns Horatio's greeting without realizing from whom it comes; then in a split second, "Horatio, or I don't recognize myself."
I'll change that name with you: Hamlet insists that Horatio is not his *servant* but his *good friend,* a name he is ready to exchange with Horatio (i.e., each calls the other friend).
make you, etc.: What are you doing away from Wittenberg?
truant disposition: an inclination to waste time away from studies.

Although Hamlet speaks superficially in jest, he makes it clear that he regards Horatio as a special person, one whom he trusts and respects as well as likes. As a result he is not restrained or inhibited from revealing obliquely feelings which would otherwise be kept hidden. If this is the right assumption, then Marcellus and Bernardo are not near enough to the two speakers to overhear what they say. Even so, Horatio will not permit himself anything more critical of Claudius and Gertrude than that the wedding followed *hard upon* the funeral.
hard upon: closely after.
Thrift, thrift, Horatio, etc.: Hamlet allows himself to say what he has thought and felt for a long time. "Economy, economy, Horatio. It was all done so swiftly so that the food left over from the hot funeral meal could be served up cold for the wedding breakfast." The reference to his *dearest foe* (deepest enemy) gains force from the fact that the last thing he would want is to meet one whom he hates so intensely in heaven. This bitterest enemy is almost certainly Claudius, whose image is in Hamlet's mind as he speaks.
methinks: it seems to me.
Season your admiration, etc.: Dilute your amazement by listening carefully.
deliver: give an account of.
together: (1) in succession, (2) together.

on their watch, etc.: had been met like this during their tour of guard duty in the inert *(dead)* and deserted time in the *middle of the night.*
at point exactly: to the teeth in every detail.
cap-a-pe: head to foot.
solemn: impressive, ceremonious.
truncheon: field marshal's baton.
distill'd: melted.
jelly: boneless and quivering.
dreadful: very frightened.
form of the thing: the thing's appearance.

Note that Horatio does not call it "the ghost," but even to Hamlet, *the thing.*

kept the watch: stood guard; stayed awake.
address itself to motion: prepared itself to accompany speech with action, as if it were about to speak.

Elizabethan works on acting use the words "action" and "motion" as synonyms in the sense of body language as distinct from voice. The picture is one of the apparition standing with arm and hand upraised in what Elizabethans called the action, motion or gesture with which a speaker asks for attention before actually letting words come from his mouth.

I have dealt with this moment more fully in *Elizabethan Acting* (1951, pp. 133 ff.). Horatio remembers having waited for the words to come, having heard the cock crow, having seen the spirit change into something like a guilty thing. He does not tell Hamlet this part.

strange: uncanny.

Horatio concentrates on convincing Hamlet that what he says really happened. Hamlet is more concerned with getting an accurate account so that he can come to some valid conclusion as to the importance of the apparition.

Then saw you not his face? This might be an alert interrogation to see if he is being told the truth. But Hamlet's confidence in Horatio is such that he is more probably disappointed to think that they could not see its face (*his* means "its" as well as "his").

Having heard everything, Hamlet resolves to watch tonight to confront the apparition. Notice he says, *If it assume.* This means that he has taken it for granted that they did not see his father's ghost, but a spirit (good or evil) which has put on itself the appearance of his father. He will speak to it even if there is no doubt that it is a devil. It is important to note in addition that Horatio, Marcellus and Bernardo do not attempt to suggest that the apparition might not be evil.

Hamlet does not know if they have spoken about the apparition to anybody else. He asks them, if they have not, to continue to preserve secrecy. As they do not tell him they have told anybody else, either they show that silently, or he takes their silence as a sign that nobody else knows.

My father's spirit: Hamlet vacillates, at times unconsciously, between belief and disbelief in the honesty of the *ghost.* A moment ago he reacted as if it were evil. Now he thinks of it as honest.

doubt: fear.

Hamlet now expresses his certainty that foul deeds will become known whenever they have been committed, even if they are covered over by the whole mass of the world.

to men's eyes: This can mean that the deeds will rise to men's sight; or that the deeds will rise even if they are completely covered so far as men's eyes are concerned.

Act One, Scene Five

Whither wilt thou lead me . . . remember me.

To play the Ghost in this scene the actor must remember that in Act One, Scene One, it was caught above ground by the cockcrow. This was such a painful experience that it is determined to be back underground this time before the cock crows. The Ghost is therefore under double pressure; it wants to tell its story and incite Hamlet to vengeance, but it is always aware of time passing and is anxious to be safely underground again before the day is announced. The Ghost's first task, therefore, is to make sure that Hamlet will listen carefully and will not delay it. In fact, so great is the Ghost's need for speed that it does not even assure Hamlet that it is his father's spirit until he has agreed to listen seriously.

Mark me: Listen to me carefully.

Although Hamlet is not certain of the Ghost's honesty, proximity to what is so like his dead father and which speaks with the dead man's dear voice disposes him to accept it.

render up: surrender, present myself.

My hour is almost come, etc.: The Ghost is concerned chiefly at this moment with impressing on Hamlet that the time has almost come for it to return, that it cannot stay with him long. But mention of its torments affects Hamlet with pity. The ghost does not want pity but concentrated attention to its story, followed by a promise of vengeance. Only when it is sure of Hamlet's *serious hearing* does it assert, *I am thy father's spirit.* Now it can start to tell its story and move Hamlet to pity and anger.

unfold: disclose, reveal.

The statement *I am thy father's spirit* is made as an insistence that this is not a spirit clothed in air in the father's shape. It *is* honest. The Ghost's intention is to convince Hamlet of its honesty.

doom'd for a certain term: sentenced for a definite stretch of time.

fast: dry, wither.

days of nature: life in the mortal flesh.

The Ghost reexperiences the torments while concentrating on communicating to Hamlet their nature, if not precise details of what they entail. Notice the image clearly here: *lightest word . . . harrow up.* Figuratively, it means that the slightest account of reality, a mere hint, would be enough to cause appalling distress. But the image has a surprising literal meaning; a harrow, which is used to break ploughed earth into a small tilth, is a very heavy implement, much of the effect of which comes from that weight. The lightest word of the Ghost's tale would be heavy enough to act as a harrow.

The effect of the lightest word is communicated in another image of accurate literal detail. Figuratively, *freeze thy young blood, etc.*, indicates how Hamlet's warm energy would be chilled with horror. But, literally, *start* is a word used of the pressure made by liquid frozen in a corked bottle. The expansion of the ice forces the cork out. The Ghost's image has the blood in Hamlet's young veins turn cold, freeze so that the expansion makes his eyes start like a cork from a bottle.

Thy knotty and combined locks: hair curled and tangled thickly.
part: separate itself, themselves.
particular: individual.
fretful: enraged.
eternal blazon: revelation, account of eternity.
strange: horrifying, chilling.
dull: apathetic.
fat: sluggish (making others sluggish).
Lethe wharf: bank of Lethe, the river in the Classical underworld whose water induces forgetfulness in those who drink it.
forged process: fabricated (false) account.
rankly: foully.
abus'd: deceived.
O my prophetic soul: Hamlet is not referring to any particular moment when he suspected his uncle of murder. But he has had a strong sense of something seriously wrong. He means chiefly, however, that his reaction to the description of the Ghost given by Horatio, Marcellus and Bernardo, was to *doubt some foul play*. Then he feared something like murder may have been committed. The actual moment came at the end of Act One, Scene Two:

> My father's spirit in arms! All is not well;
> I doubt some foul play: would the night were come!
> Till then sit still, my soul.

This is when his soul was "prophetic."
incestuous, adulterate beast: When this play was written mar-

riage with a dead brother's widow was regarded as committing the sin of incest, one of bestial quality. Adultery was not restricted to meaning fornication of a married person; the word was used of any sexual irregularity, even between husband and wife. *Adulterate*, therefore, does not mean that Claudius copulated with Gertrude while her husband was alive. To commit incest was to commit adultery; for the Ghost and for Hamlet, to be incestuous is necessarily to be adulterate. We must not make the mistake of thinking that they accuse Gertrude of betraying her husband before his death.

wits: intelligence.

falling off: (1) change of direction, course; going off course, in the wrong direction; (2) decline.

natural gifts: constitutional physical and psychological qualities.

sate: lose inclination for.

prey on: devour.

garbage: refuse, what has been rejected.

scent: sniff, smell.

But soft, etc.: The Ghost is under great pressure, wants to pour out its story to sympathetic human hearing, but knows that with dawn it must leave. It is very apprehensive that dawn may come before it has told Hamlet and convinced him, and received assurance of vengeance. The Ghost is indeed *brief* from now on.

secure: falsely assumed to be secure.

hebonon: henbane.

porch: entrance.

distilment: distillation.

natural gates and alleys: blood vessels; literally, physiological and anatomical roads and streets.

posset: curdle.

eager droppings: drops of vinegar dropped into.

wholesome: healthy.

with . . . tetter bak'd about: covered with a hard skin of blotches.

cut off: despatched.

blossoms: full flowering. Notice the literal sense of *cut off* in relation to blossoms.

unhousel'd: without having taken the last sacrament. *Housel* means the Eucharist.
disappointed: not prepared.
unanneal'd: Anneal is to temper. *Unanneal'd,* figuratively, unstrengthened by having been anointed with the last unction.
reckoning: making an account; figuratively, last confession. "Sent to give my final account of myself still responsible for all I did wrong."
if thou hast nature in thee: if you react psychologically and physiologically like a human being with natural ties as well as impulses.
luxury: lechery.
taint not: do not pollute.
contrive: plan.
Fare thee well at once: Good-bye, I must go at once.
matin: morning.
uneffectual: ineffective.

The Ghost departs in a great hurry. This is due to terror of being caught by the dawn, as happened the previous night; at this moment the Ghost does not know if Hamlet will swear vengeance or not; nevertheless, it goes because it believes it must.

O all you host of heaven . . . I have sworn't.

Hamlet has complete confidence in the Ghost now. So complete that he dismisses his former doubts as shameful. *And shall I couple hell? O, fie!* "And shall I add hell? Oh, for shame!"
sinews: muscles.
distracted globe: distracted head.
trivial fond records: unimportant, foolish memories.
saws of books: memorable generalizations memorized from books.
pressures: impressions.

Hamlet's image of his brain is of (1) a waxen tablet, (2) a commonplace book into which memorable matters are copied, written. Hamlet has an image of his smiling uncle, the smile, literally and figuratively, concealing the reality of evil. He has banished all other images from his brain, but he can use the image of Claudius as a way of ensuring that he does not forget the Ghost's request and his oath. When Hamlet has written on his writing table that *one may smile, etc.*, the image of his uncle will always be associated with this certainty, and both will bring to his mind his *word;* he will remember the Ghost's disappearance and request to be remembered.

The actor should notice the sequence: Hamlet's oath is associated with *remember me.* Those words are associated with the knowledge that *one may smile, etc.*, which has become inseparable from the image of the smiling Claudius. To imagine Claudius smiling is to start the chain reaction of conditioned reflexes which end with the oath of vengeance.

What news, my lord? . . . Indeed, upon my sword, indeed.

Horatio and Marcellus have caught up with Hamlet. Marcellus wants to know how Hamlet is. Horatio asks, *What news?*

Hamlet evades the question. He answers Horatio's remark that they could have guessed what he tells them without any need for a Ghost to come from the grave. Hamlet continues to cover up with the suggestion that they go their separate ways. Eventually Hamlet allows himself to assure them of one thing only: *It is an honest ghost, that let me tell you* (I'll tell you that one thing). They swear not to make known what they have seen tonight. Then he asks for another oath upon his sword; they demur.

Swear . . . let's go together.

Before playing Hamlet at this moment the actor has to recall when the Ghost left swiftly to go back to its prison house because it feared that day was about to dawn. Alone, Hamlet assumes that it has indeed returned to that prison for the day, and to think of the *poor Ghost* is to assume that it is now somewhere beneath the earth, *confin'd to fast in fires,* not that it is within earshot.

As a result, when Hamlet hears the voice beneath him cry,

Swear, he is surprised that it is so near. He knows it did not go back to its place of confinement; it did not have to leave so swiftly. From this it follows that the Ghost lied about the need to go; its word is no longer to be trusted. What now seems definitely an evil spirit succeeded in deceiving Hamlet into swearing an oath of vengeance. If the Ghost is not honest, in keeping that oath Hamlet will damn himself.

From thinking of the Ghost as his father, from feeling filial reverence and affection, Hamlet thinks of it as a sort of confidence trickster, who has just fallen short of success. Now there is derision in Hamlet's mind, a derision expressed in the words he uses to the Ghost: *aha, boy . . . truepenny . . . fellow in the cellarage. Art thou there?* is virtually, "Is that where you really are?" The Ghost said it was going much farther, to an entirely different place.

Hamlet's *Hic et ubique?* (Here and everywhere?) shows his suspicion that he is addressing the Devil. Only God and the Devil are regarded by the theologians as being capable of being present in one place and every other place simultaneously. This must be the Devil.

As all this is happening Hamlet realizes not only that his certainty about the Ghost's honesty has vanished, but that until he is sure one way or the other, he will be tormented by the thought that it might be honest, and that he ought to keep his oath of vengeance.

His problem is easily stated: Protestant theology teaches that the spirits of the dead do not come back. Any such apparition as the Ghost is evil. Catholic theology teaches that the spirit of a dead man might return, but it is much more likely that the apparition is an evil spirit in a shape resembling that of the dead man. Therefore, nobody ought to expose himself to the consequences of committing a sin (certainly not a mortal sin) at the instigation of the apparition.

All this is fine in theory; this is what philosophy teaches (both *your* and *our*). But it does not really help a Prince in this situation, who has talked with and loved the apparition; whose uncle is committing incest, has corrupted a whole nation.

Not long ago the apparition convinced Hamlet of its honesty, persuaded him to swear vengeance, then left him hastily, insisting that it must return immediately to its prison for the day. But hearing its voice come from the ground beneath him, Hamlet knows that it did not go to its *prison-house,* and deduces that it did not need to leave so hastily. Apparently it lied to him.

What is Hamlet to make of an apparition which did not tell him the truth, which left him in haste but did not go back at once to its prison? If this was a lie, how much of its story was truth? Ought he to dismiss it as false? But if the lie is proof of the apparition's dishonesty, what is Hamlet to make of its revelation that it did not return to the prison but stayed in the ground just beneath him? What kind of an evil spirit deceives a man and then lets him know of the deception before any harm is done? An honest spirit does not leave with a lie; on the other hand, an evil spirit does not reveal itself so easily as a liar. Which is this, honest or false? Here lies Hamlet's problem.

Hamlet knows that he will have no peace until he has certainty about the honesty or dishonesty of the Ghost. His awareness of his situation is expressed in the lines to Horatio. Then he considers feigning madness in the weeks to come to account for strangeness of manner while uncertainty absorbs his energies and concentration. In an earlier scene Polonius has forbidden Ophelia to *Slander any moment leisure* by spending it with Hamlet. The actor can therefore assume that in obedience she has already rebuffed Hamlet.

Hamlet's demand is that Horatio and Marcellus will swear upon his sword not to speak of what they have seen and heard. But once he has thought of feigning madness he asks for a different oath. Now it is that if he should bear himself oddly, they will give not the slightest indication of any kind that they are in a position to cast any light on his conduct.

As the Ghost persists in supporting him with the demand *Swear,* and as he remembers it looking and sounding so like his beloved father, Hamlet addresses it as such: *Rest, rest, perturbed spirit.* Necessarily, he must swing between trust and distrust as he remembers the beloved features and then the sudden disappearance which seems not to have been needed.

Why does the Ghost leave so quickly? In genuine fear of

being caught by daylight. Why does it not return to its prison? Day still has not dawned. Beneath the ground the Ghost is not exposed to daylight; it lingers there in the dark as long as possible to find out what Hamlet will do. It left before he could give the assurance it needs.

The time is out of joint, etc.

Shakespeare's language is very exact here, and the actor must respond with equal accuracy. The word *set* is used in the sense in which modern surgeons talk of setting a fracture; it is not a vague synonym for put or place, but means to place firmly and accurately in the right position so that strained or broken tissue may rest, knit and regain its function. Elizabethan surgeons regarded a dislocation as a form of fracture; it is an interference in the continuity of the bony framework of the body.

Hamlet uses the image well aware of the fact that to *set* (in modern terminology, reduce) a dislocation (without anaesthesia, then) involves violence and pain, which the afflicted person would prefer to avoid. Eventually the surgeon will be thanked; but first he may well be resented. The Danes do not recognize that their age is *out of joint;* the distortion does not disturb them. They will not welcome Hamlet's efforts to *set* what is wrong.

That is why he regrets the *cursed spite.* Spite, here, means something to be deplored, regretted. Hamlet recognizes clearly the unfortunate situation in which he has been placed; it is not of his own choice, but he recognizes his duty to *set* what is *out of joint.* His regret that he should have been born to do this in no way weakens his resolution to fulfill his duty as son and Prince of Denmark.

Act Two, Scene One

How now, Ophelia! . . . hate to utter love.

As Ophelia enters she remembers what has just happened in her closet. Her immediate objective is to tell her father about Hamlet's state of mind. In addition there may be a wish to be allowed to help Hamlet, a wish to reproach Polonius for what has happened, a wish for him to find some way of saving the Prince's sanity.

The actress must imagine herself sitting down, engaged in sewing; she must imagine her room round her; then her first sight of Hamlet as he came in. Obviously she must imagine herself reexperiencing the scene as she recounts it to her father.

doublet all unbrac'd: The laces attaching the doublet to the hose are all loose, not pulled taut and tied.
no hat upon his head: The hat is part of a nobleman's ensemble. He wears it indoors except in the presence of superiors. The Prince of Denmark, declared heir to the throne, would not normally enter Ophelia's room without his hat on his head.
foul'd: entangled.
down-gyved to his ankle: The stockings have slipped down to his ankles, where they act like fetters, preventing him from walking freely; he can only shuffle as if he were really fettered with his feet wide apart. Ophelia sees him not only pale, but shuffling along, feet wide apart, yet in such a grotesque attitude that his knees knock together.
purport: intention.

This is a disturbing picture of mental derangement. Polonius immediately asks if it is what he suspects, madness for her love. Her description of Hamlet's actions is very detailed, very exact, and she wishes she had not been an unintentional agent of such harm upon him.
hard: close (as well as tight). Then he stretches his arm out, moving an arm's length from her, still holding her.
perusal: careful reading of.
end his being: destroy him.
bended their light on: aimed their beams at. The Elizabethans believed that sight was the result of rays proceeding from the eyes and hitting the object seen.

Polonius is more and more disturbed as he listens. He is afraid that the Prince's madness may lead to his destruction, possibly by suicide. The old man is essentially a loyal subject of the Danish crown. He does not attempt to evade a very unpleasant duty.

Hamlet is dangerously ill. Polonius feels responsible. Something must be done to alleviate the Prince's malady which may well threaten his life.

ecstasy: trance.
foredoes: destroys.
afflict our natures: act detrimentally upon our mental and physical health.

Notice that Polonius admits his responsibility; he does not try to hide from his daughter his sense of having made a mistake, a very bad, even costly mistake.

When Ophelia says that she has merely refused to see Hamlet and to accept his letters, Polonius feels sure that this is what has sent him mad with unrequited love.
I am sorry that with better, etc.: I am sorry that I did not make comments on him with more attention and better balanced reason.
did but trifle: completely lacked sincerity.
beshrew: curse.
jealousy: This has no sense of modern envy or sexual jealousy. It means an overcautious alertness to possible danger, which takes measures well ahead to forestall what may never be threatening. This is what Polonius sees he has done. He is quite devoid of false pride and has nothing to stop him confessing openly to his daughter (to whom he was so scathing on this subject) that he thought himself too clever.
proper to: the typical characteristic of.
cast beyond ourselves: throw beyond our reach.

Polonius is determined to tell the King what has happened. His loyalty is stronger than any fear of the consequences to himself and Ophelia. The Prince must be saved from disaster.
this must be known: This must not be kept secret.
which being kept close: which, if it is not disclosed.
might move: might initiate, might lead to.

more grief to hide: more misery in hiding.
than hate to utter love: than it will lead to hate in revealing (speaking about) the existence of love.

In modern English the statement can be rendered as follows: "We must give a full account of what has happened. To keep our knowledge of Hamlet's love secret could lead to misery more devastating than the intense displeasure to which we expose ourselves by revealing it."

He also shows love by revealing this love of Hamlet and Ophelia. Polonius is now certain that Hamlet loves Ophelia honorably.

Act Three, Scene Two

(PART ONE OF PLAY SCENE)

Although this scene is written in heroic couplets, the actor should concentrate on the same aspects of the lines as when he has to play prose or blank verse. His tasks are first to be certain that he understands every word and can think it as the character's thought. Precise, accurate thinking of each of the words lets us be more accurate in recognizing the intention. And from the intention in the context we discover the emotion. As with prose and blank verse, the actor will find that the images in the lines relate to the character's intentions respectively. Every word in these rhyming couplets is a part of the action of the character.

If we are to be guided by the account given in the dumb show, this King and Queen behave very affectionately to one another.

Enter a King and a Queen, the Queen embracing him, and he her; he takes her up, and declines his head upon her neck.

Full thirty times hath Phoebus' cart gone round
Neptune's salt wash and Tellus' orbed ground,
And thirty dozen moons with borrow'd sheen
About the world have times twelve thirties been,

Since love our hearts and Hymen did our hands
Unite commutual in most sacred bands.

Phoebus' cart: The chariot of the sun god, Phoebus Apollo.
Neptune's salt wash: The salt water of Neptune, the ruler of the seas.
Tellus' orbed ground: The land of the globe of the world, the domain of Tellus, mother goddess of the earth.

The sun has made its annual journey round the seas and land of the world thirty times.
sheen: shine, light.

And in that time there have been thirty dozen new moons with their reflected light circling the world twelve multiplied by thirty times.
Hymen: the Roman god of marriage.
commutual: in harmony with one another.
bands: ties, bonds.

"Since our hearts and hands were united in common harmony by love and marriage respectively."

The King's intention is to prepare his wife for the painful information that he does not expect to live much longer. He knows that when he has told her this he will have the much more painful task of persuading her to take a second husband when he is dead. He looks back over the thirty years of their marriage and love, and has an image of the world in space with its seas and land masses, around which go the sun and moon.

So many journeys may the Sun and Moon
Make us again count o'er ere love be done.

The Queen has had her own misgivings about his health and does not want to admit to him how ill she fears he is. She hopes that as many months and years will pass for them to count up before their love ends.

But woe is me, you are so sick of late
So far from cheer and from your former state,
That I distrust you;

cheer: happy health.
distrust: feel doubtful about.
That I distrust you: that I have fears on your behalf.

She cannot hold back her fears for his health, but immediately wishes she had been able to, and tries not to disconcert him, insisting that the intensity of her alarm comes from the depth of her love which leads her to exaggerate.

> yet though I distrust,
> Discomfort you, my lord, it nothing must.

"Yet, although I have fears, that must not discomfort you in the slightest."

> For women's fear and love hold quantity
> In neither aught, or in extremity.

"For the fear of women is as much as their love, there is nothing of either, or both are exaggerated."

> Now what my love is, proof hath made you know
> And as my love is siz'd my fear is so.

"Now you have had proof of the nature of my love, and my fear equals my love in its size."

> Where love is great, the littlest doubts are fear,
> Where little fears grow great, great love is there.

She continues to belittle her fears as baseless, deriving only from the intensity of her love, in which the slightest uncertainty becomes a fear, and because of her great love, these little fears are exaggerated. But he must not be frightened by her fears.

> Faith, I must leave thee, love, and shortly too,
> My operant powers their functions leave to do.

Faith: This is the truth.
operant powers: vital strengths.

He plays wryly on the word *leave*. "I have to part from you, leave you; *my operant powers* have already left, stopped functioning, so it will not be long before I follow them."

> And thou shalt live in this fair world behind
> Honour'd, belov'd, and haply, one as kind
> For husband shall thou—

The King loves his wife so much that he wants to protect her from the lonely miseries of widowhood. He emphasizes that while his powers are failing, she will live on, and she must not mourn him forever. She will need a protector in the society which they both know; he does not want her to lose "commutual" unity with another person for the isolation of widowhood; she must marry again.

> O confound the rest!
> Such love must needs be treason, in my breast:
> In second husband let me be accurst!
> None wed the second but who kill'd the first.

She interrupts him with the wish that what he was going to add should never happen. For her to harbor such love could not be anything but treason to her husband as both man and king.

At this point the King has achieved exactly the opposite of his intention. Instead of beginning to persuade his wife to promise not to cut herself off from life after his death, he has provoked an intensity of grief at the thought of losing him, so that she cannot believe she could ever want another husband. In addition, she feels that her husband could make such a shocking suggestion only if he had doubts of her love. In her sincere love for him, desolate at the thought of his death, the Queen does all she can now to convince him (mistaking his intention) that she loves him and cannot contemplate taking a second husband.

> The instances that second marriage move
> Are base respects of thrift, but none of love.

"The actual facts which lead to second marriage are dishonorable considerations of economy, but there are never any which involve love." Her argument had substance in Elizabethan society. A rich widow required a man to protect her interests and manage her estate, while, on the other hand, a man would regard an alliance with her primarily as one of mutual material interest. The Queen's next two lines express the force of her anguish that her husband could imagine her behaving in this way:

> A second time I kill my husband dead,
> When second husband kisses me in bed.

my husband dead: my dead husband.

> I do believe you think what now you speak;
> But what we do determine oft we break.

The King realizes that he will not be able to make any headway until he has reassured her that he has no doubt of her sincerity. He says: "I really believe that you mean what you are saying now. But we do not always carry out our decisions," literally, "but often we break what we have made up our mind to do."

Note that the first line is enough to silence this volubly unhappy woman. It satisfies her that he knows how deeply she loves him. As he sees that he has calmed her, he proceeds to his next point, that people do not always do what they have determined to do. Here the intention is still to convince her that he trusts her, and at the same time to make her admit to herself that what he is saying has some truth in it. He can now continue to remind her of the general truth, that it is only human to change one's mind with changing circumstances.

> Purpose is but the slave of memory,
> Of violent birth, but poor validity:
> Which now, like fruit unripe, sticks on the tree;
> But fall unshaken when they mellow be.

Purpose (intention) is dependent completely on memory; it

exists only so long as it is not forgotten; it is violent when it first sees the light of day, but its quality soon deteriorates. Like the unripe fruit on an apple tree, *Purpose* cannot be dislodged by shaking. Even so the King cannot remove his wife's determination. But later, when the right time comes, the fruit needs no shaking; it falls of its own accord. At the right time the Queen will give up her intention because it will have disappeared of its own accord, with no effort from anybody else (but then, he, her husband, will no longer be there).

During this speech the Queen is silent, but she is reacting to him, and her reaction determines to some extent what he is saying and how he says it.

> Most necessary 'tis that we forget
> To pay ourselves what to ourselves is debt:
> What to ourselves in passion we propose,
> The passion ending, doth the purpose lose.

He builds on the foundation he has laid, reminding her of what she will acknowledge from her own experience. He is going to emphasize that nothing in this life remains constant; she, therefore, should not become upset to be reminded that she will change. The first two of these lines assure her that it is essential for men and women to forget to carry out promises which they have made to themselves. The next two lines can be modernized as: "Whatever we put forward as a course of action when we feel deeply and want something very much, that intention is lost when the feeling and wanting come to an end."

> The violence of either grief or joy
> Their own enactures with themselves destroy:
> Where joy most revels, grief doth most lament;
> Grief joys, joy grieves, on slender accident.

enacture: enactment, putting into effect.
accident: chance happening, event.

When the violence of joy or grief comes to an end, an end is also put to the carrying out of their purposes. In a situation in which joy is most happy, grief is most miserable; joy becomes sad, grief becomes happy as the result of a slight chance happening.

> This world is not for aye, nor 'tis not strange
> That even our loves should with our fortunes change

aye: ever.
strange: unusual, startling.

The King begins to develop another stage of his argument by reminding his wife that the world itself will not last forever (at the Second Coming it and all in and on it will disappear and, in Prospero's words, *leave not a wrack behind*). This being so, there is nothing startling in the admission that, like the world, our loves are not constant, but change with fortune.

> For 'tis a question left us yet to prove,
> Whether love lead fortune, or else fortune love.

"For a problem which has not yet been solved definitively is whether fortune follows love, or love follows fortune."

The King now allows himself some bitterness at the certain knowledge that after his death, not only will he have a successor in his wife's love and bed, but he will be supplanted in the hearts of his subjects; another will reign and they will forget him. He recalls the behavior of court society as he and his Queen have both had much opportunity to observe from above:

> The great man down, you mark, his favourite flies;
> The poor advanc'd makes friends of enemies.
> And hitherto doth love on fortune tend;
> For who not needs shall never lack a friend,
> And who in want a hollow friend doth try,
> Directly seasons him his enemy.

down: fallen from power.
you mark: you notice.
advanc'd: promoted.
hitherto: up to the present.
on fortune tend: pay attendance to; follow.

seasons him his enemy: adds the ingredients which make him an enemy.

In his bitterness the King gives his definitive answer to the *question:* love follows fortune. After his death he will be forgotten.

The King realizes that his emotion has led him to digress from his main topic, which is that there is nothing outrageous in his insistence that his wife shall remarry after his death.

> But, orderly to end where I begun,
> Our wills and fates do so contrary run
> That our devices still are overthrown;
> Our thoughts are ours, their ends none of our own.

orderly: systematically, correctly.
contrary run: proceed in opposite directions.
devices: what we plan.
still: always.
overthrown: ruined, destroyed, broken down.
thoughts: intentions.

"To end systematically at the point with which I started, what we want and what happens to us are so completely opposed to one another, that our plans are always ruined; our intentions belong to us, their achievement is utterly outside our control."

The King is remembering the Queen's last two lines:

> A second time I kill my husband dead,
> When second husband kisses me in bed.

He answers them directly now:

> So think thou wilt no second husband wed;
> But die thy thoughts, when thy first lord is dead.

die thy thoughts: let your thoughts die. He requests her to let her thoughts, intention, die.

The Queen cannot accept this. Her grief at the thought of his death, her anguish that he can think she loves him so little as to remarry, return. Almost desperately she tries to convince him as if he doubted her (she thinks he does).

> Nor earth to me give food, nor heaven light,
> Sport and repose lock from me day and night!

"Let the earth give me no food, nor the sky give me light; bar me from recreation by day and from rest by night."

> To desperation turn my trust and hope!
> An anchor's cheer in prison be my scope!

"Let all my confidence and hope for the future be turned into despair, may I be restricted to what is available to a hermit in a cell."

> Each opposite that blanks the face of joy
> Meet what I would have well and it destroy!

"May every reverse which wipes joy from the face meet every undertaking which I wish to prosper and destroy it."

> Both here and hence pursue me lasting strife,
> If, once a widow, ever I be wife!

"May perpetual conflict pursue me in this life and the next, if ever I marry again, once I am a widow."

The King realizes he cannot persuade her. He is too weak and frail to continue this harrowing scene. Again he gives her the satisfaction of showing that he believes she means it:

> 'Tis deeply sworn. Sweet, leave me here awhile;
> My spirits grow dull, and fain I would beguile
> The tedious day with sleep.

fain I would beguile: I very much want to overcome the tediousness of the day.

The Queen is content to leave him, hoping that sleep will

restore some of his strength. She hopes sleep will put his brain to sleep as a baby is rocked in a cradle:

> Sleep rock thy brain;
> And never come mischance between us twain!

"And may we two never be separated by misfortune!" These notes have treated the Queen as sincere in her love for her husband and in her desolation at the thought of his death and the irremediable emptiness of her subsequent life without him. If we are to be guided by the account of the dumb show, her love and grief are genuine, for there, when she finds him dead, she *makes passionate action*, and only after others *seem to condole with her*, and after rejecting the poisoner's wooing at first, does she accept *love*.

Nevertheless, there are grounds for playing the Queen as insincere and unfaithful to her husband. Her reaction to the King's words are then to be taken as dissembling, aiming at convincing him of sincerity because she is false. The actress will still have to appear so sincere as to deceive the King.

Today, the second of these two possibilities may be chosen by directors and actors who misunderstand Gertrude's *The lady doth protest too much*. This is misunderstood as meaning: "The lady overobjects, objects more than is necessary." But, in fact, to *protest* means in Elizabethan English to "insist." Gertrude means that the Queen is insisting that she will do more than she will be able to. She will not be able to carry out her intention; in her lonely misery she will find consolation in the real need which another man has for her, forgetting her promise to herself in the fulfillment of a second unexpected love which seems to her as splendid as the first that is now over. Gertrude knows, for this is what has happened to her. She thought her life was over when her first lord died; she was determined never to look at another man. But she has found in Claudius a substitute for Hamlet's dead father, and has come miraculously young and alive again in his love.

What about the King? He can be played as resenting more bitterly the fact that he will die and be forgotten. But he does not suspect his wife or try to hurt her. For in fact he emphasizes the need for her to take a second husband. He shows himself unselfish in his love for her, in his wish to make life as easy as possible for her after his death. This unselfish man is chosen by Hamlet to represent his beloved father, who was

so loving to my mother
That he might not beteen the winds of heaven
Visit her face too roughly.

And the Player Queen, like Gertrude, would

hang on him
As if increase of appetite had grown
By what it fed on.

In deciding exactly what are the intentions of the Player Queen we might be guided, however, by the fact that when Hamlet decides to have *The Murder of Gonzago* performed, he believes his mother to be guilty of plotting his father's death, and therefore of only dissembling when she hung on him and followed his body *Like Niobe, all tears*.

In conclusion, we cannot be sure whether the Player Queen is sincere or is a hypocrite only appearing to love her husband, working hard to seem upset. The result for him will be the same, it should be noticed.

Act Three, Scene Four

(THE CLOSET SCENE)

Before attempting to rehearse this scene the actor must consider Hamlet's intention when he comes to his mother's room. He now believes her to be implicated in his father's murder, but is determined to leave her to heaven. He will *speak daggers to her, but use none*. The aim is twofold: to tell her how disgusting he finds her, and to open her eyes to her sin, to make her repent, if possible.

He knows that she believes him to be mad. That means that he must not do anything to strengthen her belief, for she can ignore him the more easily if convinced he is insane.

The actor must also notice that whatever happens in the interview, when Hamlet leaves his mother she is firmly convinced of his sanity and of his love for her. There have been touchingly tender moments between them. Do not let her statement to Claudius later (that Hamlet is mad) influence you. For at the same time she describes Hamlet as leaving her closet weeping for what he has done to Polonius (Act Four, Scene One). This is not true; he does not leave weeping, quite the opposite. Gertrude lies about his "madness" and his tears to protect him.

The difficulty for Hamlet is that he might lose control, as a result of which his mother is likely to ignore his words. Keep this danger in mind, and notice where Gertrude accepts him as sane, where she is inclined to see madness, where she definitely finds him mad.

'A will come straight . . . A king of shreds and patches.

The situation is as follows: Having listened to Hamlet speaking to Ophelia in the "nunnery scene," Claudius has come to the conclusion that his nephew is not mad from unrequited love. But Polonius still thinks that this was the origin of Hamlet's illness and has asked Claudius for a last opportunity to find out if his belief is true or false. Polonius regards it as so important for Hamlet and for Denmark, that he does not want harm to come to the Prince for the lack of a true diagnosis. If he finds himself mistaken about Hamlet's love, he has agreed that Claudius should do whatever he might consider best for Hamlet and for the state. But Polonius has no reason to suspect Claudius of any need to take his nephew's life to save his own. Neither has Gertrude.

Gertrude and Polonius do not realize that since Claudius agreed to the interview in Gertrude's room with Polonius behind the arras, the Prince has learned from the play scene that Claudius killed his father; and Claudius knows that Hamlet is aware of his guilt. Polonius is therefore unwittingly placing himself in great danger, purely out of loyalty to the royal family. He and Gertrude hope to provoke Hamlet into complaining that Ophelia has rejected him. If this happens they will know how to cure him (by assuring him of her love, of everybody's willingness for them to marry). In Act III, Scene One, Gertrude tells Ophelia:

I do wish
That your good beauties be the happy cause
Of Hamlet's wildness: so shall I hope your virtues
Shall bring him to his wonted way again,
To both your honours.

Here is a hope that Hamlet is ill with love for Ophelia, and an assurance to Ophelia that if that proves the case, she can have an honorable relationship with Hamlet, ending in marriage.

Polonius and Gertrude believe themselves to be acting honorably in the best interests of Hamlet. Later, when Ophelia is dead, Gertrude declares at her funeral: *I hop'd thou should'st have been my Hamlet's wife.*

too broad to bear with: too crude to be tolerated.
hath screen'd etc.: The image comes from the English practice of heating rooms with great fires which were too hot for the eyes and face of anyone sitting too near. As a result fire screens were used; some of these were on stands and could be placed between a person and the fire. Some screens, like large ping-pong bats, could be held in the hand.
be round: be plain, don't be restrained.

By *thy father* Gertrude means Claudius. By *my father* Hamlet means his dead father. At this moment he believes her guilty of his father's murder, of knowing about it, wanting it. To the Queen it seems that Hamlet is talking nonsense; she has not offended Claudius.
idle: empty, meaningless.
Have you forgot me?: Gertrude has never experienced such

hostility from Hamlet. As she thinks him mad, she really wonders if he might not know who she is.

She realizes that she cannot deal with him; he is uncontrollable, and she is too upset at seeing him in this state (to her he is hopelessly mad). As she is about to rise from her chair he stands over her, places his hands on her shoulders to press her down.
budge: move.

Naturally she is afraid that in his madness, not recognizing her he mistakes her for an enemy and has laid hands on her to kill her, possibly to strangle her.

When Hamlet hears Polonius behind the arras his reflexes take over. He knows that with Claudius alerted to his own danger, there may be an attack at any moment and from any direction. The voice within the arras means sudden attack. Hamlet reacts by attacking swiftly in his own defense. Without rational thought as to who might be there, he thrusts before he is himself struck down. When Gertrude asks rhetorically, *What hast thou done?* Hamlet does not know whom he has killed. Then, as he has time to think for a moment, he asks, hoping to be told yes, *Is it the king?*

Only when Hamlet says *As kill a king* does Gertrude realize why he is so hostile. But she is not guilty. She was not involved in her husband's murder. Her innocence protects her from Hamlet's accusation; it also adds to her distress that he could be mad enough to suspect her and, apparently, to suspect Polonius, and to have killed him in revenge.

braz'd: hardened it.
proof and bulwark, etc.: invulnerable to and fortified (or a fortification) to repel human feeling.
wring: to wring the hands is to clasp them together with fingers interlaced. If wet clothes are pressed or wrung in this way, the liquid is forced from them. Hamlet has an image of Gertrude's heart wrung by his hands, until tears of contrition result. But Gertrude is innocent of his father's murder, and in her innocence can ask, *What have I done?* in justified outrage.

Hamlet now attacks her, not for murder of his father, but for her incest, a false form of marriage followed by bestial debauchery. She does not realize this, and responds to what she thinks is an accusation of murder *(as kill a king).* As she does not yield to his accusations they become more intense, but no more effective; for she did not murder his father.

blur: efface.

Hamlet's image of the rose displaced by a blister, with its overtones of sexual disease, is prompted by his indignation that his mother should have fallen from the glory of marriage with his father to the sordid incest with his uncle; he wishes it had never happened; he is determined to make her stop it.

as dicers' oaths: as oaths sworn by gamblers.

from the body of contraction plucks the soul: removes the living spirit from every act enjoining binding agreement.

a rhapsody of words: the incoherence of superstitious enthusiasm.

solidity and compound mass: the solid vast body (the sun).

as against the doom: as if confronted with the end of the world. The reference is to the eclipse of the sun prophesied as to take place on the Day of Judgment.

index: (1) in the list of contents, (2) in the list of things censured.

Hamlet realizes that he has not got through to her; that she is completely untouched by any awareness of her horrible sin in "marriage" with Claudius. He now decides to try to touch her by making her compare his father physically with Claudius.

counterfeit presentment: painted imitation.

He is determined to awaken in her a live memory of the reality of his father.

Hyperion: the sun god.

front: forehead.

station: posture, stance, attitude.

Mercury: the flying messenger of the gods, who had winged sandals. Obviously, Mercury has lightness and grace of stance and movement.

a combination and a form: a proportioned body and a shape.

set his seal: guarantee.

mildew'd ear, etc.: diseased ear of wheat infecting and destroying its healthy and health-giving brother.

could you on this fair mountain, etc.: Were you able to give up grazing decently on the heights of this beautiful mountain, and gorge yourself frantically like an animal on this low-lying swamp?

(The mountain is Hamlet's father; the swamp, his uncle.)

heyday in the blood: state of excited passions in the blood.

"It is obedient and lets itself be led by judgment."

Sense sure you have: You are endowed with sense to perceive and react.

apoplex'd: overthrown (by a brainstorm) and nullified.

would not err: would not want to make this mistake.

nor sense to ecstasy, etc.: nor was the sense ever so enslaved in a trance to such an extent that it did not preserve some ability to select which would operate on its behalf in so great a distinction between two alternatives.

cozen'd at hoodman blind: deceived at blindman's buff.

sans: without.

or but a sickly part, etc.: or no more than a diseased part of one real sense could not become as oblivious of reality as this.

mutine: flare up.

matron: middle-aged woman; "let virtue be as wax to flaming youth and melt in its own fire" (the fire which it kindles).

proclaim no shame, etc.: Do not call it publicly a shame when the compelling lust (heat) attacks, since frost burns as actively as fire, and reason panders to will.

Gertrude's eyes have been opened to her sin in living with Claudius as man and wife. She now admits to herself that she was blinded by lust as if she had taken leave of her senses.

black and grained spots, etc.: such black and deeply ingrained spots that will not lose their color.

Hamlet has been so carried away by the effort to make her understand her sin that he does not realize his success. He cannot control his revulsion to what she has done, his aversion to Claudius for all that he is and has done and is doing.

rank: luxurious, abundant, foul smelling.

enseamed: running with fat.

His words cut her so bitterly that she uses the image of daggers spontaneously to beg him to desist.

villain: man without honor.
tithe: tenth.
precedent: earlier, preceding.
lord: husband.
vice: caricature of.
precious diadem: crown.
shreds and patches: like a clown in a play.

The Ghost now enters, revealing itself only to Hamlet, not to the Queen; it is dressed in its ordinary clothes now, not in armor. As Gertrude sees nothing and can hear nothing she thinks that Hamlet is suffering from a hallucination and tries to console him, to soothe him, wanting him not to be too upset by what she is sure he is imagining.

This is the very coinage . . . Good night, mother.

coinage: fabrication.
ecstasy: hallucinatory trance.
cunning: skilled, powerful.

This appalls Hamlet, who is now afraid that his mother will discount all that he has said and ignore him as insane. He wants deeply to save her soul, reclaim her from bestiality. He offers to repeat every word that has passed between them, a feat which would be impossible for a madman.
temperately: moderately.
keep time: maintain its rhythm (beat).
gambol from: dance away from.
flattering unction: ointment which makes things seem better than they are. He uses the word *unction* deliberately, as it is the oil used to anoint a repentant sinner before death. Hamlet wants her to make a true confession, not to think that her sin has disappeared, because her attention was directed to it by one who is insane and can be discounted.

The ointment will grow an unhealthy skin over the infected spot, "while foul corruption undermining everything inside infects without being seen." The compost (manure) like the false unction will make the weeds grow more luxuriant and fouler.
pursy: obese (from self-indulgence).
curb and woo: bend and beg.

Gertrude perceives her son's true feeling for her. She also realizes that she must abandon her dream of a repetition with Claudius and Hamlet of the family life once enjoyed with Hamlet and his father. Her heart can no longer hold equal love for Claudius and her son. That is why she uses the image of her heart cut in two. It cannot hold equal love for both within itself any more. And she will not abandon Hamlet; but she loves Claudius.

Hamlet now wants to make sure that she will not succumb to Claudius again.

assume: steal and wear.

custom: habit.

all sense doth eat: dominates every sense.

of habits devil: the devil of habitual behavior acts like an angel in this way.

use: practice.

aptly: easily.

stamp of nature: what has been imprinted physically and psychologically from heredity and environment.

Early texts of *Hamlet* have him saying *either the devil.* In Elizabethan English the verb "to either" meant to make things easy for. Hamlet is saying that practice can either make things easy for the devil or throw him out altogether.

wondrous potency: magical efficacy.

He tells her that when she has meditated on her sins and is in a state of contrition he will come to her for her blessing as his mother.

I must be their scourge and minister: Since losing faith in the Ghost when it called out *Swear* beneath him, Hamlet has told himself that if he could be sure of its honesty his difficulties would be over. But now, certain that it is honest, that Claudius is guilty, he finds himself in greater difficulties than before. He has unintentionally killed Polonius; he will have little chance of catching Claudius unawares; he has missed an opportunity of killing him. It seems to Hamlet that, like all human beings, he is used by God in His inscrutable ways for inscrutable purposes. Hamlet knows this intellectually, but has not yet reconciled himself to it emotionally. He knows that much unpleasantness is ahead of him; that it will all be under the control of Provi-

dence and wishes it could be avoided. He sees himself functioning as a surgeon who must cut infection out of Denmark to heal the body politic.
bad begins and worse remains behind: this almost certainly means: "thus the beginning is bad, but worse is restrained as a result." But it could also mean: "thus things are bad at the beginning and are going to get worse before they are over."

Hamlet suddenly remembers that his mother might unintentionally betray him to Claudius. As she has not been involved in the murder of his brother, Claudius might well decide on her death for fear that she might denounce him or try to avenge the murdered man. Hamlet now warns her of her danger as well as his.

He now speaks ironically (but emphasizes the fact, saying explicitly not to do "what I bid you do").

bloat: self-indulgent, gross.
wanton: amorously (or, by pinching make you wanton).
reechy: grimy, smelly.
ravel out: search out, interrogate, disentangle, make plain.
mad in craft: mad as a clever policy.
paddock: toad.
gib: tomcat.
in despite of: in contradiction of, to the destruction of.
unpeg the basket, etc.: This must refer to a proverb, since lost, involving an ape which insisted on opening up a secret and lost its life as a result.

There is no need for Hamlet to worry. Gertrude has already reached the same conclusion in her own way. When she told him he had cleft her *heart in twain*, she realized that she must choose between him and his uncle. His warning may alert her to her own possible danger, a matter which she might have overlooked; but she is determined not to expose her son by a careless word.
bear the mandate: carry the order (from superior to lesser authority).

marshall me to knavery: lead me unsuspecting into a criminal trap.

Hamlet is already thinking ahead; looking forward to outwitting them; the advantage will be his in that they regard him to be foolishly unaware of danger.

engineer hoist, etc.: the sapper blown up with his own explosive charge.

mine: explosive charge placed in a tunnel dug beneath a wall which is to be breached. Hamlet talks of digging another tunnel underneath that of his opponents, and blowing them up first.

Notice the similarity of sound between *below* and *blow.*

crafts: (1) ships, (2) opposing cunnings.

This man shall set me packing: This man might be Claudius, but is more probably Polonius. Hamlet resents the fact that he is powerless and must leave Denmark as directed. With Polonius dead there is even less possibility of staying in defiance of the King.

Good night, mother: A sincere statement. But now Hamlet must return to his "antic mood." He begins to take on the madness which he must contrive to maintain if he is to get away (from the court) with his life. As he leaves her room, however, he drops the mad pose and wishes Gertrude a last good night.

Act Four, Scene Seven

Laertes has returned recently from France to find not only that his father has been killed by Hamlet, but that the Prince has got away scot-free, and that Polonius has been buried dishonorably without the heraldic ceremony which his rank and the honor of his family demand. Laertes is more enraged to find his sister has lost her sanity as the result of these events, particularly in that Hamlet is the killer of her father. Laertes left Denmark warning her against Hamlet, and mistakenly assumes that the Prince has "trifled with" her.

conscience: knowledge of right and wrong. Claudius means

that Laertes must find him guiltless by absolute standards.
acquittance: release from responsibility.
pursued my life: sought my death.

Claudius intends to convince Laertes of his innocence, of his own disapproval of Hamlet. When he is certain of Laertes as an ally, the King intends to tell him of the order for Hamlet's execution the moment he reaches England. Laertes can believe that Claudius is innocent, but wants to know why no action has been taken against the Prince.

capital in nature: punishable by death.
crimeful: criminal.
mainly: copiously, in so many respects.
unsinew'd: weak.
virtue: good quality.
plague: source of destruction.
conjunctive to: inseparable from.
as the star moves, etc.: It has already been explained that Elizabethan cosmology envisages the stars held in the sky on great circles of crystalline substance, spheres. A star moves only as the result of the sphere moving.
I could not but by her: I had to let her take me with her.
public count: public reckoning; trial.
general gender: common people.
gyves: fetters, symbols of degeneracy.
graces: signs of nobility.
too slightly timber'd: not made of heavy enough wood.
loud: strong, noisy.
reverted: turned back.
into desp'rate terms: into despair.
Whose worth, if praises, etc.: whose value (dignity), if praises can be recalled (given over again), made claims above all contemporaries for her perfections.
break not your sleeps: lose no sleep.
to imagine: Claudius means to imagine the kind of action that he is likely to take or have taken against somebody as guilty of so many crimes as Hamlet.
naked: stripped of possessions.
abuse: deception, trick.

Claudius is deeply disturbed by Hamlet's letter. Does Hamlet know of the intention to have him executed? How has he managed to return, by chance in ignorance, or by chance and contrivance in the knowledge of his uncle's ruthlessness? What has happened to his companions, to the strong guard sent to take him to his death? Have they betrayed Claudius?

advise me: give me any suggestion.

Laertes' reaction, his delight at the possibility of confronting Hamlet, sets the King planning another move against his nephew, the last, he hopes. But first Laertes must be persuaded to use cunning, for, while Hamlet must be killed, his death must not compromise Claudius.

to thine own peace: to your own satisfaction.

checking at: not going on; refusing to proceed.

work him: get him to.

ripe in my device: fully developed as a plan in my mind.

choose but fall: He will have no choice but to be laid low.

no wind of: no breath of.

uncharge the practice: make the trick seem innocent; exonerate from treachery.

organ: agent.

falls out: works itself out of its own accord (the fruit does not have to be shaken, but drops out of the tree).

sum of parts: all your good qualities totaled.

of the unworthiest siege: of the least importance (*siege* means seat, place).

riband: ribbon, decoration.

becomes: fits.

sables: black clothes.

importing: expressing.

can well: perform well, are skilled.

incorps'd: incorporated, shared the body of.

demi-natur'd: took of the nature (body, physiology).

topp'd my thought: outdid what I thought possible.

forgery: imagining, devising.

shapes: maneuvers.

brooch indeed and gem: highest adornment.

made confession of: said he knew.

match you: equal, fight a bout against.
scrimers: fencers.
play: fence in sport.

When Claudius asks Laertes if he really loved his father and really grieves for him, the young man is indignant; dares the King to doubt him. Claudius deliberately stirs him up to want to show his love in revenge.

passages of proof: occurrences which confirm my uncertainty.
time qualifies, etc.: reduces the intensity.
wick or snuff: The image is of a candle flame; the longer it burns, the greater amount of charred wick is produced inside it; this will not burn, and thus reduces the clarity of the flame.
growing to a pleurisy: increasing to excess.
abatements: reductions.
that we would do . . . when we would: What we want to do, we ought to do when we want to.
accidents: chance happenings.
hurts by easing: It hurts to sigh, yet the sigh eases the physical and psychological pressure on the afflicted person.
spendthrift: It was believed that with each sigh, the heart loses a drop of precious blood. That makes the sigh *spendthrift*, wasteful.
quick of the ulcer: the sound flesh inside the corrupt flesh, which hurts when touched.
in deed: in fact, in action.
sanctuarize: give sanctuary to.
close: secluded.
varnish: gloss.
in fine: in brief, in the end.
remiss: unsuspicious.
peruse: examine closely.
contriving: treacherous planning.
unbated: not blunted.
pass of practice: treacherous manipulation.
requite: pay back.
anoint: rub oil or grease on.
unction: ointment.
mortal: causing death, deadly.

cataplasm: plaster.
simples: herbs, medicinal plants.
virtue: healing power.
contagion: source of poison through touch.
gall: rub raw, rub skin off.
may be: can be, has the power of.
fit us to our shape: make us capable of carrying out our plan.
drift: intention.
assay'd: attempted.
back or second: reinforcement.
blast in proof: fail when tried.
cunnings: skills.
preferr'd: offered.
for the nonce: by chance for this occasion.
venom'd stuck: poisoned thrust.
our purpose may hold there: Our intention may be achieved there.

Laertes' *Drown'd! O, where?* comes from his need to know how it could have happened, where has she been drowned; he wants to be taken to her. Gertrude describes the place in order to explain how it happened. Her main object is to convince Laertes that it was an accident, and that his sister died peacefully, with no terror and no struggle, not even realizing her own danger. She wants to spare him distress, both for his own sake and in an effort to stop another emotional outburst from him. Claudius has managed to calm Laertes. Gertrude is afraid that the new sorrow might stir him up against both her husband and her son.

First, Gertrude describes the place, as one well-known to her as a haunt of the unhappy girl.

shows his hoar leaves: whose gray leaves are reflected in.
crowflowers: water-buttercups.
long purples: As she mentions the long purples, Gertrude realizes that Laertes does not like to be told of his sister decorating herself with obscene flowers. The Queen therefore observes that while coarse shepherds have an obscene name for

the flowers, *our cold maids* call them *dead men's fingers*—an innocuous name which explains Ophelia's preoccupation with them.

Gertrude now describes how the girl climbed on the overhanging boughs, and when a branch broke, fell with her flowers into the water. Gertrude now explains that Ophelia does not sink. Her clothes spread out (with a farthingale they are held out) and the air trapped beneath them keeps her afloat. Ophelia is indeed *mermaid-like,* out of water from the waist up and singing. She has no conception of her danger and enjoys floating downstream on the current *incapable of her own distress* or *native and indued* (born to and inured to) the water.
lauds: hymns.

Eventually, when her clothes are saturated with water, their weight pulls her suddenly under. The *poor wretch* goes swiftly to her death, with no anxiety, with no struggle. Gertrude impresses these facts on Laertes. It is uncertain whether the Queen believes her story, or tells it only to shield him from too traumatic a shock. But the description is what an onlooker might easily have seen from a distance. Such a person might well make much of the fact that Ophelia did not struggle, made no call for help, seemed content with what was happening to her. This description lays the foundation for the suspicion of suicide which so outrages Laertes at her funeral. Gertrude's account awakens no suspicion in Laertes, but it could waken suspicion in other ears. Gertrude obviously wants to keep him calm, to alleviate his distress as much as she can.

it is our trick: It is our characteristic; "nature does not forsake her custom, however shameful it might be." "When all my tears have gone, the woman in me will have been expelled."

douts: puts out.

Laertes leaves to be alone, to think over his troubles and decide what to do. He would like to denounce Hamlet in public. Claudius does not want this. He wants Hamlet to be murdered in accordance with the plan which will hide his murderer's guilt.

MACBETH

Act One, Scene One

TO PLAY THE THREE witches we need to know what Shakespeare assumed them to be. In his day the word "witch" was used of human beings, dedicated to serving Satan by doing evil, who were believed to have the power of flight and of making themselves invisible. But the word was also used of evil spirits which were normally invisible and had the power to appear to human beings by taking on a shape of air. In Act One, Scene Three, Banquo declares that the witches are bubbles of air. He believes them to be evil spirits, the *instruments of darkness.*

Each actress playing a witch may therefore imagine herself either a human being who can be invisible or a spirit making itself visible. In each case the witch's intention is to destroy as much of God's creation as possible. Macbeth is just one human being the witches intend to destroy; they know that he is vulnerable because he has longed to murder Duncan for the throne, and they hope to use him to cause much more destruction to human society, especially by undermining Scotland. At this point the most important task for the actress is to concentrate on wanting to destroy Macbeth, on looking forward to doing it and on extending the havoc to human society as far as possible.

The witches are believed in Shakespeare's day to be able to foretell the future to a limited extent. They know about the fighting to be done before sunset today. They know that Duncan is going to give Macbeth the title of Thane of Cawdor, which is to be forfeit for the treason of its present owner. They also know that Macbeth wants the crown and has considered murder to gain it. The scene opens just as they have made their plans, which they are looking forward to putting into execution before nightfall. The first witch asks her question as one who knows the answer; it is rhetorical, expressing her satisfaction at the arrangements.

hurlyburly: tumult.

The use of this word to describe the serious fighting which is about to take place suggests that the witch does not think it as important as the Scots and their enemies. The witches know the exact place where they will meet Macbeth.

Reference to Act One, Scene Three, will show that they meet Macbeth after the battle, after Duncan has sent his messengers with news of a new battle, but just before those messengers meet the returning leaders. As a result, immediately after the witches disappear, Ross and Angus come with news which confirms the second of the prophecies. In Scene One the witches are planning this encounter.

Graymalkin: gray cat. The witch hears the mew of a familiar spirit which shows itself as a cat (this may be inaudible to human ears).
paddock: toad. This witch similarly addresses a familiar spirit in the shape of a toad.
anon: in a moment.

As two of the witches are about to leave at the call of the familiars, the third detains them, saying, *Anon* ("wait a moment"). Obediently they join hands with her and circle round with the last two lines of the scene.

Fair is foul: Good is evil, beauty is ugly.

The witches exult in their power to confuse good and evil, beauty and ugliness, so that human beings can be deceived into mistaking each for its opposite.

Act One, Scene Three

In this scene as in the first scene there is no need for the witches to assume a false voice or to chant, except, of course, when they are actually laying their spell. They can be played as old women. The fact that they are called *weird sisters* means simply that they are evil and concerned with the supernatural. Some commentators have been misled by the word and by their number, into taking them for the three Fates, as in classical and Norse mythology. But these witches have no absolute power over the lives of men, unlike the Fates; also, unlike the Fates, they are associated with Satan and try their hardest to do evil. They do not know all of the future; the Fates and Norns do.

Aroint thee: begone.
rump-fed: fat-rumped, fed on offal.
ronyon: fat creature (sheathed in fat).
the shipman's card: the compass.

The witches focus their hatred on their images of the sailor and his fat wife.

drain him dry as hay: wither him, press all the moist life out of him.
pent-house lid: overhanging eyebrows, worn from lack of sleep.
peak: lose energy.

The witch knows that they are not able to sink the ship.

forbid: on whom a ban has been laid.

Now the witches join hands and incant their spell as they move in their circle.

posters, etc: who move ultra-swiftly about the sea and land.
weird: evil and supernatural.
about: around.
wound up: locked up in circling.
foul and fair: literally, this means with both good and bad weather. It also means with such a mixture of bad and good fortune. Macbeth speaks as a man who knows that he has faced very great dangers and overcome them.
aught: anything, anybody.

Banquo immediately recognizes the uncanniness of the witches once he has asked his first question. They direct one another to say nothing, putting a finger to closed lips.

choppy: chapped.

They look like women in every way, except for the fact that they have beards.

should be: ought to be.

interpret: understand.

The witches are determined not to answer Banquo. Their business is with Macbeth; their silence provokes him into speaking.

hereafter: later, in the end.

As the aim of the witches is to convince Macbeth that their greetings are true, that they are sure he will be Cawdor and King, their manner must be that of underlings greeting a superior person with pleasure.

start: jump with fright.

Looking at Macbeth, Banquo notices that the witches' greetings seem to terrify him. The question in modern English is: "Why do you jump with terror and appear to be frightened by things which sound so benign (or favorable, auspicious)?" Banquo now addresses the witches.

truth: (1) truth, (2) God.

fantastical: imaginary.

outwardly . . . ye show: appear from the outside.

present grace: favor immediately.

great prediction: foretelling future grandeur.

Present grace is related to *noble having, great prediction* to *royal hope.*

rapt: oblivious of the present, entranced.

Banquo neither begs their favors nor fears their hate.

get: beget.

imperfect: incomplete, fragmentary.

Macbeth knows that his father's death has made him Thane of Glamis. He cannot believe he is Thane of Cawdor. If, however, he were Cawdor, it would be possible for him to believe he might become King. Macbeth has often wanted the crown, has imagined himself killing Duncan to gain it, has thought about ways of doing this. But he is speaking in front of witnesses, particularly Banquo.

within the prospect of belief: something which might be considered or rejected by belief. Too remote even to be considered.

No more than to be Cawdor: The witches have manipulated

Macbeth into conceding that if he were to find himself Cawdor he would be able to believe that he might be King eventually.
strange: uncanny.
intelligence: secret advance information.

As the witches have disappeared Banquo points out that they were spirits in a shape of air which can be found in the earth as in the water.
corporal: physical.
would they had: I wish they had.

Macbeth also believes the witches to be spirits which have made themselves visible in a shape of air.
insane root: drug ground from a plant root which causes insanity.

At this point Macbeth tests Banquo to see how far he accepts the prophecy of the witches concerning himself as the ancestor of many kings. Necessarily, Macbeth will now be developing envy and antagonism to the thought of Banquo or his family having the coveted throne. It is not appropriate to insist on intention and manner for these two at this moment. Much depends upon the relationship which the two actors have developed as they create men who have trusted each other, friends for years, who have recently overcome fearful odds together in two battles. The uncertainty is less about Macbeth than about Banquo. Macbeth is uneasy, afraid that his companion's descendants might be kings, but he must not show this. Banquo, with a clear conscience, not having contemplated such events is less affected. Almost certainly he does not yet experience any ambition, does not see himself a rival to Macbeth, does not suspect any danger to himself or Duncan from Macbeth. His remark *to th' self-same tune and words* suggests a refusal to take the greetings as serious prophecy. His *You shall be king* may be equally a light refusal to be impressed, in answer to a dissembling statement by Macbeth, *Your children shall be kings,* made in a way which suggests he does not take the whole matter seriously. If actors feel called on to play the two men as already suspicious of each other, they must reconcile what Banquo does now with his evident lack of suspicion of Macbeth immediately before and after Duncan's murder.

The witches disappeared after awakening in Macbeth an intense wish to interrogate them, to test the possible truth of the prophecies. Very soon after the disappearance, messengers come from Duncan to confirm the prophecy about Cawdor.

The messengers, Ross and Angus, are both delighted to have been given the task of passing to Macbeth the news of the King's pleasure and of rewards to come. They regard both Banquo and Macbeth with admiration, but regard the latter as the more important of the two. The admiration and liking for him which Ross and Angus exude help to persuade Macbeth that possibly Duncan means to name him as heir to the throne. This is possible at this time in Scotland, which has what is known as an elective monarchy. Each king has the right of naming his successor, who is then elected by the college of electors when the appropriate time arrives. It is therefore possible for Duncan to name Macbeth instead of Malcolm as his successor.

thy personal venture, etc.: the personal risks which you took in the fight against the rebels.
His wonders and his praises . . . thine or his: There is a conflict between the wonder which he feels and the praises he wishes to give you.

Ross points out that Duncan, reduced to silence by praise and amazement, reviews the second battle fought the same day, this time against a fresh force of Norwegian invaders.
stout: solid, formidable.
strange images of death: death in unusual and deterring forms.

Notice the image of the post boys carrying bags full of letters to be emptied on the ground in front of Duncan.

Angus insists that they have not come to reward Macbeth but only as forerunners of the reception which he can expect when he finally reaches the King. Angus adds that the honor they have brought is not Macbeth's reward, but only a foretaste, some small fraction of it given now as a binding promise of what is to come in full.
addition: title, style of address.

When Ross's words confirm the witches' second prophecy, Banquo's reaction is typical of him; he does not doubt their evil nature.

borrowed robes: robes belonging to somebody else.
line: support.
vantage: reinforcement at a critical time.
wreck: destruction.
treasons capital: treasons punishable by death.

Now Macbeth's reaction is to hope that the kingship will come later.
is behind: remains to follow.

Again, Macbeth sounds Banquo wanting to find his reaction. Almost certainly this question is disguised as something casual, as if he were still not taking the witches seriously, but underneath there is some anxiety caused by the prophecies about Banquo and his children. Notice that Macbeth says, *gave the Thane of Cawdor;* he stresses the fact that this second *All hail* has come true. In fact, the witches have promised much more than *no less* to Banquo's descendants.

trusted: Notice how near this sounds to "thrusted."
home: all the way, to the hilt.
enkindle: set alight.
strange: uncanny.

Banquo has been thinking about the possibility of the devil speaking true. He has come to the conclusion that there may well be some unholy trap in all that has been happening. He concentrates on warning his friend not to be deceived.
instruments of darkness: servants of Satan.
honest trifles: honest facts which are trivial, worthless.
in deepest consequence: into the deepest depths as a result, into the most evil consequences.

Macbeth rejects Banquo's warning, insisting the witches have told two truths (he is Glamis and Cawdor) as happy introductions to the developing action of a play concerned with the theme of monarchy and the yielding of power.
soliciting: inciting to lawlessness, urging.

No sooner has he insisted to himself that the *soliciting* cannot be ill than he realizes that the soliciting is also to lawlessness. The ambiguity is inherent in the word he uses.
earnest: advance payment to bind the contract.

horrid image: image of horror.
unfix: disturb (stand his hair on end).
seated: firmly fixed.
against the use of nature: in a manner abnormal to human physiology and anatomy.

Macbeth is aware of his heart beating fiercely, with enormous contraction and expansion, as a result of which it knocks against his ribs, while firmly fixed in its correct anatomical position (i.e., it doesn't knock itself by moving, but it expands enough to hit the ribs).

Present fears, etc.: Things feared that are present are less than horrible things imagined before they take place.
my thought: What I am thinking, what is in my mind.
whose murder: the murder which it contains.
but fantastical: only imaginary.
single state of man: Elizabethan pre-Descartian belief was that a living human being is not a dual state of body controlled by mind, but a single unified state of both body and soul.

(For a fuller account of the part played by the substance spirit in the single state, see J. B. Bamborough, *The Little World of Man*, pp. 54–57, and *Shakespeare's Eden*, pp. 251 ff.)

function: ability of body-soul to operate simultaneously.
smother'd: choked.
surmise: imagining.

Macbeth says: "My thought which is of a murder as yet only imaginary so upsets the unified state of body-soul, which I consist in, that the ability of body and soul to cooperate is nullified, and nothing exists for me except what does not really exist."

He knows that he is imagining the murder so powerfully that it dominates his consciousness and excludes his perception of reality. Nothing exists for him except the nonexistent imaginary murder. The fact that Macbeth knows that the murder he sees is merely imaginary does not stop him seeing it or stop his senses responding as if it were real (that is what he means by *function is smother'd in surmise*).

rapt: absorbed in his thoughts, or imagining.

Macbeth recollects that Duncan has the right to make him

his successor, and that the manner and messages brought by Ross and Angus suggest that the King intends some unusual reward. Macbeth is horrified by imagining the murder and hopes he can gain the crown without any such crime.

If chance will have me king, etc.: If Fortune wants me to be king, why, Fortune may make me king without my having to make any move on my own behalf.

strange: unaccustomed.

cleave not to their mould: do not preserve a comfortable fit.

but with: except with.

use: (1) being used, (2) custom.

Macbeth consoles himself that let whatever come that can come, every day comes to an end, sooner or later, even the roughest.

give me your favour: give me your indulgence.

dull: tired.

wrought: was occupied by.

regist'red: recorded.

The image is of a book in which their *pains* are set down accessibly to be reread every day. The last two and a half lines are for Banquo.

at more time: when we have more time.

interim: the time which has passed.

having weigh'd it: having given some reason to show how much weight to be placed on what has *chanc'd*.

our free hearts: our innermost thoughts without constraint.

Act One, Scene Five

In this scene the actress must consider what Lady Macbeth knows, or is mistaken in thinking, about her husband. She knows that he wants the crown, not only for wealth, obedience, power, but for the admiration, love and honor which he sees go with it in the case of Duncan. She and her husband have discussed ways of seizing the crown by force; they have contemplated murder, and he has wished he could contrive an opportunity. But when it comes down to details, to discussing a real attempt, he has shown hesitation. This she ascribes to a weakness in him, to an inability to be inhuman enough when it comes to the push. (Later in the play it is apparent to her that she has been mistaken.) He is a man ready to take enormous risks when he has calculated them and can see a chance of success. In the case of the crown, however, he feels that the risk of failure is so great that he cannot resolve to act. In their discussion in the past he has never brought himself to the point of agreeing to put a plan to murder Duncan into action. As a result, in this scene she still thinks he is not evil enough to murder the King, unless she urges him on.

An actress has the choice of imagining that Lady Macbeth is reading the letter for the first time, or that she is going over it again after having read it once or more. In any case, she has read far enough to know that *they* are the witches, and that they have *all-hailed* Macbeth (and probably Banquo) three times.

more in them than mortal knowledge: have more knowledge than is given to a mortal.
made themselves air: Spirits were believed to make themselves visible in a shape of air; by dissipating this they become invisible again.
rapt: oblivious of everything else.
missives: messengers.
saluted: greeted, hailed.
referr'd: directed.
coming on of time: future, time to come.
the dues of rejoicing: the rejoicing which ought to be yours.
nature: She means specifically the physiological composition on which depend psychological and spiritual characteristics.
milk of human kindness: softening secretion which belongs to the human race (as distinct from beasts or fiends). Her words may be paraphrased as: "not inhuman enough to be as ruthless as is necessary."
kindness: here does not mean benevolence, but belonging to human kind, to the human species.
wouldst be: want to be.
illness should attend it: evil which should accompany and support it. "What you want very much you would like to attain

without sinning." "You do not like playing false, but you have no objection to having won illegally or sinfully."
thou'dst have: You would like to have.
that which cries, etc.: something which insists there is one way in which you must act if you are to have it; and that is something which you are merely afraid of doing, rather than that you would want it undone if it were to be done by somebody else for you.

At this moment she is convinced that Macbeth would raise no objection if somebody else were to do it, or to present him with it as a *fait accompli.* She has now decided to do it herself, because she is sure he will not do it.
spirits: (1) literally, vital spirits through which physical actions are performed; (2) figuratively, courage.

She pours them in his ear by exhorting him.
golden round: golden circle, the crown.
fate: Fortune, speaking through the witches.
metaphysical aid: with the help of metaphysical beings (the witches).

She calls the messenger mad because she cannot believe that the King is coming unannounced. Her other motives are all present, but satisfactorily masked by appropriate amazement at the unexpected and apparently unannounced visit.
He brings great news: As the servant is leaving she considers how really great the news is for her. She recognizes an opportunity which may never return if not taken now, and determines to take it.
The raven, etc.: A raven is a bird of ill omen. Its voice is naturally hoarse. As a result a raven which is hoarse on top of its natural tone would sound very hoarse, and is therefore to be seen as a bird of extraordinary ill omen.
fatal: that will cause his death.
you spirits: She means evil, invisible supernatural beings, which exist to do harm to human beings, which lie in wait for every opportunity to carry out their purposes.
tend on: wait to serve, to act as servants to.
mortal thoughts: thoughts of killing.
unsex me here: She may well mean her head (the place of

thoughts). On the other hand, the heart is often referred to as the seat of thoughts when these imply intentions (as here). Whichever the actress chooses, she must imagine the place she touches to be the seat of emotions and wishes which must be transformed into a masculine ruthlessness.

direest: most horrible.

make thick my blood: She means this literally; she wants it to flow more slowly, so that what is soft in her female physiology will not interfere with her male determination to shed blood.

access and passage to: Again, she is speaking literally of blood vessels, through which the blood carries the secretions which result in her feeling pity and repulsion for the deed.

nature: her female physiological composition. If these flow normally with the blood round her body, into heart and brain, they will bring with them a feminine compunction, an inability to do the deed.

fell: fierce.

it: i.e., her *fell purpose.*

the effect: the carrying out of the purpose.

gall: bitter black bile.

take for: (1) take to make into gall, (2) take and replace it with.

ministers: servants (of Satan).

sightless: invisible.

substances: Spirits were thought to be made of a substance more pure and ethereal than air.

nature: unregenerate natural forces, turned evil by the Fall of Adam and Eve.

She invokes night because she recognizes that her natural repugnance to committing the deed which she can plan is derived from God and Heaven. Even to imagine the murder is to feel the ability to do it begin to drain from her. She therefore asks to be cut off by darkness, by the power of evil, from the benign power of Heaven.

pall: cover.

dun: dark.

keen: The word suggests sharp sight as well as sharp edge.

blanket: cover.

Lady Macbeth is begging the forces of evil to overcome in

her everything which as a woman prevents her committing murder herself. She asks for a darkness so intense that if a knife possessed sight it would not be able to see the wound it is actually engaged in making. It cannot be closer than that to the flesh it wounds. Yet that must be too far for the knife's vision. The image communicates her stress, the violence she is doing to herself psychologically.

The most important point to remember is that Lady Macbeth invokes darkness, not because she is afraid of her crime being discovered, but because she needs to be given the remorseless ability to commit it with her own hand. She regards *thick night* as a source on which she can draw to maintain her resolution when the moment comes in fact, because she finds it so unnerving in fantasy.

She greets Macbeth by the greetings used by the witches.

the all-hail hereafter: the last greeting, the greeting which comes last of all.
in the instant: at this moment.

Remember that Macbeth had very high (and justifiable) hopes that Duncan might name him as successor. These hopes were dashed when, instead, Malcolm was named, with the title of Prince of Cumberland. Duncan a few moments earlier had assured Macbeth that more was his due *than more than all can pay.* As a result, the naming of Malcolm was an unexpected shock. Now he knew that *chance* did not intend him to be King without having to make a move himself. He also recognized that Malcolm is now in his way. A few moments later Duncan had announced his intention of being Macbeth's guest. Macbeth recognized that he had been given an opportunity to seize the crown. He admits to himself that he wants the deed done, Duncan murdered, even though he cannot bear to imagine it fully.

Riding ahead of the royal party, ostensibly to prepare his household to give appropriate entertainment, Macbeth has been unable to come to a decision, whether to take the opportunity provided or whether to neglect it as everything has happened too swiftly, and without careful planning a deed of this quality is bound to fail; he is also afraid that even if it were to succeed at the beginning, sooner or later regicide, especially when the monarch is a guest, will be punished by God.

He is still undecided when his wife greets him. His announcement to her, followed by her question and his answer *Tomorrow, as he purposes* are noncommittal. There is scope for actor and actress to convey much while making nothing in the way of commitment. Then she commits herself.

His reaction to *O, never/Shall sun that morrow see!* shows in his face. As a result, she warns him not to show his true feelings and intentions in it.

beguile: enchant, deceive.
the time: society, contemporaries.
th' innocent flower: The image is related to sentiments and illustrations stretching back to the story of the Fall, in which Satan is disguised as a serpent with a beautiful face, discovered by Eve amid the flowers of Eden.
provided for: have arrangements made for him (again, a noncommittal, two-edged statement).
into my despatch: into my execution. The word suggests not only carrying into effect, but with speed, and killing.

She insists that all he must do is look innocent; she will make all arrangements and do the deed herself.

solely sovereign: (1) we two the only sovereigns, (2) complete as belongs to a sovereign.
sway: power, rule.

Macbeth is still undecided. She has not persuaded him that the murder must be committed tonight. On the other hand, he cannot make up his mind not to do it or not to let her do it.

clear: innocently.
alter favour: change expression.
ever is to fear: (1) always shows fear, (2) means to be afraid forever (the first is more probable).

Act One, Scene Seven

Macbeth still has not made up his mind. He has just come from the feast with which he is entertaining the King and his court. Macbeth has been appearing innocent, showing himself full of loyal happiness at having his monarch as his guest. But all the time it has been becoming harder to keep up the show; every time he looks at Duncan and Malcolm he feels envy and intends treachery. When the conflict within him becomes too great he leaves the chamber, his manner suggesting that he is an anxious host who himself makes certain that there is no flaw in his hospitality. This whole scene is played with an awareness of Duncan and his court feasting not far away, with servants moving back and forth in the background serving the revelers.

If it were done: if it would really be done with forever. "If it would be really done with once and for all when it is done (the deed), then it would be well if it were done quickly (i.e., to-night)."

But Macbeth is not convinced that it would be done with once and for all. He wishes that he could believe that there would be no repercussions, simply one blow and nothing more for the rest of his life.

trammel up: catch the smallest particle in a threefold, fine-meshed net. *Trammel* was also the name for the tasseled cord used to tie a shroud round the feet of a corpse.

surcease: death.

Notice how Macbeth's cruel humor expresses itself in the sound play of *surcease—success.*

but this blow: only this blow, this single blow.

bank and shoal of time: this short life which seems so much more substantial than it is in the flow of time.

Macbeth's image is of a sandbank which, when compared with the water, is solid, but, compared to dry land, is insubstantial. In the same way, human life seems substantial compared with the seemingly endless movement of time; but it is revealed as transitory when contrasted with the endlessness of eternity. Macbeth says he would do it *quickly* if he were sure of enjoying the throne for the seeming length of transitory human life.

jump: risk.

He knows that there would be punishment in the life after

death, but he is ready to risk that if he could be certain that the crown would be his to enjoy for the whole of his natural life.

The actor playing Macbeth must imagine himself believing in the theology of the Fall, the existence of Satan and evil spirits, the Last Judgment, at which the dead arise and are divided into those to be punished eternally and those to be received into eternal life in Heaven. Macbeth firmly believes that he cannot escape punishment indefinitely; he wishes that his could be delayed until after his death. But he is afraid that his punishment will take place here in this life. He now considers his chances, taking into account the nature of the sin he is contemplating.

these cases: cases such as this (i.e., killing a king).
still: always.
have judgement here: Sentence is passed in this life.

The punishment takes the form of the criminal being killed by the same method as he used in his crime, which he has stimulated somebody else to copy.

but: only.
plague: kill.
inventor: the person who first devised it.
even-handed: impartial; the scales of justice are perfectly balanced.
commends: proffers (with recommendation).
ingredients: mixture.
chalice: cup.

Macbeth has thought about the fact that Duncan is his King. Now he contemplates the fact that he owes the King loyalty on two grounds, that of being a kinsman as well as subject, and of being host to a guest.

trust: He can expect protection from me or can trust me on two counts.
strong both against the deed: Macbeth thinks in one sense that they should work on him strongly against the deed, and, in another, that they will speak strongly against it when he has judgment.

In a split second before he says *Besides*, he realizes something which he has overlooked, and the significance of this fact reduces him to a terrified imagining of being discovered attempting the murder. This fact is simple: Elizabethans believed that when we are awake our Reason can control the impulses coming from Imagination, which is particularly subject to sin. In sleep, however, Reason rests and Imagination is at liberty to imagine evil deeds. As a result a man who dies in his sleep may well die in a state of mortal sin and this may lead to his consequent damnation. It has dawned on Macbeth that Duncan's life has been so comparatively without sin that God will not leave him exposed to damnation by being assassinated in his sleep. This means that his would-be murderer must fail, and must himself be exposed in his attempt. He therefore imagines supernatural powers at work against him.

borne his faculties so meek: has carried the great powers of his office with so little arrogance.
clear: innocent, sinless.

A clear image of the admirable and lovable Duncan is essential here, with the accompanying feeling of reverence.

Macbeth has a vision of a special Judgment being held for Duncan before he can be killed. If he is included with the rest of humanity in the Last Judgment, it will be too late, death in a state of mortal sin will have given cause for his damnation. At this special preliminary Judgment Duncan's virtues will testify on his side; indeed, their testifying will function like the trumpeting which precedes the Last Judgment; they will awaken a sleeping, not a dead, world. And when all the world is roused from sleep, Macbeth will be found for the would-be murderer he is.

like angels trumpet-tongu'd: a visual image of angels, mouths open wide, from which protrude not tongues, but trumpets. This is also an auditory image of both the cries of the virtues and the trumpet sounds awakening the sleeping.
his taking-off: his assassination. The virtues plead for him not to be assassinated, so that he will not be damned.
pity, like a naked new-born babe: Divine pity is imagined in the shape of the newly born Jesus. The second person of the

Trinity is sometimes shown iconographically as a naked baby holding a sword.
or heaven's cherubin: Editors sometimes print *cherubim* in error for *cherubin. Cherubin* is the English word for cherub, a member of the second of the nine orders of angels. *Cherubim* is the anglicized form of the Hebrew word for angels. It is plural; *cherubin* is singular.

In Macbeth's vision the naked baby is succeeded by a similar image, that of a cherubic face, with head and wings. There are innumerable representations of the infant Jesus, often with Mary, attended by babylike angelic presences. But the cherubins are also frequently shown and imagined as fearsome creatures with six wings. Body and wings are covered with eyes like those in the markings of a peacock's feathers. In this manifestation the cherubin is usually blue green, not unlike that of the peacock. The cherubin is an angel of light, very watchful and alert. In the heavenly choir its order is entrusted with the care of the firmament, the sphere of the fixed stars.

From the image of the *new-born babe* astride the *blast* of air that comes from the angel-like *trumpet-tongu'd* virtues, Macbeth's mind moves to a babylike *cherubin,* with which is associated the terror of the six-winged creature of many eyes which also sits astride the invisible winds.

hors'd: seated astride and borne along by.
sightless couriers of the air: invisible runners of the air (i.e., the winds).

Macbeth now considers what Duncan's virtues will achieve with their pleading. An awareness of his *horrid deed* will be blown into every eye, those of *heaven's cherubin* and those of the awakened sleepers. There is an image of a speck of grit blown into an eye, both visual and tactile. Intellectually, this is a statement that the knowledge of the deed will reduce everyone to tears of pity. The aim of the virtues was to save Duncan by evoking pity. When that is evoked they stop their pleading, the trumpets cease to blow, the wind ends. Tears come. As a result the wind is "drowned." With everything else

Macbeth has had a vision of a special Day of Judgment. It has two objects: one, to save Duncan, the other, to sentence his would-be murderer. Macbeth is telling himself that he cannot expect to evade judgment in this life, that he will have to face it *here,* that any attempt to kill Duncan will arouse supernatural opposition and exposure. It follows that Macbeth cannot make up his mind to do the deed *quickly,* i.e., tonight. On the other hand he is equally incapable of giving up his hopes. He would still like to kill the King; he is stopped only by his certainty that the assassination will not *trammel up the consequence.* This conflict between an ineradicable wish to act and an equally strong refusal to resolve to act is expressed in the image of the horse and the vaulter. To "vault" was the name for an exercise of Elizabethan superior horsemanship; the rider takes his horse to the barrier, stops it there and vaults over from the saddle, leaving his steed where it stands.

In the image *intent* (resolution to act) is the horse. Ambition, the rider, does not need his steed to jump, but vaults over alone, falling on the other side. For Macbeth to gain the crown, it is not enough for him to have fantasies of acting, for his ambition to make him want to have acted. He must resolve and act. His horse must go over beneath its rider; the fantasies of murder can be turned into reality only if they are supported by a resolution to act.

Macbeth is dissatisfied with himself for not being able to decide to act, but knows that he cannot so long as he knows that he cannot evade *judgement here.* He is equally dissatisfied in that he cannot put the whole matter out of his mind. As long as he is not King he will want the crown; but for all that, there is nothing to make him decide to seize it.

For the whole of the scene that follows, the actor and actress have to be aware that not far away is the dining hall which they have just left, with the King and his subjects finishing their meal, served by Macbeth's servants who pass to and fro in the background on their way from kitchen to dining tables and vice versa.

Lady Macbeth has followed her husband partly to bring him back to the King before too much comment is caused by his absence, which may be recalled later after the murder (which she intends to commit), and direct suspicion at him. She is also seriously disturbed by the length of his absence, for fear that it means that he has decided not to let her act tonight.

Macbeth would still like Duncan to be killed tonight; but he has made up his mind that it would be too dangerous. He is not afraid of the deed in itself. He is a man of great courage, experienced in taking great risks and succeeding, as any general must be in warfare of personal combat. But he always calculates the risks; and this time his calculation tells him the risk is too great; there is no chance of success as he understands it, that is, just one blow and nothing more, with no *judgement here.*

Lady Macbeth does not really see as clearly as her husband; she is certain that success tonight means success for all their *days and nights to come.*

Know you not he has? Either we must imagine that servants have been sent to find him, or she is speaking with sarcasm (how can you be so stupid as to think he would not have by this time?).

Macbeth is determined not to kill Duncan in his house tonight. The reason he gives her is partly true. He is convinced that an attempt will fail and that they will be exposed, so that he will lose all the honor his recent victories have brought him. Although he enjoys admiration and love much less than those given to Duncan, yet they are enormous; under the King he is outstanding. He wants to enjoy what he has gained; he is certain that an attempt on the King will merely lose all that has been gained. That is why he argues in the image of providing oneself with better clothes before the most recent purchases have been worn, let alone worn out.

She thinks that he is frightened and tries to shame him.

Was the hope drunk, etc? When you imagined yourself dressed in this most golden of golden opinions, was that the expectation of a drunken man? Has it changed to the nausea and despair of awaking sober with a hangover, faced with the results of its own excess?

such I account thy love: I value your love as of the same kind

as the resolutions you made when you wanted the crown, and which you give up when you face difficult reality.
act and valour: courageous action.
esteem'st the ornament of life: value as the element which most enhances life (i.e., *golden opinion*).
live a coward in thine own esteem: live with your own opinion of yourself as a coward.

Mistakenly thinking him afraid, she argues that while other people admire him for courage, he will live with the frustration of knowing that he has missed the crown in his cowardice.
adage: proverb.

She ridicules him by comparing him to a cat that would like to catch a fish but is afraid to get its paws wet.

She does not succeed in doing more than exasperating him. He knows that she has no real idea of what is involved in fighting and gaining victory against enormous odds, as he has just done twice in one day. It is a side of him that she completely underestimates in her ignorance of the realities of fighting and warfare. He will not argue with her. He knows that he is right not to take this risk, much as he wants the crown.

break this enterprize: suggest this undertaking (i.e., seizing the crown, as an idea in itself).
durst: dared.
adhere: were added. (We had the will but not the time or place.)
made themselves: created themselves for us.
fitness: appropriateness.
unmake: undoes your ability. This is a play on *you would make, they have made themselves.*

As Lady Macbeth sees that he is impervious to her taunting, still assuming that he is scared, she tries more intensely to shame him, by saying that if she had sworn as resolutely as he has in the past, nothing would force her to break the oath. She says that before breaking such an oath, she would do the thing that she finds it least possible to do. She insists that she knows how incapable of violence to her baby she feels when suckling it. The assertion does not reveal her as one to whom violence comes easily, but the opposite. Her aim is to shame him with her resolution, to make him remember how determinedly he has sworn, how much he has wanted to do this.

Macbeth still wants to, just as much. As a result he is provoked by her utter unawareness of the impossibility of succeeding tonight. His *If we should fail?* is another way of saying, "And what if we don't succeed, what are you going to do about that?"

Now his conviction of failure becomes apparent to her for the first time. She sees now that he is not afraid of the idea as she has been thinking, that he wants to seize the crown as much as ever, that he has some rational motive for his decision not to do so tonight. She now changes her tack; instead of trying to shame him by calling him a coward, she sets herself to convince him that they cannot fail.

We fail!: Some modern editors print the words this way. But others prefer *We fail?* This is because no definitive Elizabethan text exists to tell us which was intended originally. Whichever an editor decides to print, all that matters for the actress is that Lady Macbeth is determined not to admit the possibility of failure. To say to her husband at this point, "We fail, and that's all there is to it," is to reinforce his determination not to act. Her *We fail!* or *We fail?* must communicate her assurance that failure is impossible.

screw . . . to the sticking place: This image could be (1) of screwing one thing to another, just enough to hold without facing a great strain; (2) of tuning a stringed instrument to the right point without making sure the string will stay at the right tension for very long; (3) of screwing a crossbow to the point at which it can shoot, but not do the shooting; somebody else does that.

rather: more swiftly (and more easily).

soundly: healthily, deeply.

wassail: drinking.

convince: conquer.

warder: warden (to guard its treasure).

fume: vapor.

receipt: receptacle.
receipt of reason: cranium.
limbeck: a retort, used in alchemy to turn a solid into a vapor.

Her image is of the insides of the skulls of the grooms swirling with vapor, of the heads themselves converted into instruments designed to turn solids into gas (i.e., certainties into an inability to remember anything with any kind of clarity).

drenched: sodden, drowned.
nature: physiological processes.
as in a death: as inert as if overtaken by death.

Nature in this context has almost the sense of *life*, and she is playing on "life"—"death."

put upon: lay the blame on.

Notice how she says *perform upon—put upon.*

spongy: sodden; rotten.
quell: murder, killing.

When she begins this speech he is determined not to change his mind. With every actor there will be a point at which he finds himself listening to her, then giving her full attention, because she is saying what he wants to hear, putting forward what strikes him as a foolproof way of killing Duncan without being discovered. As it dawns on him that his belief in certain failure was premature, as he is flooded with relief, as he listens to her practical and efficient plan, there is a relaxation of his enormous tension. He is delighted to be shown a way which cannot go wrong. His relief and delight are expressed in his next words.

undaunted: able to triumph over difficulty and danger.
mettle: (1) tempering, (2) metal of which she is made.
receiv'd: accepted.
their very daggers: actually their daggers.
other: differently.
clamour: cries of outrage.
settled: resolved, unchangeable.
bend up: tense.
corporal agent: every physical part involved.
mock the time: deceive and make fun of everybody.

fairest show: most beautiful (and deceptive) appearance.

His final speech accepts her earlier exhortation *only look up clear* and *bear welcome in your hand, your eye, your tongue* with the insistence that he should be *like the innocent flower, but be the serpent under it.* Naturally, she is delighted by his acceptance of her plan and by his readiness to put on the *fairest show.*

By this time each is certain of the crown as the result of tonight's murder.

Act Two, Scene One

Banquo's remark made a few minutes after the scene opens *(There's husbandry in heaven; their candles are all out)* may indicate the fact that the courtyard is ablaze with torches. Or it may be that they have just come from a hall still ablaze with candles lit in the "feasting presence" in honor of Duncan. If Banquo is to be interpreted as contrasting the darkness of heaven with Macbeth's abandoning of husbandry for extravagance, then the scene may well be fairly full of lights. If we take the reference as one to the lights in the hall, the scene may be dark.

I take't, 'tis later, sir: Fleance agrees with, does not contradict, his father. Banquo is not content with the utter darkness of Heaven. He looks in vain for some sign that dawn is not too far off. He does not want to fall asleep, because then (for reasons explained above, p. 197) his imagination will be out of the control of his reason, and can tempt him to evil with *wicked dreams.*
would not: do not want to.
cursed thoughts: evil ideas in the mind.
nature: physical powers of the mortal body.

It was believed that imagination and dreams are part of the physical body, not the rational soul.

Banquo hears somebody coming and is very much aware of the King sleeping nearby. He gives his challenge with the sword ready for action, as it is not usual to meet somebody moving, apparently stealthily, about the castle at this time of night.

Macbeth's reply to the challenge must have some impact on Banquo. Remember, he has just challenged his friend (who is his host) most suspiciously for going about his business in his own household. Banquo assumes that Macbeth is still making certain that nothing is left undone for the royal entertainment of this special guest and his court. He wants to convince Macbeth that everything has been arranged superbly and that there is no need to be worried.

largess: generous gifts of money.
officers: servants.
shut up: enclosed, asleep in bed.
measureless content: satisfaction, or happiness beyond measure.
servant to defect: forced to be less than perfect.
else should free have wrought: would otherwise have worked without any restriction (inhibition).

First, Banquo assures Macbeth once more that there is nothing to worry about. Then he brings up the matter to which he has referred in his words to Fleance earlier. He is perturbed by dreams of the witches. At this moment he still regards Macbeth as a friend with whom many great dangers have been shared and in whom he can confide. He is honest and does not like the effect of the dreams on his desires. What happens in his sleep tends to tinge his hopes when he is awake.

we: Macbeth is probably thinking of himself and Banquo. But he may be using the royal *we* unconsciously. "When we can get hold of an hour for our use, we ought to (or would like to) . . . if you have time to devote to it."
At your kind'st leisure: whenever you are most kind to have the leisure.
cleave to my consent: stick to what I want; do exactly as I want.
when 'tis: when the time comes (for discussion).
It shall make honour for you: It will bring you honor.
augment: increase.
bosom franchis'd: conscience free.

allegiance: loyalty to king.
clear: innocent, unspotted.
shall be counsell'd: shall take the advice I am given.
repose: rest.
the while: in the meantime.

When his servant has left him, Macbeth, alone, contemplates the night's work. He has made up his mind to kill Duncan, and as he imagines himself using his dagger, his strong imagination exerts itself, with the result that there seems to be a dagger floating in the air in front of him. The fact that his determination is unweakened is shown by his attempt to *clutch* the dagger. Fear, or irresolution, would show themselves in an attempt to avoid the dagger or deny its existence, rather than in one to seize it.

fatal: deadly.
vision: something seen; *fatal vision:* manifestation of something deadly.

At this moment he is not sure whether he is confronted with a supernaturally produced, but insubstantial dagger, or whether it is a delusion. A *vision* which really existed might affect all or some of the senses; he asks if this is one which affects only sight and not feeling.

false creation: delusion.
yet: still.
in form as palpable: in a shape which looks as solid (capable of being touched).
marshall'st: direct, indicate the way.

Because he is still determined to kill Duncan and intends to go to Duncan's room, Macbeth imagines the dagger pointing out the way and directing him to proceed.

instrument: weapon.
made the fools of: are shown to be fools compared with.

Still determined to kill Duncan, he regards the *vision* as a delusion, or concludes that his sight is the only sense which is responding to what is really there, a supernaturally produced weapon, intended to encourage him as a portent of success. The knowledge that he is going to use his own dagger on Duncan makes him imagine it dripping with the royal blood. As a result

his imagination responds by showing him blood on the *vision*.
dudgeon: wooden hilt.

He thinks of the imaginary dagger and realizes that he has not yet used the real one; it follows that without his concentrating on using the dagger he no longer imagines it so strongly. It disappears and he knows it was an image from his *heat-oppressed brain*.

informs thus to mine eyes: provides my eyes with this sort of information.

nature: physiological processes of living in all mortal creatures.

abuse: deceive. See above (p. 197) for an account of the working of the uncontrolled, and therefore evil, imagination in sleep.

curtain'd: (1) in darkness, (2) behind eyelashes, (3) behind the curtains of the bed.

Pale Hecate: the goddess of magic, associated with the moon.

alarum'd: awakened to action.

whose howl's his watch: whose howl acts for him as the cry of the night watchman, announcing the passing of time and the state of the peace.

Tarquin: The Roman tyrant who stealthily broke into the apartment of Lucrece and raped her; she was the wife of one of his subjects, Collatine.

design: purpose.

like a ghost: silently.

firm-set: solid.

prate of: betray.

take the present horror from the time: deprive the hour of the horror now in it.

suits with it: is appropriate to it.

Macbeth is afraid that if his footsteps are heard as they touch the ground the noise will destroy the intense silence which he finds so in tune with what he has to do; the silence adds to the horrifying quality in which he is reveling with the thought of killing Duncan and seizing the throne.

threat: threaten.

The cold breath of words cools the heat of deeds; the longer he stays there speaking, the longer the deed remains undone.

Earlier in this same night, Macbeth agonized about *if it were done,* and decided not to do it. Now, nothing seems able to shake his determination; he is looking forward to when *it is done.*

invites: summons, bids come.
knell: bell rung when a human being dies; passing bell.

Act Two, Scene Four

volume: unrolling.
strange: terrifying.
sore: grievous.
trifled: made trifles of. "Has made everything known before seem trivial."
knowings: knowledge, things known.
act: action. Ross picks up another sense of act and develops it in the reference to *bloody stage* (i.e., bloodstained kingdom where the act is performed).
strangles: extinguishes.
travelling lamp: the sun.
predominance: conquest, victory.
entomb: make dark in a grave.
unnatural: monstrous, contradictory to the laws of nature.
the deed that's done: He assumes that Duncan has been killed by his sons.
tow'ring: high up.
pride of place: supremely elevated position.
mousing owl: owl that usually hunts mice (on the ground).
hawk'd at: attacked as if by a hawk, in the manner of a hawk.
minions: darlings (beautifully bred and tended).
flung out: dashed out.
contending 'gainst obedience: at war with the very principle of obedience (refusing to obey).
as they would: as if they wanted to.

Macduff has no definite suspicions. He is shattered by two things; first, the death of Duncan, and second, the absence of

Duncan or one of his sons from the throne. Macduff is committed in loyalty to Duncan and his family. His world is destroyed by what seems to have happened; he cannot reconcile himself to a world in which one or both of Duncan's sons must be his murderer, a world in which anybody else has the throne. For Macduff, Macbeth or anyone else on the throne must be offensive for the very fact of not being Duncan or Duncan's son.

pretend: claim, hope for.
suborn'd: bribed.
ravin up: devour like a beast of prey.
He is already nam'd: Scotland in this play is an elective monarchy. Each king is elected. The reigning monarch has the right to name his successor, who is then always elected. In Act One, Scene Four, Duncan names Malcolm as his successor. After the murder, suspicion has been thrown on Malcolm and Donalbain; their flight leaves the way open for the notables of the kingdom to name Macbeth, who will be elected and crowned at Scone. This is the place where the kings of Scotland were crowned.
Fife: Macduff is Thane of Fife. He goes home rather than witness the crowning of someone who is not son to Duncan. He hopes that whatever is done at Scone will be *well done* (i.e., beneficial, not detrimental, to the common good). He hopes that people will not look back with longing to the days of Duncan as infinitely preferable to those of Macbeth.
sit: fit, be worn.
benison: blessing.
would: want to.
make good of bad, etc.: turn bad into good, and convert enemies into friends.

Act Three, Scene Two

By this time Banquo is almost certain that Macbeth murdered Duncan and cannot put out of his mind the fact that the witches also prophesied that his children would be kings.

For his part Macbeth has never fully recovered from imagining the voice crying that he would sleep no more, immediately after the death of Duncan. Macbeth almost did not commit the murder because he was afraid of *judgement here;* and he envisaged that judgment as taking the form of somebody else having learned from his example to kill him as he killed Duncan. The man of whom he is terrified as the agent of his punishment is Banquo.

Earlier in the afternoon on which this scene takes place Macbeth has found out that Banquo and his son, Fleance, will spend the time out riding, that they will return at nightfall to be punctual for the feast which he is giving in Banquo's honor.

Macbeth has also convinced two men that their many misfortunes come from Banquo who has made it his business to ruin them. They are ready to murder in revenge. Macbeth tells them he will send a messenger to tell them the exact time and place to be in ambush.

In this scene Lady Macbeth is disturbed by her husband's brooding; she assumes that he is troubled by thinking about his murder of Duncan. Her aim is to persuade him to give up dwelling on what is over. In fact, of course, he is thinking about the future, about the murder to be done tonight, after which he will feel safe to enjoy his crown and *love, obedience, honour, troops of friends.* He is trying to tell her not to worry about the future. They are thus at cross purposes.

attend his leisure: wait for him if he has the leisure, wait until he has the leisure.
naught's had, etc.: We have nothing, everything is dissipated, when we have gained what we wanted without happiness.

Before the murder she was sure that everything would be easy. Even after it she assured Macbeth *a little water clears us of this deed.* A little water would wash away the bloody traces, making them to all intents and purposes innocent of it. But by this time she has found that success has not brought *content,* and that without happiness, the deed might just as well have not been done. As much as anything, her husband's unhappiness is on her mind. And his unhappiness comes from his inability to enjoy what he has gained unless he feels safe from *judgement here*.

doubtful: fearful, insecure.
keep: stay; "in the company of nothing but miserable (and misery-making) thoughts and fantasies."
using: habitually having.
without regard: go unregarded.
scorch'd: incised, cut, gashed.
close: hide, coil up, heal. All three ideas are present. The snake drags itself into refuge, coils itself up, resting, or hibernating, while it heals.
poor malice: ineffectual wish to harm.
her former tooth: the ability to bite which she retains.
disjoint: go to pieces.
both the worlds: the natural and supernatural worlds.
restless ecstasy: state of unconsciousness which gives no rest.
his: its.

Macbeth's self-love and self-pity are so strong that he envies his victim's freedom from fear and unhappiness. There is the possibility that we should imagine him wryly aware of the irony of the situation, objectively seeing what a mess he has made for himself.

malice domestic: harm from inside the country.
foreign levy: armies raised against him outside.
touch: have the slightest effect on.
sleek: smooth, polish.
Let your remembrance apply to: Do not forget to give attention to.
present him eminence both in eye and tongue: Pay special respect to him in seeing him and in the way you look at him, as well as in addressing him.
unsafe the while: the time is still unsafe so long as.
lave: immerse.

He is saying either (1) we must steep our honors in these streams which make them look better than they are; or (2) we must immerse our honors in these streams which flatter possible enemies.

vizards: masks.

scorpions: bitter stinging. Scorpion can mean (1) the reptile, (2) a very sharp whip, which draws blood.
nature: vital forces of a human being.
copy's not eterne: Right to possess is not endless. (Nature has only right of possession for a limited time.) *Copy* might mean imitation. Each human being is an example of nature.
assailable: vulnerable to attack.
jocund: cheerful.
cloister'd: through cloisters (of church, monastery or convent).
black Hecate: the goddess of witchcraft.
shard-borne: borne on scaly wings. Some texts read *shard-born*. This means born in dung.
hums: The note made by the beetle.
hath rung night's yawning peal: has rung the peal of bells with which night makes everyone yawn for sleep.
dreadful note: (1) of dreadful quality; (2) (with a play on a different sense of *note*) dreadful.

Macbeth is anticipating happily the murder of Banquo and Fleance, just before the full darkness of night has descended. He is also trying to encourage his wife to be happy without giving her exact details.
chuck: term of endearment.

Have innocence and ignorance of the knowledge until both disappear when you approve of what has been done.

The following images must be imagined precisely and used with precision to communicate Macbeth's intention, which is to make himself safe from death at the hands of Banquo or his children. He also wants to be sure that this particular murder will never be traced back to him, that it is done in complete secrecy, and that his murder of Duncan will similarly stay secret. He wants to be safe from exposure, because he must enjoy the love and admiration of his subjects in addition to feeling safe from punishment.

Macbeth imagines night as a falconer who hoodwinks a hawk. In this case there is no bird to be plunged into darkness. Macbeth is afraid of being observed and punished by God. He associates divine mercy and justice (exercised in *judgement*) with an eye in heaven with the wings of a hawk. This is what the falconer, *night*, is asked to hoodwink.

seeling: To seel involved taking a thread, knotting one end and passing the other through the hard insensitive lower eyelid of the bird, moving from the inner corner; the thread is taken over the top of the head, passed through the other lower eyelid, this time from the outer corner. It is then tied off in another knot. By twisting the thread on top of the bird's head, the falconer forces the upper and lower eyelids to close, though not completely.
scarf up: This is the next phase of hoodwinking. The bird is now in twilight. A bandage or scarf is wound round its head, blindfolding it completely. Eventually it becomes accustomed to darkness and is trained to sit on its master's wrist wearing a hood, which is removed for it to fly after game.

Macbeth wants night to come for the murder. But he also wants spiritual darkness, evil, to hide him and his misdeeds from the mercy and justice of God. The eye of day is that of a hawk as a symbol of justice, but it is tender and pitiful in its merciful functions. For Macbeth it is justice; for his victims it is mercy.

The next image is again very detailed and concrete.
that great bond: A bond is a legal agreement arranging for the disposal of property otherwise than to a man's natural heirs. In this case the witches have announced a *bond* by which Duncan's property goes first to Macbeth, but after his death, not to his children, or to Banquo, but to Banquo's children. Ever since the prophecies respecting himself have come true, Macbeth has been frightened by that concerning Banquo's children. In this sense the *great bond* has kept him *pale* (i.e., with fright).

The image visually concerns a parchment document over which an invisible hand moves dripping blood, putting a pen stroke through the writing *(cancel);* then the document is taken up and torn to pieces. Some actors will have their individual tactile and auditory images in addition. For Macbeth this image communicates intense longing for Banquo and Fleance to be killed to make him safe.

Macbeth now exults in the fact that night is beginning to descend with daylight departing.

thickens: becomes dark.
makes wing: begins to fly.
agents: active servants.
rouse: awaken, stir for action.

Lady Macbeth has no idea what he is talking about. He has kept his fears of *judgement here* secret from her; and consequently she cannot imagine why he is so tense, and what he is contemplating with such happy anticipation now.
hold thee still: say nothing (ask no questions).
Things bad begun, etc.: Things which have begun by doing evil increase their strength by doing more evil.

Do not forget when studying this scene that Lady Macbeth and Macbeth are married, love one another deeply, and each is unhappy at the other's unhappiness or anguish.

Act Four, Scene Three

Let us seek out . . . 'Tis hard to reconcile.

When this scene starts Macduff's wife and children have been murdered in Scotland, but the news has not yet reached him. The murders have been performed by Macbeth's servants as punishment for Macduff's having fled to England to join Malcolm, son of the late King of Scotland.

Although Malcolm has been suspected of the death of his father, it is now clear that Macbeth was the murderer. Macduff, who is virtually unshakable in his loyalty to the royal family of Scotland, has come to England to put himself at the disposal of Malcolm, whom he wants to persuade to return and liberate his country.

But in coming to England, Macduff has left his wife and family at the mercy of Macbeth. As the news of their murder has not arrived, Malcolm has every reason to suspect the honesty and good faith of Macduff, reasoning that he would not turn so openly against Macbeth with his dear ones exposed in Scotland as hostages. Nevertheless, this is exactly what Macduff has done.

weep our sad bosoms empty: sad means heavy as well as unhappy. The sense "heavy" refers literally to the secretions and "fumes" which in Elizabethan physiology were supposed to press on the area of the chest containing the heart as a result of strong emotion. To some extent the pressure could be relieved by sighing, it was thought; but this weakened the heart of its blood. The best remedy was to give way and talk and weep the results of grief away.
fast: firmly.
bestride: The image is of a fighting man standing astride a fallen comrade and beating off the enemy in battle. Macduff wants to do that for his country.
like syllable of dolour: similar, the same syllable of grief (i.e., the sky echoes the cry of dolor; figuratively, Heaven responds with equal grief on Scotland's behalf).
redress: set right, undo wrongs.
to friend: helpful.
whose sole name: merely to speak whose name alone.
and wisdom: and it is prudent.

Malcolm speaks of himself as the lamb to be sacrificed to appease Macbeth. To Macduff's angry repudiation of the charge of disloyalty, Malcolm points out that the treacherous plan may not be his, but may come from Macbeth who has control of Lady Macduff and the children.
recoil: give way to the weight of royal pressure.
transpose: reverse, change
Angels are bright still, etc.: The reference is to the Fall of the Angels who deserted God with Satan before the Creation of the Earth and human beings. The Fallen Angels fell into Hell to become the dark and evil devils of Christian tradition. Although these lost their brightness, unfallen angels look as they did before the Fall from Heaven.

Until recently Macbeth hid his treachery under an honest appearance. This fact leads Malcolm to observe that merely to look honest is to run the risk of being judged treacherous. He realizes that he must not be prompted by the case of Macbeth to insist that an honest appearance necessarily hides treachery. Although the brightest of the angels hid pride and treachery beneath his shining exterior, those angels which remained true to God in Heaven have continued to be bright in appearance. The actor of Malcolm might give himself an image of a host of bright red angels (seraphins, the highest order), one of which is brighter than the others. This angel reaches upward wearing a crown. This image can give place to another of the same angel falling through space toward Hell, his color faded and dark. Above, in Heaven, the unfallen angels are still as bright as before, but Lucifer's companions in the Fall to Hell have changed from shining angels to black, repulsive devils. Malcolm has something of this sort in mind.

in that rawness: in such exposure, open to infection.
motives: justifications for action.
jealousy: acute suspicion which anticipates harm or malice long before it is planned.

"Do not let my acute suspicions be a source of your dishonor but of my safety"; i.e., my suspicions should be regarded as the result of my own caution rather than as my certainty that you are treacherous.

just: honest.

Macduff may be played here either as wanting to persuade Malcolm by feigning despair, or as really desperate.

lay thou thy basis sure: make your foundation rock firm.
check: (1) reprove, (2) stop.
title is afeer'd: rightful owner (ruler) is scared.
would not: do not want to.
to boot: in addition.

Malcolm is affected enough by Macduff's apparent honesty to decide to test him further. He is about to accuse himself of sins and crimes. If Macduff ignores them and still wants him as a King, Malcolm's suspicions are well-founded. That is the way his reasoning runs.

in absolute fear: in complete (undiluted) fear.
in my right: to support my true claim.
gracious England: the gracious King of England.

what should he be?: of whom are you talking?
particulars: individual kinds.
grafted: so inseparably grown into.
open'd: revealed; what has been inoculated will show itself later.
poor state: the poor state of Scotland.
confineless harms: unlimited evils.

Macduff refuses to believe that anyone can be worse than Macbeth. The refusal strengthens Malcolm's doubts. He tries once more to disgust Macduff.

grant him: admit him to be.
sudden: swift and unsuspected in attack.
smacking of: tainted with.
continent impediments: obstructions that contain or hold it back.
o'erbear: push down.

Again Macduff's loyalty overcomes his repugnance for this man.

you may convey your pleasures, etc.: You can have abundant scope to conduct your pleasures.
hoodwink: blind, deceive.

"You cannot have in you a greed of such voraciousness as to devour the large number of women prepared to offer themselves to a person of high rank, finding him inclined to take advantage of them."

Malcolm is still not certain whether Macduff's readiness to overlook his apparent failings comes from sincere loyalty or from a hypocritical wish to lead him into Macbeth's trap. He adds avarice to the failings of which he accuses himself.

ill-compos'd affection: wish which is made up of evil.
stanchless: unstoppable.
forge: fabricate something false.

This time Macduff is nearer to being deterred; but he overcomes his disgust yet again; loyalty to the royal house combines with hatred of Macbeth, both as tyrant and man.

summer-seeming: appearing naturally in physical maturity.
the sword of our slain kings: (1) the sword which has slain our kings; (2) like a sword wielded by our dead kings.
foisons: abundance.

your mere own: What is purely your own; what you may grasp for your rightful possession.
portable: bearable.
graces: virtues.
weigh'd: balanced.

The image is of a heavy burden carried by a beast or a man on back or shoulders when counterbalanced by a similar weight.

king-becoming: appropriate to a king, suiting a king.
verity: truth, honesty.
lowliness: humility, lack of arrogance.
relish: (1) slightest taste, hint; (2) enjoyment.
division of each several crime: different possible forms of each individual crime.
acting: carrying out, performing.
concord: harmony, order.
uproar: turn into uproar.

To have this on top of everything else that Malcolm has asserted against himself is too much for Macduff. His loyalty cannot control his disgust. He repudiates Malcolm.

untitled: without legal right.
issue: child.
interdiction: repudiation, accusation.
blaspheme his breed: asserts the unholiness of his birth.

When Malcolm hears himself denounced his doubts in Macduff are conquered.

scruples: slight doubts which destroy confidence.
trains: traps, tricks.
modest: moderating, moderate.
to thy direction: to being directed by you.
abjure: deny under oath.
for: as.
upon: about.
here-approach: arrival.
at point: fully prepared, ready to leave.
chance of goodness: possibility of success.
as our warranted quarrel: as certain as our quarrel.

In order to convince himself of Macduff's honesty, Malcolm

has severely shaken Macduff's ability to support him. Macduff is now thoroughly confused, not wanting to distrust, but unable to trust. In fact, he stays uncertain until news arrives from Scotland of the death of his wife and family, after which he cares about nothing but the opportunity for revenge upon Macbeth.

Act Five, Scene One

The actor should know that a Doctor of Physic is of a much lower rank than a Gentlewoman. She is of the elite honored with personal service to the Queen.

watched: stayed awake to observe.

The Doctor's skepticism makes the Gentlewoman determined to convince him of the truth of her story. While the Queen's health is at stake, individual actresses might wish to act varying degrees of personal wish to be vindicated or dislike of being doubted.

She is distressed by the fact that the Queen does each of the things mentioned while fast asleep.

perturbation: disturbance of the mind by passion.

nature: physiological processes.

The Doctor says that such a psychological upheaval comes from a psychophysiological malady.

The Queen at one and the same time performs actions as if awake *(do the effects of watching)* while receiving the beneficial results of sleep. He wants to know if apart from what she has seen the Queen doing, the Gentlewoman has actually heard her say anything.

Lo you: look there.

to satisfy my remembrance the more strongly: to make sure that I remember what she says more completely.

Lady Macbeth's fantasy in her sleep of having blood on her hands derives from her earlier certainty that she and her husband needed no more than a little water to clear them of this deed. Later she has found that much more than water is needed; and as she has found that they have been involved in ever-increasing murder, accompanied by hatred and distrust, her conscience has asserted itself, terrifying her with physical images.

Hell is murky: literally, Hell is dark. But earlier she invoked darkness to come to her aid, to cut her off from Heaven peeping through the blanket of the dark. Now darkness terrifies her.
fie: for shame.
call our power to account: a memory of her exultation that nobody dare question their grief and outrage.
mar: spoil.
starting: jumping with terror. A memory of Macbeth's behavior when he imagined Banquo's ghost at his feast to accuse him.
sorely: grievously, heavily.
charged: burdened, loaded.

Here is an example of belief that extreme emotion brings blood and vapors to the heart. The pressure is relieved to some extent by breathing away the "fumes" in a sigh.
practice: medical experience.
nightgown: dressing gown. Elizabethans slept naked.
discharge their secrets: Diseased minds unburden themselves of their secrets by confessing them to their pillows which cannot hear what is said.
divine: priest.
annoyance: harm, destruction.
mated: confounded, reduced to misery.

ROMEO AND JULIET

Modern actors of this play have to imagine themselves in a society closely resembling that of the last decade of the sixteenth century in England. Above all, it is Christian. Ordinary men and women (among whom we include both Romeo and Juliet) might not be conscious of their faith every moment of the day, but if catechized, or if the occasion arose to make them consider it, they would assume the biblical story of the creation of the world and of the Fall of Adam and Eve to be true. Even those who admitted themselves sinners ascribed their sins and those of others to the power of Satan, perpetually at war with God, a war in which humanity must suffer until the end of the world at Doomsday. The characters of this play assume that God is in control of the world, acting through what is called Providence. To them Providence is the aspect of God which is aware of everything that occurs and will occur, down to the smallest action of the least significant element of creation. Taking into account what will happen, Providence works through human beings and through Fortune ultimately to circumvent the worst malice and cunning of Satan. Men and women do not have control over the situations in which they are involved, but ideally they have control of themselves. The human will is left free. Romeo is free to refuse to fight Tybalt. He controls himself and does not fight. But he cannot control Mercutio or Tybalt, nor the chance that Mercutio is killed as the result of an attempt to stop the killing. Still free to spare Tybalt when he returns, Romeo has already decided to kill him and does so.

The people of Verona, like those of Shakespeare's England, think of a human being as simultaneously body and soul. The body they know to be subject to Fortune; but the soul, perfect and eternal, is free; and Will, which is part of the human soul, is also free. Providence acts through Fortune as through human beings with Free Will. Fortune affects everything beneath the moon which is physical and mortal, which includes the human body and its passions but excludes the soul.

One of the ways in which Fortune works is through the stars. Romeo and his fellow citizens (like Francis Bacon, Sir Walter Raleigh, and their sovereign, Queen Elizabeth) believe that the stars exert an influence on our bodies and passions, but not on our souls. The stars can incline a human being toward a certain action, but he or she has the power to resist the inclination and overcome it. The influence of the stars does not determine human action.

The actor or actress who imagines himself or herself to be a person possessed of such information, accepting and not questioning it, will understand what is meant by two lines of the Chorus:

> From forth the fatal loins of these two foes
> A pair of star-cross'd lovers take their life.

Fatal means "death-dealing" (not fateful or tying to fate). *Star-cross'd* means "obstructed by the stars" (not destroyed by the stars or bound by the stars). As a result of the influence of the stars, Romeo and Juliet are "crossed" in their love; this means that their love meets obstacles. What will result depends upon the decisions taken in Free Will by the human beings concerned. In modern English these two lines could be expressed as follows: "From (out of) the life-giving parts *(loins)* of these two enemies which cause death *(fatal)*, a pair of lovers come to life, who are obstructed in their course by the influence of the stars."

Romeo twice refers to the stars. First in Act One, Scene Four, when he says that his mind:

> misgives
> Some consequence yet hanging in the stars
> Shall bitterly begin his fearful date
> With this night's revels.

His mind has a misgiving that "some future event, the result of stellar influences which have not yet been exerted, will bitterly begin the terrifying period of its existence at the time of tonight's amusements." Nevertheless, Romeo decides to put his trust in God and to accompany his friends to the Capulet house.

> But he that hath the steerage of my course
> Direct my sail!

So long as he is able to maintain this frame of mind, Romeo comes to no harm. Only when he loses control and kills Tybalt do the "crosses," the obstacles caused by the stars, begin to take real effect. And then he recognizes how stupid he has been in exposing himself to Fortune with the death of Tybalt: *O, I am Fortune's fool.*

Romeo refers to the stars the second time at the beginning of Act Five. Told that Juliet is dead, he says, *then I defy you, stars!* He means that they have done their worst to him, he will not worry about anything else they can do to him. This is his mistake. His defiance, with his hasty reaction, leads him to kill himself a few short minutes before the arrival of the Friar and the awakening of Juliet from her drugged sleep. If Romeo waits, does not kill himself (a matter of his own free will) he will be reunited with her in a few minutes (when she kisses his dead lips before killing herself they are still warm). He never knows how wrong he was to defy the stars; the only way to circumvent them is to control oneself and refuse to give way to despair.

In this society, suicide is the sin of yielding to despair, virtually a denial or rejection of God's love for human beings. For such there is no prospect of reunion after death. The pagan Cleopatra can kill herself in the expectation of meeting Antony almost immediately in the after life. For Romeo and Juliet death is the only way which seems possible to avoid or put an end to the agony of living in despair. There is no thought of the future, only an appalling need to put an end to the present. They have each succumbed to the "crosses" of the stars in consequence of their own freely willed decisions.

Act One, Scene Four

An extra edge is given to this scene by the fact that here are a number of young men of the house of Montague or its sympathizers discussing going to take part (without invitation) in a festivity in the house of the head of the Capulets. There is no intention of behaving badly; and in the light of the Prince's insistence that the feud must end, these young men could argue that they are doing their best to carry out his intentions. Nevertheless, the undertaking could end in trouble.

excuse: a conventional apology for intruding (remember, they will not be recognized under their masks) which in this case can also serve to decrease animosity if their identity slips out.
the date is out of such prolixity: that sort of long-windedness is out of date.
hoodwink'd: blindfolded.
scarf: bandage.
crowkeeper: boy with a rattle to frighten crows away from seeded fields.
without-book prologue: memorized introductory speech.
measure: judge.
measure a measure: dance a dance.
ambling: dancing.
soul: play on the sense of *soles* (of shoes or feet).
stakes: fastens.
bound: (1) limit, (2) leap, jump.
sore: sharply. A play on *soar*, meaning fly above.
bound: tied, confined.
bound: jump.
pitch: height above. A bird flies a *pitch* high in the sky.
to sink in it: If you were to sink into love, you would be burdening it.
prick: spur. The word has bawdy senses as well.
case: cover, disguise.
visor for a visor: a mask to cover a mask, a bag for my mask.
curious: pedantic, finicky.
quote: list, mention.

beetle brows: bushy, overhanging eyebrows. He does not care who calls attention to his ugly details, his mask can blush for him.
betake him to his legs: begin to dance.

The plan is simply to enter, to mingle with the guests by dancing at once, with no ceremony, no formal apology, no entrance as a group, but as a number of individuals.
wantons: lighthearted persons.
rushes: Rushes were spread on the floor in lieu of rugs.
senseless: without feeling.
I am proverb'd with a grandsire phrase: An old saying makes a proverb which fits me.
candleholder: attendant holding a light.
The game, etc.: The game was never all that good and I have had enough.
dun's the mouse: Mercutio puns on "done." The mouse is silent (*dun* means dark; the word used by the constable himself). Mercutio is saying, "You are not done, the mouse is dun, be quiet now."
dun: also a name for a horse.
dun . . . from the mire: Dun was the name of a game in which the players had to haul a heavy log of wood.
sir-reverence: an expression of mock reverence as a preliminary to an insulting or bawdy joke.
burn daylight: waste time.

Romeo's *that's not so* means "that's all nonsense," referring to the admonition to be silent, and to the assertion that by delaying they are wasting time. He means that time spent on delay now is time well spent, because he feels that the uninvited visit may have unpleasant consequences.
lights: (1) torches, (2) abilities.
good meaning: good intentions. Mercutio realizes under all his fooling that Romeo is talking good sense. But if they go intending good and not harm, there is every reason to have a good time without any trouble.
that: our good meaning.
'tis no wit: It's indiscreet, tactless, unnecessarily risky.
and we mean well: even if our intention is good.

When asked why he thinks this, Romeo starts to tell Mercutio about a dream he had which has filled him with foreboding. Mercutio interrupts him, determined to take him with them to the mask (as much for Romeo's own sake as for theirs).

When Romeo asserts that dreams are true, Mercutio sets himself to prove him wrong. That is why he says, "If you believe that, then you are suffering from the influence of Queen Mab." First, he declares how small she is; and then points out that nonetheless she has only to touch any part of a sleeper for him or her to dream a dream in which it is involved and in which what he or she has uppermost in mind comes to pass. The whole point is that when Queen Mab affects a sleeper he dreams his own dream and as a result of her power believes the dream to be reality. This, says Mercutio, is what has happened to Romeo.

The actor must concentrate at first on making Queen Mab and her equipage seem actual. The intention is all the time to insist that this personage has misled Romeo, that his dream is to be ignored, not taken as a foretelling of what will truly happen.

shape: form and size. She is believed to take on a shape of air to be visible to human beings.
agate-stone: semiprecious stone.
atomies: minute creatures.
athwart: across.

To imagine how small Mab is, the actor can take a small gnat and a hazelnut as comparisons. Set beside them, she is obviously very small. When Mercutio has established her as a personage, he goes on to show that in every case when she touches a sleeper he dreams and mistakes dream for reality. Notice the speed and lightness with which she passes.

court'sy: bending of the knee obsequiously to a superior at court to gain favor and gifts. Courtiers depended on patronage of more important people, right up to the monarch, for land and money.
straight: at once.
sweetmeats: candy.
smelling out a suit: (1) finding out how to beg something from the King; (2) finding somebody who wants his help in petition-

ing the King for a gift or favor. The courtier would be paid for his help.

tithe-pig: a pig paid to the Church as a tenth (tithe) of a farmer's income.

When Mab drives over the soldier's neck, it is involved in his dreams.

elf-locks: tangles.

Mercutio is determined to go on until he provokes Romeo into arguing or giving way.

hag: fairy.

Finally Romeo is provoked into telling Mercutio that he talks *of nothing*. The latter seizes his chance and says, yes, he is talking about nothing, that is, about dreams.

idle: empty, not substantially productive.

Mercutio makes his point again.

consequence: event which will follow. Not the modern "result of." See discussion of the part played by the stars (pp. 221 f.).

Romeo has a foreboding that as a result of stellar influence this night's entertainment will set in motion a train of future events which will then run their allotted course.

expire: bring to an end.

despised: unvalued.

clos'd: enclosed.

He that hath, etc.: i.e., God; "May He who directs the course of the ship of my life keep me on my proper course."

Romeo has decided to have faith in God, to let whatever it is happen, and rely on Providence to protect him. At this moment he is ready to accept patiently whatever life may bring him.

Act Two, Scene Two

Romeo has seen Juliet dancing in her father's house. In despair because another girl, Rosaline, steadfastly refuses to respond to his love, he recognizes in Juliet a purity and generosity of nature which make her utterly superior to Rosaline; he knows that here is somebody who could give meaning to his life, who could regenerate him. Not knowing who she is, he approaches her, playing the part of a pilgrim who has come to worship at her shrine, as if she were a saint. Understanding his need, and realizing for the first time in her fourteen years how a woman can bestow meaning on a man's life in her love for him, Juliet lets him kiss her. She is committed to him, and he to her, before either knows the other's identity. Each knows the truth, however, just as he and his companions leave the Capulet house.

When this scene starts Juliet is brooding over the bitter fact that her *only love* comes from her *only hate*, and is trying to find a way of removing the obstacles between them. Romeo, equally in love, cannot go home yet; he has to stay in her vicinity. He does not know where she is in the building, but her presence there makes it a place that he treasures.

When he scales the wall Romeo has no hope of seeing Juliet. He wants to be alone to think about her, to be near her, in a place which she knows well, in which she has spent many hours.

Suddenly one of the upper windows shows a faint light. As he looks at it, whoever has just entered the room inside moves toward the window and the light grows brighter. He is reminded of the way dawn breaks, its first faint light gradually growing until it fills the sky.

But, soft! What light through yonder window breaks?

Romeo does not know that the light comes from Juliet's room; there is no reason why he should. This dark garden, an enemy's home territory, is strange to him. But, with his mind full of her and her beauty, he indulges in a little fantasy while the light grows brighter as it is brought nearer the window:

Arise, fair sun . . . cast it off.

This invocation expresses his wish that Juliet will not prove so adamant as Rosaline, will not wear the livery of the chaste Diana, but will be ready to marry and have children.

Suddenly, to his unbelievable joy, the impossible has happened. He sees that Juliet is indeed the person who has brought the light to the window; he can see her standing there illuminated by it, framed in darkness. The happiness is spoiled only by his inability to let her know of, and therefore accept and return, his love:

> It is my lady! O, it is my love!

Realizing how much stands between them which he would like to be removed, Romeo adds:

> O, that she knew she were!

Although he cannot hear what she says, he knows it is an expression of love; that is clearly to be seen in her eyes as they shine in the light. He has an impulse to reveal himself, but remembers that she does not know he is there, and that he has no reason to assume that he is the object of her reverie as she is of his. Overwhelmed with his admiration of her beauty, Romeo now consoles himself with another fantasy, that her eyes' dialogue is with *two of the fairest stars.* Like his contemporaries in Verona, Romeo assumes that there are a number of spheres in the heavens. Each sphere is hollow and is composed of invisible crystal on which a planet is fixed as a bead might be fixed on a circle of wire. And each sphere is perpetually turning, like a wheel, moving the planet in its orbit through the sky.

Every sphere has the earth as its center, with the Moon nearest, then Mercury, Venus, the Sun, Mars, Jupiter, Saturn. Immediately outside the sphere of Saturn is another, called the firmament, on which are placed the so-called fixed stars. The outermost sphere of the system is the Imperial Heaven where God and his angels dwell. Between that and the sphere of the fixed stars is another called the First Mover or *Primum Mobile.* This revolves from east to west and causes all the spheres and their stars within it to move from west to east through the heavens. The actor who knows this can imagine space and the stars as Romeo does. That part of space between the sphere of the moon and the Imperial Heaven is what Romeo envisages when he talks of the airy region. If Juliet's eyes changed places with the stars their brightness would light up the greater part of the night sky, right out past the furthermost stars that men can see, as brilliantly as the light of the sun, with the result that the birds would be misled into thinking day had come.

her maid: servant of Diana, goddess of chastity.
vestal livery: the uniform of her vestal virgins; i.e., virginity.
sick and green: Green is an appropriate color for the servants of Diana, the huntress. But there is also a reference to "greensickness" a malady peculiar to virgins.

As Romeo watches her, Juliet changes her position, leaning her cheek upon her hand, musing unhappily on her situation. Her *Ay me* expresses her want and emotion; her internal monologue is concerned with the difficulty of ever being united with the man with whom she has fallen in love. She considers the situation, wishes it were different and knowing it is not, utters a cry of distress. During Romeo's next speech she thinks of all that must happen if she is to have a happy married life with Romeo. They must not be separated by the enmity of their families; he must renounce his, she is ready to renounce hers. She assumes that he cannot love her because of her family, that as a Montague he must hate all Capulets.

Having heard her, and being able to look at her, Romeo is consumed with admiration and love; if only she would speak again. He speaks of her, as lovers do, as an angel, but as a particular kind, an angel of light, *bright angel,* illuminated by her lamp or candle, a cherub, one of the order assigned to care for the sphere of the fixed stars and regarded as powerful messengers of Heaven. Romeo's image expresses his love for her and her beauty, his awareness of a creative quality in her that makes for peace and good, his wish that they might share life together.

O Romeo, Romeo! wherefore art thou Romeo? . . . Take all myself.

wherefore: why.
but sworn: only sworn (just swear yourself to be).
though not a Montague: even if you were not a Montague.
owes: owns.
title: (1) name, (2) legal ownership.
doff: take off.

Juliet's clear recognition of her predicament makes her wish that the man with whom she has fallen in love were anyone but *Romeo,* the son of the enemy house of Montague. Her internal monologue has involved an awareness of her own conditioning to respond to him with hostility which is in conflict with her knowledge that she is committed to him in her heart. At the end of Act One, Scene Five, she lamented the fact that a *prodigious* (monstrous, unnatural, horrifying) love was being given life in her, *That I must love a loathed enemy.* She does not know that he is equally in love, and, more important, that he has no intention of being obstructed by the long-standing feud.

In her fantasy Juliet is doing her best to persuade the splendid young man, whom she met for the first time that night, that to further their love (she is really thinking only of her own, though she knows he loved her when ignorant of her identity), he should renounce his family. Afraid that he will refuse (or imagining his refusal), she adds that if he will do no more than swear his love to her, then she will renounce her family. She then concentrates on persuading him to give up his inessential name, promising herself in return.

I take thee at thy word . . . yet I know the sound.

counsel: discussion of a secret or private matter.

Romeo is beside himself with joy that not only is his love returned, but that she is ready to renounce her family for him. Happily he picks up the word she has used, *take.* If she will call him her love he will promise never to be Romeo and to be *new baptiz'd* with the name she has given instead. He has not said directly that he is Romeo, only that he will not be in future. The voice out of the darkness beneath her terrifies and confuses Juliet. It is not pleasant to think that some relative or some member of her father's household has overheard her fantasy and avowal of love for an enemy. Romeo, remembering what he called her when they met, repeats the loving nickname, *dear saint.* This confirms her memory of his voice and she knows who it is.

The rest of this scene is between two lovers separated by the distance between her window and the ground. They are ecstatic to know that love is requited. Each has been afraid that the other might not reciprocate; each has been aware of the feud; neither has known how to find the other, much less talk and exchange assurances of love. And now, most unexpectedly, against all possibility, what they want is actually happening. He has heard her avowal made in ignorance of his presence. He has the opportunity to make sure that she knows that she is his love. He wished *O, that she knew she were!* She begged him in her fantasy, *doff thy name*. Their wishes have been answered. They are young; they are each experiencing the high point of life; they do not expect to die; they do not know they are involved in a tragedy. Recognizing his voice, she asks: *Art thou not Romeo, and a Montague?* The reply gives her the assurance she has wanted: *Neither, fair maid, if either thee dislike.*

Dislike: displeases; causes dislike.

How camest thou hither . . . I should adventure for such merchandise.

o'erperch: step over; raise myself above, higher than; hop over.
stop: obstacle. Some editions have *let,* which has the same meaning.
proof against: invulnerable to; completely armored against.
prorogued: postponed, put off.
but thou love me: unless you love me.
pilot: navigator, explorer by sea.
vast: very distant.
adventure: risk all the hazards of the journey.
I am no pilot, etc.: I am not a navigator, but if you were as far away as that remote shore, the other side of the most distant sea, I would risk a voyage to bring back such priceless freight as you.

Juliet has been surprised at his ability to find her room; he assures her that it was nothing compared to the dangers and difficulties he is ready to overcome for her sake.

For most of this section she is alarmed for his safety, thinking of the risk he runs, of the consequences if he were found. He has despaired of his life for so long in his barren love for Rosaline that death has been in his thoughts as a way out of an empty anguished existence, and it really has no terrors for him compared to a life empty of Juliet. As a result, what is a theme of conventional gallantry for courtly lovers has reality for him. He wants chiefly to communicate to her the quality of his love for her, the effect of her love on his life. He really means that it would be better for his life to be ended by their hatred than for it to linger on, empty of her love until his death by natural causes. Her fears dissipated by his confidence and by the strength of his love, she next wonders how he could possibly have found where her room is. Understandably he does not say it was sheer chance. But he takes the opportunity to insist on a truth, that the danger and difficulty of exploring this hostile garden are nothing to what he is prepared to undergo in order to win her for the rest of his life.

Juliet is a young lady with a conventional upbringing who would not normally make such an avowal of love as he has heard to a man who has not already declared himself. In the next section she wants him to know two things; first, that had she known of his presence she would not have let him know her true mind; and second, that notwithstanding, it is her true mind and despite her vulnerable position she confirms what he heard to be true. Then she begs him to leave her if he is not equally serious and honest.

Thou knowest the mask of night . . . I will come again.

Fain would I: I would very much like to.
form: formal behavior, behavior in accordance with accepted conventions.
compliment: conventional courteous behavior.
mayst: are permitted to.

Jove in mythology is credited with adventures in which he disguised himself in various shapes to seduce earthly women, in falsehood to his wife, Juno. The god normally punishes perjury, but merely laughs when a lover breaks his oath.

perverse: obstinate.
fond: (1) loving, (2) foolish, i.e., foolishly loving.
'haviour: behavior.
light: trivial, wanton.

more cunning to be strange: more wit to contrive to remain distant (i.e., not involved).
ere I was ware: before I had any warning.
light love: The main sense is trivial or wanton love, but Juliet knows that she was visible to Romeo, thanks to the light she had with her. And his presence was hidden from her by the dark night. She therefore indulges in verbal play, contrasting the sense of light which is "illuminated" with the "dark" which has revealed her love in hiding Romeo.
discovered: revealed.
circled orb: sphere, orbit.
This bud of love: The bud of love refers to their admission to one another of true love. If it *prove a beauteous flow'r,* their private assurances will develop naturally into formal betrothal. This is what she wants. If she cannot have it with her parents' consent, she is prepared to leave them for this husband.
faithful vow: private exchange of oath; promise of marriage. A formal, public exchange of "faith," sworn oath, could be legally acceptable as betrothal, even as the equivalent of marriage, if the union was consummated.
Wouldst thou: Do you want to?
frank: generous.
but: only
bounty: ability to give (both wish to give and supply from which gift is made).

When Romeo asks, *But wilt thou leave me so unsatisfied?* he knows that there is no possibility of physical contact with her; he is not even asking for it. She has not let him swear his "faith"; has hoped that perhaps this will be done, or will have been done the next time they meet. She is reluctant to take this step, unused to independence, and with misgivings about *this contract tonight.* But he wants it. He wants her to do for the real Romeo what she did for the Romeo of her fantasy; and he wants to give his "faith" in return for hers. Until this has been done he feels *unsatisfied.* She points out that she gave her vow before he asked for it. For the moment, instead of doing as he asks, she gives herself up to a realization of her feeling for him, to the unaccustomed joy of being one who gives. Until now her experience has been that of a child who receives. Now she is an adult with something to give, ability to give it and delight in giving to this beloved man. But before the oath can be exchanged they are disturbed by the sound within.

O blessed, blessed night . . . toward school with heavy looks.

flattering-sweet: seeming sweeter than it is. To flatter is to make somebody or something seem better than it is.

As this whole experience takes place in night, and as he could not rationally expect it to happen, Romeo says it is like a dream, seeming sweeter than reality and therefore likely to be something dreamt, not experienced in reality *(substantial).*
thy bent of love: the aim, intention, of thy love.
if thou meanest not well: if your intention is not honorable.
strife: striving, efforts.
by and by: at once; I won't be a moment.

In the time between leaving him and appearing again Juliet has determined to face the issue. She accedes to his wish with the proviso that if he does not want to marry her he must have no more to do with her. She does not even ask for an answer now. She will send a messenger, whose return will let her know his decision. He starts to swear his honesty, but she has no time to listen: A *thousand times good night.* This is often overlooked; that with the Nurse calling for her, Juliet has not time to listen to what Romeo has to say. She must trust him.

Hist! Romeo, hist! . . . to attending ears.

tassel gentle: tercel gentle (i.e., male falcon).
hoarse: low-voiced; soft-toned. It is the word used by Lear to describe Cordelia's voice, when she is dead in his arms and he is trying to persuade himself that he hears her speaking softly.

A falconer's voice was soft but carrying, with a frequency to which the bird was responsive. Juliet wishes she could reach Romeo's ears with a piercing voice which nobody else could hear. A person in captivity, or not free to do as she wants, must be soft-voiced, otherwise she would shriek his name aloud and make Echo's voice more hoarse (in the sense of tired, sore) than her own is soft.

attending: attentive, sensitive.

Romeo comments on the fact that a lover does not need to shout at night because his or her voice, however soft, will be picked up by the sensitive ears of the other person tuned to receive it.

What o'clock to-morrow . . . good night till it be morrow.

still: always, continually.
I would have thee gone: I wish you had left.
wanton: could be read as "capricious child" or as "wanton woman."

If we take the second reading, Juliet realizes that in her fear for Romeo she wished him gone, but the thought of his absence has made her want to keep him with her. She is ashamed of her change of mind, especially as it keeps him in danger from her *kinsmen.*
loving-jealous: The word *jealous* has the sense of being afraid of a loss and trying to prevent it beforehand.
gyves: fetters between the legs.
morrow: morning (or tomorrow).

Romeo, left alone, determines to go and seek the help of his confessor. It must be remembered that Friar Laurence (Lawrence) belongs to an order (the Franciscan) dedicated to reconciling warring factions in the Italian cities. He will have often deplored the feud and will have admonished Romeo on the sin of civil war and a blood feud. Romeo knows his man, and thinks there is a strong chance that the Friar will marry him and Juliet in order to reconcile their families. This, of course, is the Friar's response.

Act Two, Scene Three

Friar Laurence is a holy Franciscan. Elsewhere I have dealt more fully with the importance of this fact for an understanding of his motives and the part played by his order, the Franciscan, in Italian cities constantly subjected to civil disorder.* For the actor it is essential to know that the Franciscans were dedicated to reconciling warring factions. At the beginning of this scene Laurence greets the dawn happily in an equivalent of the Franciscan hymn to the sun.

One part of his vocation is to do good as a physician. To collect plants to fight illness is not a chore but a pleasing occupation in the freshness of early morning before the dew is off them. As a Christian priest he is accustomed to an abundance of evidence that he lives in a fallen, sinful world, which has not been abandoned by its Creator, using man and natural objects for good, despite the onslaughts of an evil adversary Satan. Thanks to Satan and the Fall, anything and anybody, however good, can be perverted; but thanks to the grace of God, anything and anybody, no matter how evil, can be used to good effect. Laurence sees his role as one of doing all he can, with divine grace, to further the eventual victory of good. To gather medicinal plants is as much his vocation as to deliver the sacraments and to aid human souls.

Shakespeare gives the Friar a traditional image of the morn, *grey-ey'd*, and smiling in the face of the darkness of the night. He is contentedly observing the gray light of the dawn, a welcome sign that the night is as good as over.

chequ'ring: mottling.
fleckled: spotted, speckled.

Darkness staggers away from the advancing day to avoid the onset of the rising sun.

Now, ere the sun . . . precious-juiced flowers.

osier cage: willow wicker basket.
baleful: harmful, poisonous.
juice: sap.
Now, ere the sun, etc.: Now, before the sun lifts up his burning eye to make the day pleasant and to dry off the damp dew of night, I have to fill up this willow basket of ours with poisonous weeds and with flowers whose sap is precious.

**Acting Shakespeare*, 1969, pp. 131 ff.

The earth . . . all different.

nature: everything that lives and dies a natural death.
virtues: good qualities; powerful influences on others.
The earth, that's nature's mother, etc.: The earth which is the mother of all natural things is also their grave; she herself is both their womb from which they are brought forth, and a grave in which they are buried. And we find different kinds of offspring, produced from her womb, drawing sustenance from her as is natural (she being their mother). Many excel in many characteristics with benevolent effects *(virtues);* there is not one without some, and yet they all have different ones.

O mickle . . . on abuse.

mickle: much, large.
grace: ability to exert a benevolent quality deriving from a divine source.
strain'd from: forced, or distorted, from.
use: function, habit.
revolts from: recoils from; rebels against; turns traitor to.
stumbling on: straying into.
abuse: misuse of true qualities.

The Friar considers what to him is a fact of life; in a fallen world under God, everything natural has the power to exert influences (even stones can affect human beings benevolently or malevolently). Good can be perverted and evil transformed into good.

O, mickle is, etc.: O, great is the power to do good left resident in plants, herbs, stones and their undistorted qualities. For there is nothing in the natural world so vile that it does not bestow some individual source of good upon the world; nor is anything so good that, distorted from its benevolent function, it does not rebel against its true nature, straying into misuse of its true qualities.

Virtue itself . . . with the heart.

infant rind: tender (because immature) skin.
medicine: medicinal.
cheers: revives, invigorates.
Slays all senses: destroys the senses (by means of which the body functions).

Some editions have *stays all senses; stays* means stops.

Virtue itself, etc.: Virtue itself becomes vice when it is misused; and sometimes vice is transcended by what is done with it. Within the immature skin of this weak flower there reside both poison and medicinal strength. When this plant is smelled, that part of it invigorates every part of the person who smells it; if it is tasted it kills (stops) the heart and all the senses.

The actor must not lose sight of the Friar's reason for this soliloquy: he is happy because he is doing God's work in his small way. He wants to see all good things functioning freely, all evil transcended. The plants which he is gathering let him play his part in his Creator's plan for the world and its inhabitants.

Two such . . . plant.

king: sovereign power; dominant strength.
still: always.
grace: divinely given ability to overcome sin.
rude will: uncontrolled determination to carry out the desires of the passions.
is predominant: overrules.
canker: canker worm; grub that eats leaves or petals.
Two such opposed kings, etc.: Two conflicting sovereign powers have ever pitched their armed camps ready for combat in man as well as herbs—grace (to overcome sin) and unredeemed will to commit evil. Where the worse of these two prevails, the canker-worm death soon devours that plant.

Although Friar Laurence knows this for an intellectual and emotional, as well as theological, truth, he speaks from a confidence in the love of God for mankind which has not been tested by experience of human littleness when assailed by the undiluted depredations of evil. This confidence enables him to resolve to end the strife between the two houses by marrying Romeo and Juliet. (By the end of the play his faith in God is in no way diminished, but his confidence in his own power to act without disastrous consequences has vanished.)

Romeo has made his way to the cell, determined to persuade the Friar to marry him and Juliet this very day. He knows his man. If Romeo can convince the Friar that here is a way to reconcile the two households, the battle is won. It is inconceivable that the younger man has not been upbraided by his confessor frequently for regarding the Capulets as enemies, as for his lusting after Rosaline, and his sinful despair with life because she has resisted every attempt at seduction.

Good morrow, father . . . where has thou been, then?

The actor has latitude in deciding the Friar's exact relationship with Romeo; how much tolerance, how much active disapproval, how much affection will be decided differently by each Romeo and each Friar in their interaction both as actors and as characters. But in each case the Friar's intention remains the same, of prevailing on Romeo to abandon a negative way of life, which can lead only to frustration, even without taking its sinfulness into account. Seeing Romeo up so early, he suspects him of having spent the night with Rosaline and is prepared to admonish him.

Benedicite: bless you.
saluteth: greets.
distempered head: a head not in perfect health.
keeps his watch: (1) looks out, (2) stays awake in.
unbruised: relaxed, at ease, suffering no hurt.
unstuff'd: free from any physical or mental sense of oppression.
couch: lay on a bed.
distemp'rature: ill-health (mental or physical).
Or if not so, then here I hit it right: Or, if this is not so, then I am sure I am not wide of the mark this time.

Romeo has his opportunity to tell what has happened. He knows that he owes to his wakeful night *the sweeter rest.* For once he is in a position honestly to deny the Friar's suspicion. He is flooded with the knowledge of how much richer his life can be, how fortunate he is in being able to rely on Juliet's open generosity in exchange for the frustration of the warped relationship with Rosaline. He manages to communicate to his companion his certainty that Rosaline belongs to his past. As he replies to Friar Laurence's *where hast thou been?* Romeo remembers the desolation of his first minutes at the Capulets, the sudden joy of seeing Juliet, their exchange of words and kisses, the knowledge that this girl can give meaning to his life and is ready to, the shock of discovering who she is, followed by the knowledge that she is prepared to marry him and will send a messenger to find out if he will marry her.

both our remedies/Within thy help and holy physic lies: Your help and holy medicine are capable of curing us both of our hurt.

Romeo works to convince the Friar that he has cast hatred out of his mind; he is making an appeal which brings equal aid to the one who is superficially his enemy.

intercession: appeal.

steads: gives succor to.

The Friar is not absolutely certain what Romeo is asking.

homely: uncomplicated.

drift: explanation of purpose.

Riddling confession, etc.: A confession which states nothing clearly will have absolution which absolves nothing clearly.

all combin'd: completely united, apart from what you must join together by means of holy marriage.

Romeo concentrates on convincing the Friar of his sincere love for Juliet, and of the strength of their determination to ignore the feud and be married, at once, today.

Holy Saint Francis . . . that run fast.

The Friar professes himself unconvinced of the durability of Romeo's change of heart. The actor has the choice, either of not taking him seriously or of beginning to see what can be done by marrying him to Juliet for peace in Verona, and therefore of testing the young man, while Friar Laurence makes up his own mind as to what he shall do.

season: (1) flavor, (2) preserve, pickle in salt water.
may fall: are permitted to succumb to temptation.
strength: durability.
pronounce: declaim formally.
sentence: sententious statement; valid generalization.

Romeo justifies himself for putting Rosaline out of his life, saying he has merely obeyed his mentor.

The Friar's reference to a grave is based on the custom of leaving the dead in their graves in the small churchyards only until all flesh had disappeared; then the bones were dug out and stored in the charnel house, and another body could be interred in the empty grave.

grace: favor.
allow: grant.

By this time the Friar has decided to do as Romeo asks, but still insists that the young man has not been able to distinguish between inordinate doting and justifiable love. While almost convinced that this time Romeo may not be making the same mistake, Friar Laurence sees clearly that he can take advantage of Romeo's passion for the eventual good of the whole city. With Romeo and Juliet united in what is to this society the sacrament of marriage, the way has been found to end the hatred separating their families.

In one respect: taking only one point into account.
rancour: hatred.
pure: utter, undiluted, nothing but.
I stand on sudden haste: My success depends upon, demands, sudden speed. (If the marriage does not take place swiftly before it can be stopped, it may never take place at all.)
They stumble that run fast: The Friar takes the more usual sense of *stand,* and observes that people who run fast stumble, i.e., trip up and fall instead of standing.

The Friar has made up his mind suddenly without much ado. His order was known for its unworldly ability to ignore obvious difficulties and undertake a course of action with an eye only to the good attending its success. He conforms to type in this.

Act Three, Scene Five

This scene contains lines of such beauty that traditional criticism can mislead actor and actress into trying to communicate "the poetry" as an end in itself. The antidote lies in a firm resolution not to attempt to act any part of even the most beautiful lines without having discovered the motive which makes the character speak it.

Wilt thou be gone . . . thou need'st not to be gone.

wilt thou: Do you want to?

Juliet asks if he wants to leave her because it is not even near day yet. Either she really thinks it is still deep night, or she does not want to admit to herself that they must soon part. But her intention is to keep him with her longer, a reluctance to separate (for how long, she dare not think). The fact that she is terrified for him a few moments later suggests that she honestly does not realize how near it is to the dawn.

fearful: scared.

She has had *the hollow* of his ear close to her all night, has caressed it, loved it as a *part* of Romeo. She must convince him that they are listening to the nightingale. Romeo knows it is the lark. He must make her understand that if they are ever to be reunited in this life, he must leave her now and save himself from certain death at the hands of the servants of the state.

herald of the morn: one who precedes and announces the imminent arrival of the morn.

Romeo sees streaks of light emanating from a rift in the darkness through which comes the light of the day. The streaks crisscross the split in the darkness like laces holding together two parts of a garment or a boot. But these streaks do not hold the severing parts together; the stronger the light, the more darkness is conquered. Romeo calls the streaks *envious* because they seem to him to begrudge him any more time with Juliet.

He adds that the *candles* (i.e., comparatively weak short-lived lights) of the night have burnt themselves out. He knows that the first imprint of light is about to be placed on the mountain tops which are still *misty* (i.e., in darkness). Romeo imagines day full of vitality and joy *(jocund)*, and resents what makes the rest of the world happy—the end of the night.

Juliet will not admit that the light in the sky comes from the sun.

meteor that the sun exhales: It was thought that a meteor was produced by the heat of the sun upon the atmosphere in the "aery region" between the earth and the moon.
stay yet: don't go yet.
needst not: you don't need to.

Romeo has been near suicide several times in the last few weeks. He almost killed himself yesterday afternoon. He really means that his life *were better ended* than for him to eke out a miserable existence without Juliet. If she wants him to stay he will do so; but he also wants her to realize what she is doing. Some actors may well decide that he does this to shock her into letting him leave. This is valid; but we must also bear in mind the fact that he does not want life without her and can be attracted by the thought of sudden death with her.

Let me be ta'en . . . dark our woes.

content, so thou, etc.: I have no objection so long as that is what you want.
reflex of Cynthia's brow: light reflected back from the face of the moon.
more care: more concern with.
will: desire.

Notice that Romeo says virtually, "*Come, death, and wel-*

come." Now Juliet realizes the truth and wants him to save himself.

straining: forcing unnaturally.

makes sweet division: divides up notes in a sweet melody. But *division* also means "sundering," the sense which Juliet takes for *This doth not so, for she divideth us*.

Folklore declared that there could be an exchange of eyes between the sweet-voiced lark and the hateful, croaking toad.

affray: frighten. The sweet song of the lark frightens them from one another; the croak of the toad would have no such effect.

hunt's-up: morning song summoning hunters to their activity.

Madam . . . But send him back.

be wary, look about: be careful, keep your eyes open.

much in years: very old in years, have lived many years.

ill-divining: foreseeing evil.

To her, from above, he glimmers in the darkness as if in the depths of a tomb. He looks up and sees her pale face reflecting the growing light: framed in the darkness round her window she, too, looks like one dead in a tomb.

dry: thirsty. It was thought that every time a person sighs, the heart loses blood.

dost thou: What business do you have?

If Fortune is changeable, what business can it have with a man who is unchangeable once he has given his oath. She hopes that if chance happenings continue, as in the recent past, they will bring Romeo back.

Ho, daughter! . . . weep the friend.

Lady Capulet comes to give Juliet the news of her wedding to Paris. The mother assumes that her daughter's grief for Tybalt will soon be dissipated by the good news of what she has to look forward to. Juliet is genuinely puzzled by a visit from her mother at this time of day. She has no inkling of the truth. Her father has always insisted that she is too young for marriage, and that in any case no arrangement will ever be made for her nuptials until she has given her consent. As a result, marriage to Paris or anyone does not enter her mind. On the other hand, the possibility of Juliet's having been married in secret cannot enter her mother's. It is even more impossible for Lady Capulet to imagine a secret marriage to, of all people, a Montague.

down so late: up so late; out of bed so late.

how now: What's the matter.

Juliet wants desperately to be alone, not knowing that her mother will ascribe her distress to grief for Tybalt. Lady Capulet interprets *I am not well* as referring to this grief. To comfort Juliet and change her grief to happiness, she must first be persuaded not to abandon herself to such intense misery.

wilt thou: Do you want to, are you trying to.

have done: stop it.

Some grief, etc.: A certain amount of grief is a witness to much love for the deceased, but a lot of grief is always a sign of being unreasonable, irrational.

Juliet uses the pretext her mother has given her, letting it be thought that her cousin's death distracts her.

feeling loss: loss which is felt so sharply.

Lady Capulet says that the reality of the grief will not bring the reality of the person for whom it is felt.

Well, girl . . . and I'll find such a man.

First, Lady Capulet now tries to stop Juliet's tears by promising her vengeance; it is necessary to remind her that she does not really love her dead cousin too much to consider marriage to Paris, and that her emotion is as much due to her wish for vengeance as to the gap caused by Tybalt's death.

runagate: renegade; outlaw.

dram: drink.

temper: blend; dilute.

wreak: (1) avenge, (2) express.

During this dialogue, Juliet's real meaning is not what her

mother assumes. The girl is able to give vent to her real grief for Romeo, knowing how it will be misconstrued.

But now I'll tell thee . . . at your hands.

Lady Capulet congratulates herself on having calmed Juliet down and turns to her *joyful tidings.*
careful: solicitous.
heaviness: sadness.
sorted out: chosen, selected.

Juliet, quite unsuspecting the truth, welcomes the prospect of some diverting sign of her father's affection to mitigate the desolation of life without Romeo.
in happy time: at a most opportune moment.

Juliet's response to her mother's news is not defiance. She has often been told she will not be married without her consent. She is merely reminding her mother of this fact, with no reason to think that her parents are determined to have her married in what to them are her own best interests. She is justified in being amazed at the speed with which her wedding day has been fixed without any visit from Paris to ask her consent, or to declare his love. Her *I pray you* is sincere; it is "Please, for my sake, tell my lord and father that I do not want to get married yet." Lady Capulet has no time for this unexpected opposition. She cannot think of any valid reason for Juliet's refusal.

When the sun sets . . . I'll not be forsworn.

Capulet enters with no inkling of what is happening. Assuming that Juliet will not refuse the marriage, he can indulge his little daughter, and tries to tease her out of her tears in a manner which has never failed when she has come to him in distress.
conduit: free-flowing water pipe.
sudden: unforeseen.

Capulet's account of *a bark, a sea, a wind* is aimed at amusing her; at catching her attention so that she will be interested in seeing how well he manages to develop the emblem.

she will none: She doesn't want any, thank you.
take me with you: I don't follow you; let me follow you.
wrought: arranged.

At first he is not enraged, but tries to make Juliet realize how lucky she is, as if the realization will put an end to her objections.

proud: delighted.

Juliet tries to explain that while she cannot be happy at what they want, she understands that it is being done in what they regard as her best interest.

meant: intended as.
chopped-logic: sophistry.
minion: minx; spoilt darling.
fettle: make ready, prepare.
hurdle: sledge on which traitors were dragged to execution.
green-sickness: paleness of a young girl with anemia.
carrion: dead flesh.
baggage: good-for-nothing girl. (The word can mean "strumpet," but Capulet does not use this of his daughter.)

It is uncertain whether Lady Capulet's *Fie, fie, what, are you mad?* is to her husband or to Juliet, who at this moment has thrown herself on her knees in a frantic effort to change his mind.

hilding: good-for-nothing.
rate: scold, denounce.
smatter: chatter.
I speak no treason: What I have to say can be said in public openly.
God-i-god-en: That's enough from you, good-bye to you.
You are too hot: (1) Don't excite yourself so much; (2) you are too harsh.
God's bread: by the Host (used in communion).
demesnes: property.
parts: qualities.
puling: whining.
mammet: puppet, doll.
I do not use to jest: I am not in the habit of making jokes.
advise: think carefully.

Capulet's rage and his wife's displeasure with Juliet are both the result of their inability to imagine why she should refuse to be married. She is two years older than most girls who are unmarried in their society. Moreover, in Act One, Scene Three, she assured her mother she would not allow herself to be involved with any young man any further than her parents approved. For them there is no explanation of her behavior but sheer, spoiled contrariness. Capulet's pride and sense of honor are involved; he is under an obligation to Paris which Juliet's capriciousness would make him break. He and his wife are certain that the girl's objection cannot be justified and expect her to surrender when she realizes the consequences of her foolishness.

Is there no pity . . . this is wisely done.

Juliet now discovers that she must rely on her own strength and courage; she can expect nothing from Father, Mother, Nurse. By marrying Romeo she has made it impossible for her normal protectors to help her.

bottom of my grief: The image is one of grief as deep as the sea; so deep that the sea bottom is apparently not visible to a beholder stationed high in the heavens. Her need is for the depth of her anguish to be given some relief by divine pity.

monument: an edifice celebrating past splendor, or glory.

With her mother gone, Juliet begs the Nurse for help, stating her predicament clearly (which she cannot do for her parents). She has sworn an oath before heaven (where it is on record) which she must keep during her husband's life (on earth). She is not free to marry again, to swear such an oath again, unless her husband dies, leaving earth for heaven, whence the oath returns to earth. Clear recognition of her situation makes it seem almost as if heaven has deliberately involved her in a tortuous trap.

The Nurse loves Juliet and wants to give her comfort, to help her. She is a fierce partisan of the Capulets who has suppressed her enmity of a Montague only out of affection for her charge. Not very intelligent, the Nurse sees clearly that Juliet is right; the marriage to Romeo makes another to Paris impossible. But where Juliet wishes that there were no Paris to upset her apple cart, the Nurse wishes there were no Romeo to make her little girl's life so difficult. If only Romeo were dead all would be simple. And because the Nurse wants to see Juliet happy, and mistakenly sees Romeo as the only bar to Juliet's happiness, she hits on what seems to her the only solution. Romeo may not be dead; but so far as Verona is concerned he is legally as good as dead, banished with his rights as a citizen forfeited. And he cannot return to claim Juliet. So in her stupidity and in her sincere wish to see Juliet happy, her Nurse advises her to marry Paris.

dishclout: dishcloth.
green: alert, full of youthful vitality.
beshrew: curse.

The Nurse has known Juliet all her short life; knows her moods, the expressions on her face, has often coaxed her out of discontent, and tries what has always worked before. She has no awareness of the woman Juliet has become, of the constancy and independence which are now part of her. Juliet realizes that her last comforter here has nothing for her, that only the Friar may be able to take some part of her burden, and decides to dissemble in order to visit him without arousing suspicion. She shows herself to the Nurse as the girl who has once more been coaxed into sensible behavior; the deception succeeds.

Ancient damnation . . . power to die.

Ancient damnation: old tempter to damnation.
forsworn: guilty of breaking a marriage vow.
Thou and my bosom, etc.: You shall never again be in my confidence.

Juliet is aghast at the Nurse's advice, hates her for her attitude to Romeo. The girl is still determined not to marry Paris. She looks on the Friar as her last resort, from whom in her recent disillusionment she really expects no solution to her problem. That being so, she sees death as her only way of avoiding the second marriage. In fact, of course, inasmuch as she and Romeo are married and the marriage has been consummated, there is another solution, an open declaration of the truth. It is therefore essential for the actress of Juliet and any actor of the Friar to imagine how stultifying on them is their awareness of the intensity of the hatred between the two families, whipped up by Tybalt's death and Romeo's banishment, so that they cannot imagine the fact of marriage being any restraint. Rather will it be further incitement to both families; to declare it, must seem to girl and priest to invite even worse agony than Juliet now suffers, worse and more prolonged, involving private vengeance, litigation, the mental torment of reproach and detestation from those who are outraged by the match and its secrecy.

Act Five, Scene One

If I may trust . . . I will lie with thee tonight.

flattering: making something appear better than it is.
presage: foretell.
bosom's lord: heart.
sits: rests.

Romeo translates his feeling of relaxed well-being into an image of a ruler at ease on his throne in complete control of his kingdom. Since leaving Juliet he has known no cheerful thoughts until those which are now inspired by his memory of the dream in which he was brought happily to life by Juliet's kisses.

how sweet is love, etc.: How sweet is love when experienced in reality if illusionary images (fantasies, dreams) are so rich in joy!

Romeo hopes that his dream really foretells reunion with Juliet.

monument: tomb.
took post: To take post means literally to travel by post horses; the statement therefore developed the sense of to travel as swiftly as possible. Indeed, a succession of swift post horses,

each being ridden as fast as possible until it tired, to be exchanged for another fresh horse, was the fastest way of traveling in Elizabethan England.

presently: immediately.

did leave it for my office: left it as my duty.

I defy you, stars: Some editions print *I deny you stars*.

In each case Romeo refuses to submit patiently to events which have happened as a result of the influence of the stars. He is in complete despair. With Juliet dead he no longer wants to live. He makes up his mind to see her once more before he kills himself. This is the only reason why he does not make away with himself immediately. Life has one remaining alleviation of misery for him, to see his dead wife, still untouched by the corruption of death. It is not an unmixed joy; but it is something to look forward to as an alleviation of his agonizing existence.

import, etc.: suggest some mishap threatens you.

Romeo has determined irrevocably to make his way to the tomb, to enjoy the bittersweetness of seeing Juliet again, of touching, kissing her body, of dying there with his wife.

He remembers her as he last saw her, as he left her standing above him, pale in the light of dawn, framed in her window like one in a tomb. Then she told him that as he stood beneath her he looked to her *As one dead in the bottom of a tomb,* to which his reply was *And trust me, love, in my eye so do you.* In his lonely exile this is the image of her which he carries, as he last saw her, pale, wan, *as one dead in the bottom of a tomb.* The image dominates him, drives him on to see, touch and kiss the reality before he dies.

Act Five, Scene Three

O, give me thy hand . . . with a kiss I die.

Still intent on reunion with Juliet whose image never leaves him, Romeo has fought and killed an unknown adversary in the darkness of the churchyard, promising to lay his victim in the tomb with her. When the torchlight shows him who it is, he takes hold of Paris to keep the promise, still most concerned with the expectation of seeing Juliet in a moment or so.

writ with me in sour misfortune's book: One whose fortune like mine and with mine has been a source of bitter unhappiness and misadventure.
triumphant grave: a grave which bears witness to the splendors (triumphs) of the dead.

As Romeo thinks of the darkness of the grave, he imagines how it will be transformed for him by the pale beauty of his dead wife. For him it will not be a place of dark horror, but radiant with love. His image of the dark tomb gives place to one of Juliet which lights up the confined space in the way in which a chamber or turret is bright as the result of an architectural device to admit light from above. Sometimes the word *lantern (lanthorn)* refers to the windowed structure which lets the light in, sometimes to the whole turret or room which is full of light as a result. Here Romeo seems to be thinking of the grave flooded with light from Juliet as a hall or turret is flooded with light from the window above.
feasting presence: splendid state apartment or hall in which ceremonial meals take place.

Romeo insists that Juliet's presence counteracts the dark unpleasantness of the tomb, so that its occupants, the dead (in various stages of decomposition and reduced in most cases to bones) do not oppress him any more than if they were a happy company celebrating a feast with their monarch in a blaze of light from candles and torches, the hall filled with color and excitement.

Romeo expects his despair to have some slight alleviation when he can see, hold and kiss once more the body which is so dear to him. It is like the *lightning* which those who attend on dying men *(their keepers)* often observe after many agonies have been passed through and death is only moments away. He has expected to see the pale face which he remembers; he has prepared himself to confront it without being too overwhelmed with grief. But now he sees a living girl; as the effect of the drug has almost worn off, she has regained her living color. But, as he thinks her dead, the sight is too bitter. His loss is now too painful, and so he says:

O, how may I
Call this a lightning?

ensign: flag.
advanced: raised.
beauty's ensign yet, etc.: Beauty has not yet struck its colors and allowed the pale flag of death to be raised in the conquered body.

He has intended to kill himself here ever since hearing the false news in Mantua. Now he repeats his resolution, having found it impossible not to linger and gaze on the beauty which he knows so well, but which he has not expected ever to see again. Unnerved by the sight, he reaffirms his purpose. In his despair he can think of only one way of overcoming the influence of the stars on his mortal, irrational part. If he were not in despair he would know that patience, reconciliation to the will of God, is the way of overcoming stellar influence. (See above, pp. 221 f., for an account of stellar influence on the flesh but not the soul.) Romeo can see nothing for him in life with Juliet dead. He kills himself because oblivion is better than *death prorogued, wanting of thy love.* There is no expectation of reunion after death, of love triumphing over death, merely a desperate refusal to endure more pain in this life.

dateless: perpetual, with rights which never expire.
engrossing: buying up the whole market.
righteous: lawful, legal.
bitter conduct: (1) bitter tasting guide (poison); (2) painful, sad guide (guide with unhappy consequences).
unsavory: bitter, ill-tasting.
pilot: the guide, i.e., the phial of poison (the pilot who guides in despair).
at once: swiftly.
dashing rocks: destroying rocks, destructive rocks.

quick: (1) swift, (2) full of life. Romeo is aware of both senses.
He indulges in a flash of dark humor: The drugs are lively, or full of life, to make him die.
Thus with a kiss I die: Romeo does not kiss Juliet until he has taken the poison, so that his last sensation will be the touch of his lips on hers as he dies. As a result he does not realize that she looks as if she were alive because she is alive. Now that her circulation has restored color to her cheeks and lips it has also given them warmth. But Romeo is dead before he can be conscious of the warmth. Had he kissed her before taking poison he would almost certainly have noticed that her lips were warm, and then the tragedy would have been averted.

Romeo!/Alack, alack . . . let me die.

The Friar first calls out Romeo's name, then notices the blood, the swords, then Romeo and Paris, both dead.
unkind: (1) unnatural, (2) malevolent. The reference is to the astrological hour, in which the relative positions of heavenly bodies resulted in *this lamentable chance.*
comfortable: giving comfort. She says, virtually: "What a comfort you are."
contagion: infection from the corrupting bodies.
unnatural sleep: death. (Natural sleep is the sleep of the physical powers of a human being, a restorative of vitality. Death is a sleep unlike that, one in which the vital forces are quenched, never to recover.)
contradict: overrule, gainsay.
in thy bosom: cherished, very dear (not "lying in, or on, thy bosom").
timeless: untimely.

Juliet's despair is equal to that which drove Romeo to his death. Before taking the drug she was prepared for death if even this expedient failed to unite her with him. It would be a mistake to interpret her resolution now as a bid to be united with him in death. Unlike Cleopatra, a pagan (who expects to meet Antony immediately after death), Juliet is a Christian. She has no such expectation. In her despair she rejects life without Romeo. Like him she prefers oblivion to enduring more misery.

churl: selfish, ungenerous, impolite fellow.
die with a restorative: Her bitterness is similar to Romeo's quip that *quick* (live) drugs make him die. To kiss Romeo has been for her a *restorative,* a source of life: now she hopes the kiss will kill her. Contact with his lips allows her to realize that he has only just died; this gives her intolerable anguish.
sheath . . . rust: another bitter joke. There is a Renaissance saying that weapons left unused in their sheaths tend to rust. When Juliet places her dagger in her own body as its sheath, her blood will redden (i.e., rust) it.